IMAGES
of America

BANNING

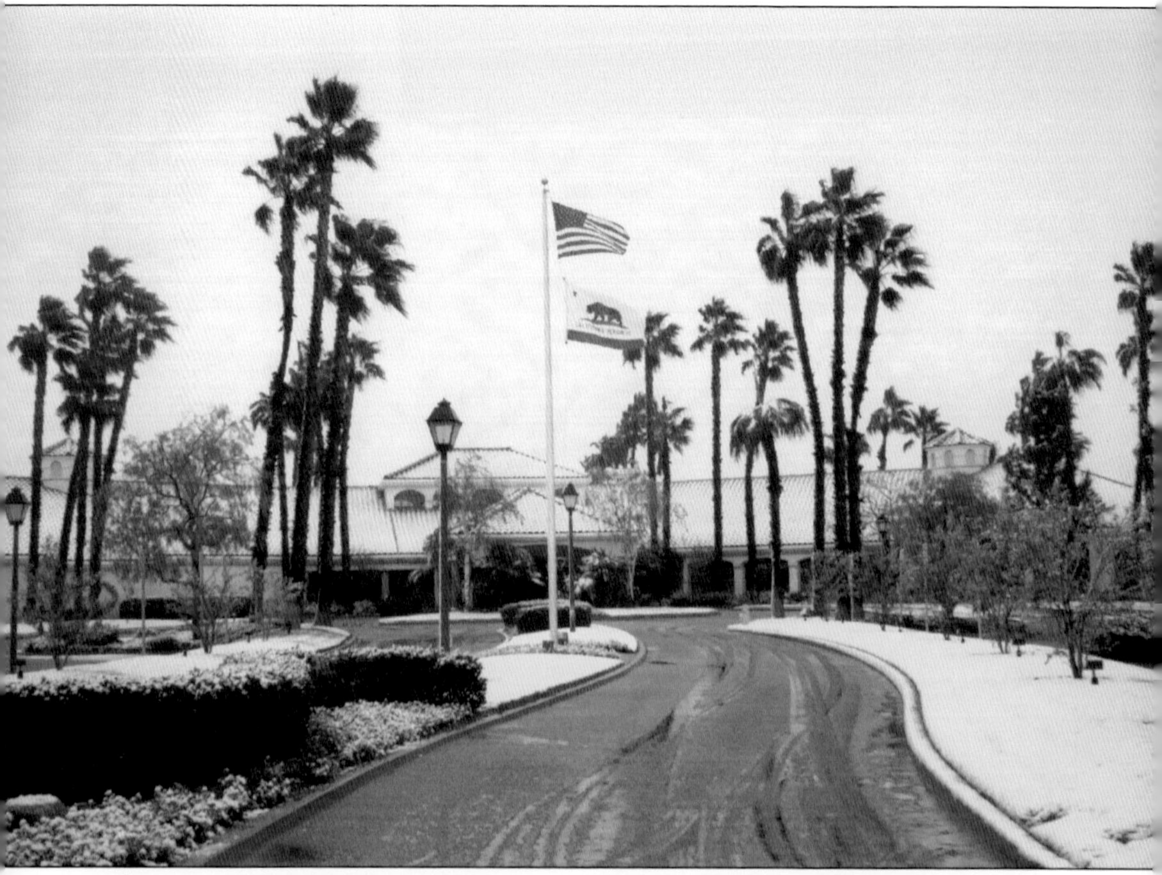

This picture was taken the morning after an unusual snowstorm at Sun Lakes Country Club that turned its two 18-hole golf greens white. Featuring a large auditorium, the clubhouse is the seat of many activities at Sun Lakes. Around 57 different clubs have been established on the grounds, with the Friendship Club having over 900 members at present. (Courtesy of the author.)

IMAGES
of America

BANNING

Kenneth M. Holtzclaw

ARCADIA
PUBLISHING

ISBN 978-0-7385-2992-9

Published by Arcadia Publishing
Charleston, South Carolina

Printed in the United States of America

Library of Congress Control Number: 2005923148

For all general information, please contact Arcadia Publishing:
Telephone 843-853-2070
Fax 843-853-0044
E-mail sales@arcadiapublishing.com
For customer service and orders:
Toll-Free 1-888-313-2665

Visit us on the Internet at www.arcadiapublishing.com

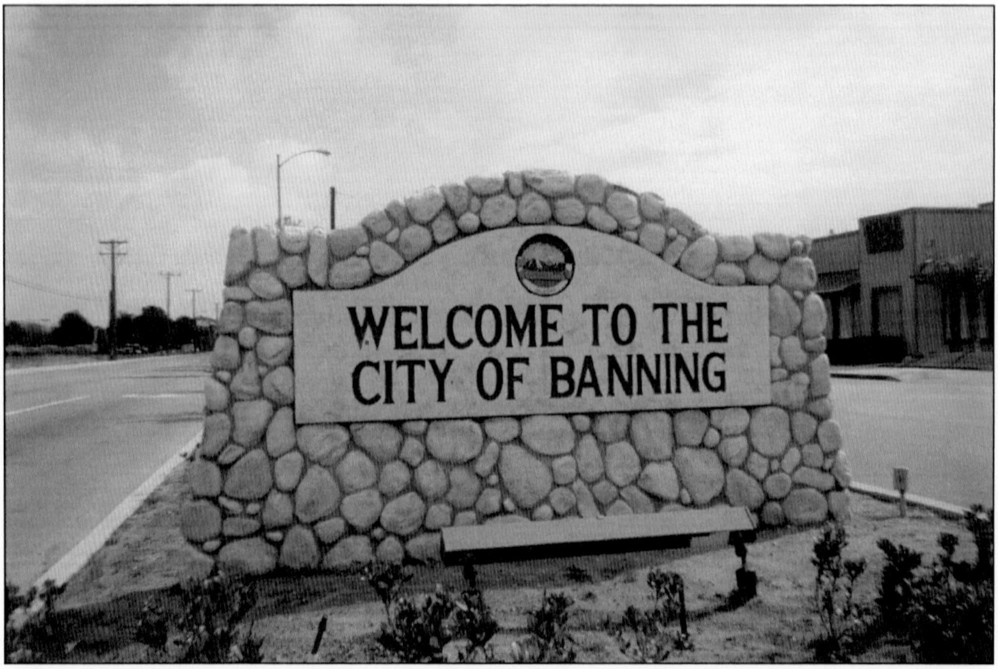

This monument has replaced the large white arch that once beckoned everyone entering the city of Banning. The arch was razed to make way for the development of more modern, wider roads. (Courtesy of the author.)

CONTENTS

ACKNOWLEDGMENTS

The preparation of this book involved many people, all of whom were of great assistance and support during its compilation. I thankfully acknowledge these wonderful people with great gratitude and also thank the various institutions and personal friends who helped and encouraged me.

First, I would like to thank the Banning Public Library, where this book got its start under the encouragement of Bill Bell, head of interlibrary loan and reference, and Lisa Rutherford, library director. Bill often took time out of his busy schedule to give me valuable assistance. And certainly not to be overlooked is the great advice and encouragement that was given by author Maria Webster Weisbrod of Banning. Joan Coombs, longtime resident of Banning and affiliate of the Gilman Historical Ranch and Wagon Museum, provided useful vintage photographs, including the one for this book's cover. Marianne Bailiff, another longtime resident, provided numerous other photographs. Nara Haskell, member and ex-president of the San Gorgonio Pass Historical Society and the last owner, along with her husband, Jim, of the historical Haskell Ranch in San Timoteo Canyon, is also to be thanked for giving her time, advice, and numerous photographs to this publication. Thanks are also given to Katherine Siva Saubel, cofounder of the Malki Museum on the Morongo Indian Reservation, for providing photographs and Native American history and culture that was very helpful.

Steve Lech, Riverside County historian and author, provided additional photographs and helpful advice. Marilyn Vonderheide, program manager of the Laura May Stewart Foundation, supplied vintage photographs of the Stewart Ranch, a portion of which is now covered by Sun Lakes Country Club and golf courses. Homer Shockey, ex-president of the San Gorgonio Historical Society, related his experiences of years ago while stationed at one of General Patton's hospitals and also provided pictures of that era. Bud Mathewson, Banning businessman and longtime resident, provided information from his store of knowledge of local history as well as photographs that were helpful in the book's preparation. Linda Fisk, registrar of the San Diego Museum of Man, provided several photographic contributions. Banning mayor John Machisic's help is also appreciated.

Helpful during the book's development was advice given by Debra Garcia, press editor of the Malki Museum, and photograph preparation done by Sahara Quinn of Sahara Design, owned and operated by Sahara Quinn and Rebekah Wheat. Others to thank are Brenda Focht, curator of collections and exhibitions of the Riverside Municipal Museum; Dorothy Bailey, another longtime Banning resident; Christie Mitchell, curator of the Gilman Historical Ranch and Wagon Museum; Michael Frydrych, owner of the Fox Cineplex Theater; Diane Fisher of the Corda Art Gallery for loaning pictures; Susan Phillips, receptionist of the Malki Museum; and others too numerous to mention. And last but not least, thanks to my wife, Margaret, for her encouragement, support, and advice during the preparation of this book. Thanks to everyone concerned!

INTRODUCTION

While men on the eastern coast of a future United States of America were busy putting together a democratic government, the area where the town of Banning now stands was still a remote section of the San Gorgonio Pass, inhabited by indigenous Native Americans who had lived there for ages. It was not until about 75 years later that the serenity of the Native Americans, who resided peacefully there, was threatened when their land was invaded by foreign intruders.

In 1851, Perfecto Abillar, a Spaniard, drifted over into the San Gorgonio Pass and returned to it several times. Two more of his countrymen, Miguel Bustamente and Juan Garcia, came in 1853. In the same year, Newton Noble, a North American white man, first visited the San Gorgonio Pass area as a lad of 18. He later settled in the nearby San Timoteo Canyon with his wife, Rosa Sansavine, a Cahuilla woman.

When Bustamente first arrived in the San Gorgonio Pass, he found Paulino Weaver living with the Native Americans at their summit rancheria northwest of today's Banning. Thus, we come upon the major crises in San Gorgonio Pass's human history, for we may say with some assurance that through the hands of Paulino Weaver and Newton Noble the rod of the empire, so to speak, passed from the red man to the white man. Weaver, born in Tennessee about 1800, had perhaps come to California with Kit Carson in the Ewing Young party in the early 1830s.

The influx of foreign adventurers increased throughout the years, as many came to realize the great opportunities that the lucrative San Gorgonio Pass offered. The Native Americans in the area were friendly, which was a further incentive to homestead there. Fur trappers, miners, and timber cutters soon added to the population. Eventually farms and cattle herds were established, houses and buildings erected, fruit orchards planted, and a path to the beginning of a small town in the San Gorgonio Pass became a gleam in many a man's eye.

Eventually, a small town began to emerge that was later named Banning, reportedly in honor of Phineas Banning, promoter of the town of Wilmington, California, and inaugurator of its railroads. When the Southern Pacific Railroad arrived through the San Gorgonio Pass in 1878, it spelled the demise of the stage lines through the Banning area.

However, growth that had begun because of the stagecoach lines only became stronger with the railroad's appearance and further strengthened when the railroad established a station there. Then the bust of the real estate boom of the 1880s evolved and stymied growth. Nevertheless, on February 6, 1913, the little settlement that had been growing apace in the cradle of the San Gorgonio and San Jacinto Mountains officially became the city of Banning.

A number of years later, the Metropolitan Water Company began the massive California aqueduct construction from the Colorado River, past Banning via a 17-foot diameter, over-a-mile-long tunnel, through its southern Mount San Jacinto mountain range, which again spurred growth to the area—especially because its headquarters were located in the heart of Banning. Several years later, during the early years of World War II, Gen. George Patton built a hospital complex in Banning for his large desert tank-training operation to the east, further enhancing growth.

However, growth was slowed once again with the bypass of Banning by the installation of Interstate 10, which took away traffic through the downtown area. Regardless, new businesses and many new homes are being built in Banning today, and in 2004, it had a population of over 27,000 inhabitants. One retirement community alone, Sun Lakes Country Club, makes up over one-fifth of Banning's population. Because Banning once maintained a prominent stagecoach stop at the Gilman ranch adobe in north Banning, it became well-known as "Stagecoach Town USA," and the Banning Chamber of Commerce hosts a yearly Stagecoach Days celebration with a parade and numerous other activities.

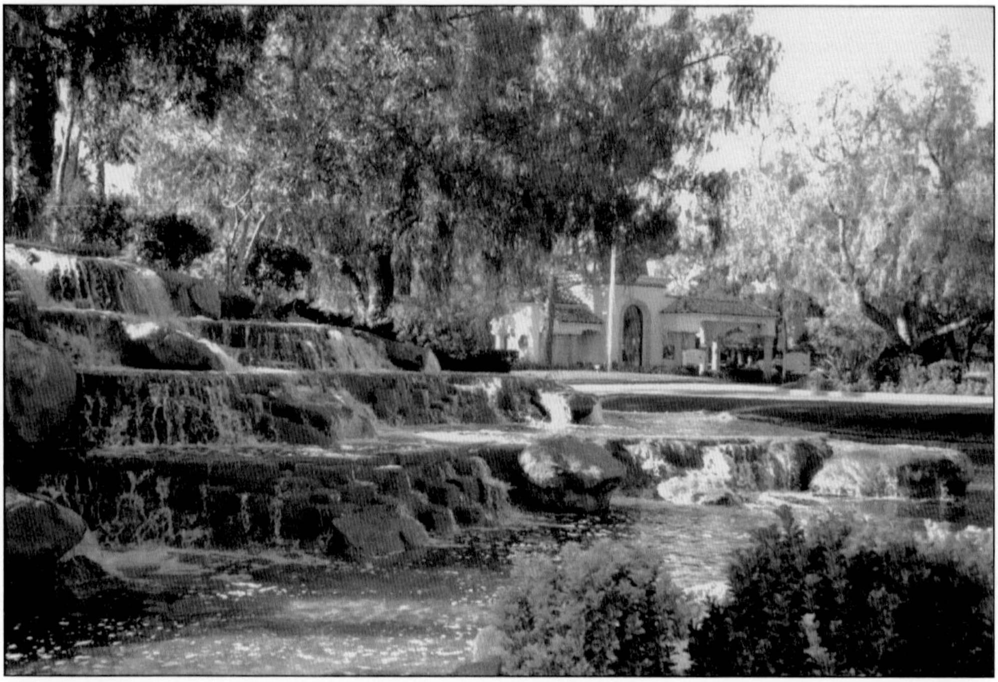

Pictured here is the main gate and entrance to Sun Lakes Country Club in Banning. Begun in the late 1980s, the retirement community is spread over part of what was once the large Stewart farm. At present, it has 3,400 residences and a population of over 6,000. The grounds contain two 18-hole golf courses with beautiful lakes, two tennis courts, one indoor lap pool, and two outdoor pools. The numerous officially organized clubs keep its community active. (Courtesy of the author.)

One

First Inhabitants of the Banning Area

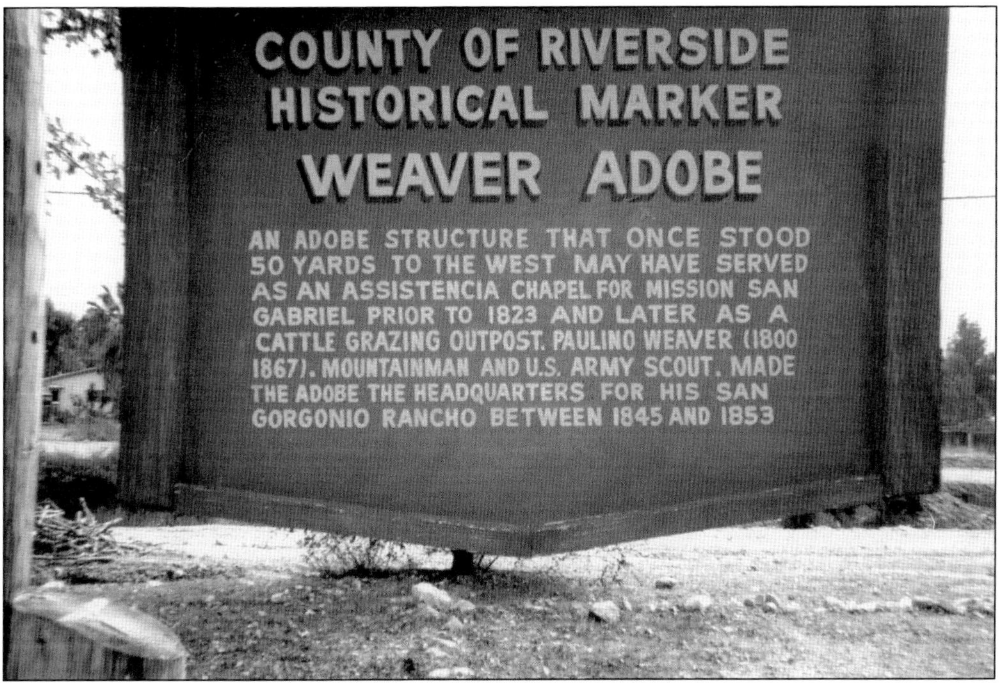

Paulino Weaver may have come to California with Kit Carson. A naturalized Mexican citizen, Weaver was a man of some standing, being one of two grantees upon which Gov. Pio Pico bestowed the deserted San Gorgonio Rancho. Weaver occupied the abandoned adobe there and claimed the rancho. During the Civil War, he served as a scout for the U.S. Army and, in 1862, discovered gold on the Colorado. (Courtesy of the author.)

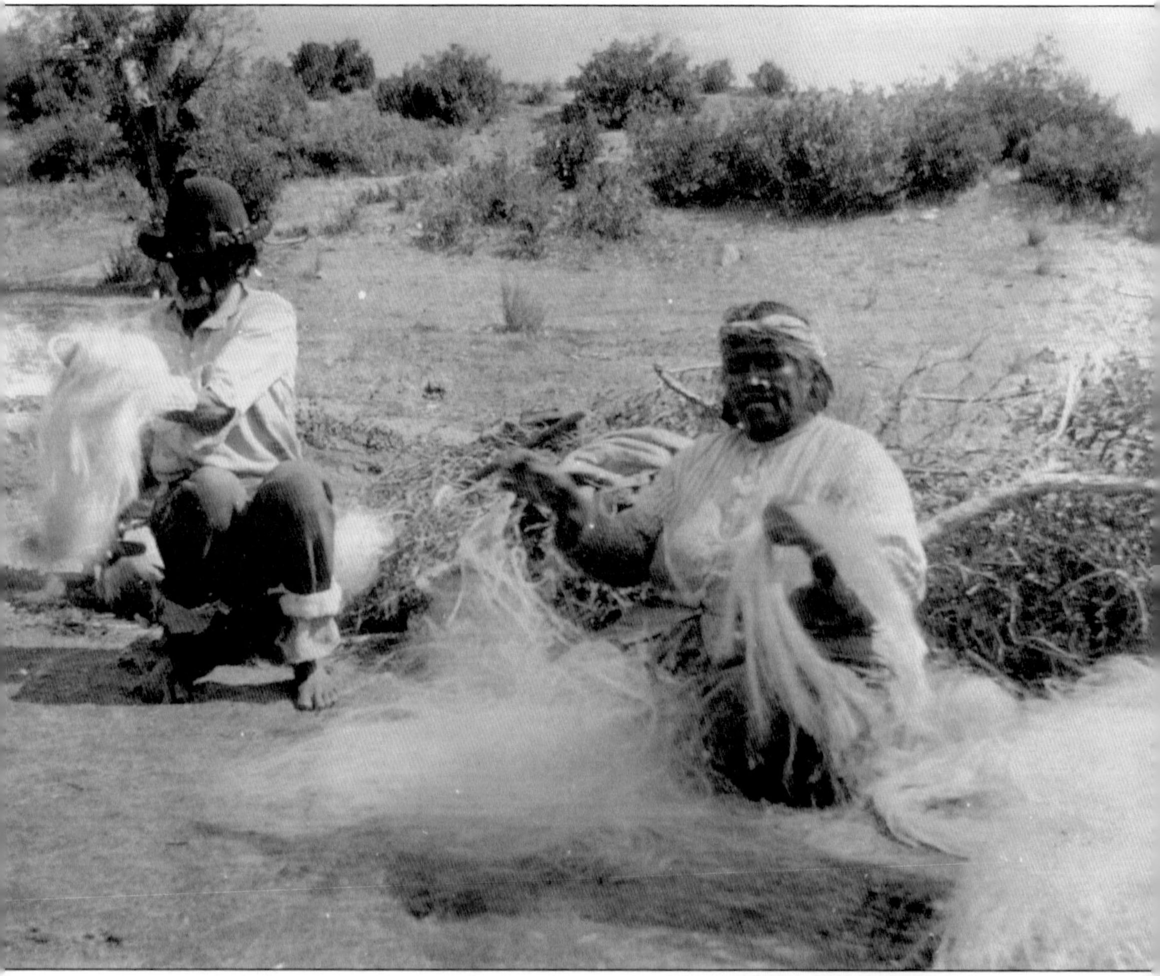

These Native Americans are working with yucca fiber, which was used for making many things, especially mats and rope. Piles of fiber are in front of them, and a pile of brush is behind. (Photo by Ned Gillette; courtesy of the San Diego Museum of Man, DuBois, Constance Goddard collection.)

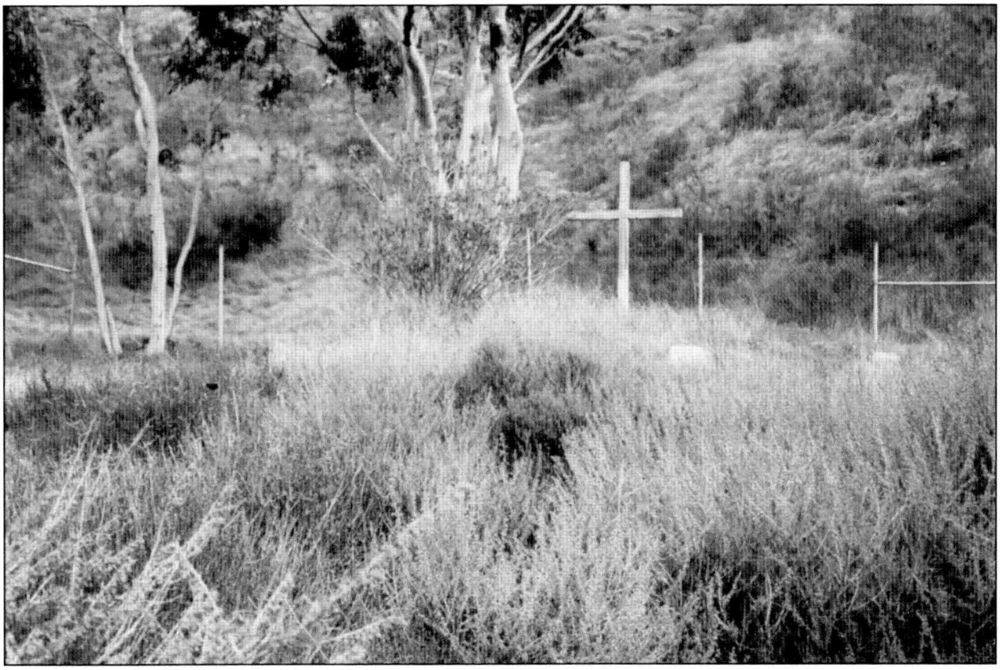

When the last buildings of the St. Boniface School in Banning were demolished, only the grounds, rock-lined walkways, and cemetery on the back of the property remained. This is how the cemetery appears today in its run-down condition. Some graves have been exhumed and moved to other established cemeteries, but a few still remain. A housing development is scheduled to soon surround the small cemetery. (Courtesy of the author.)

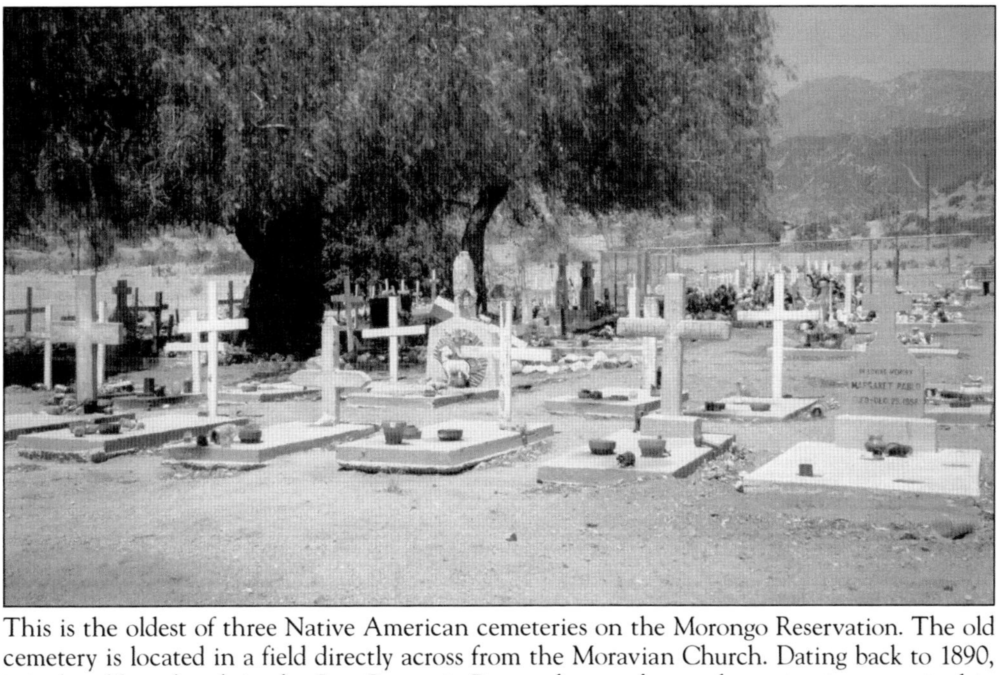

This is the oldest of three Native American cemeteries on the Morongo Reservation. The old cemetery is located in a field directly across from the Moravian Church. Dating back to 1890, it is the oldest church in the San Gorgonio Pass and stems from a denomination organized in Germany in 1722. (Courtesy of the author.)

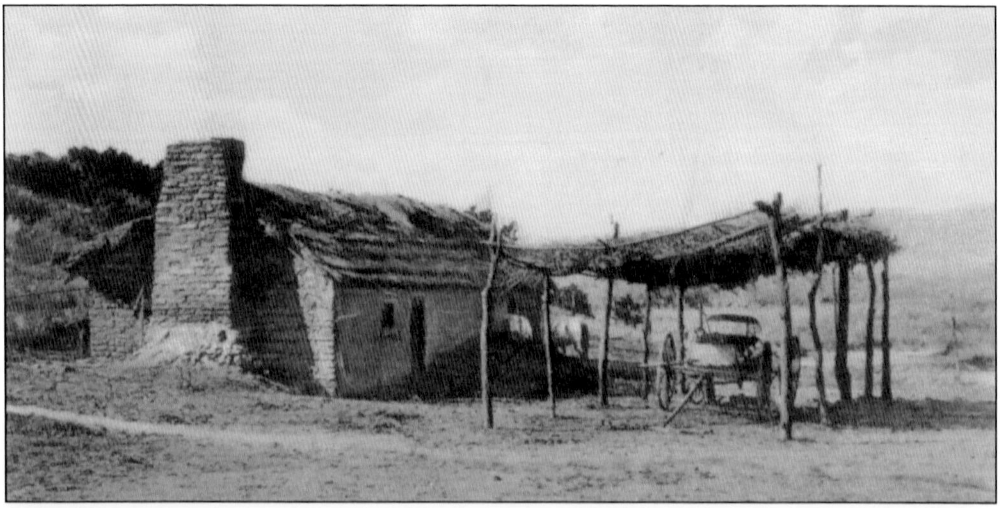

This more modern Native American home is equipped with a garage for a small buggy. When the Spaniards arrived, some of the natives took note of their building techniques and began to move away from their own antiquated and flimsy houses to adobe structures like the one shown here. Note that the garage still uses the familiar pole construction, though, and that the house roof is thatch. (Courtesy of the San Diego Museum of Man.)

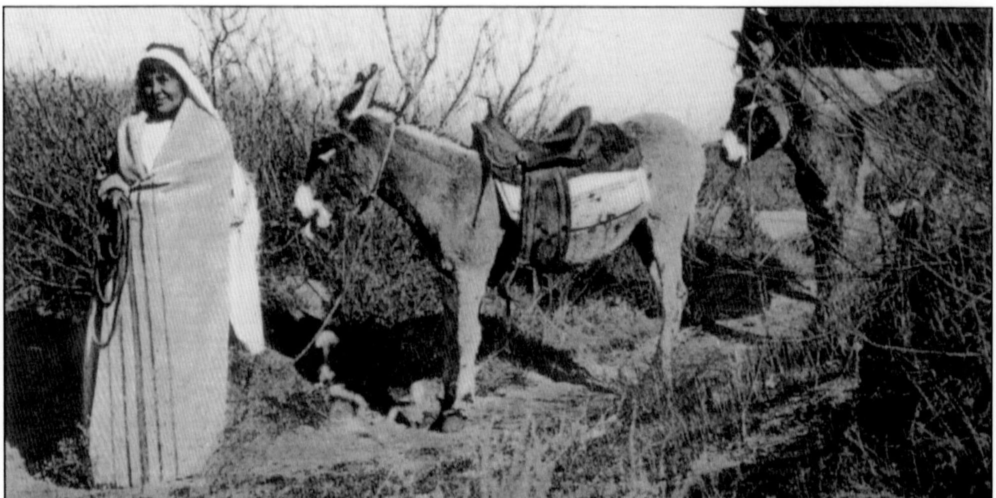

Donkeys were a popular form of transportation for Native Americans and were often used to travel short distances. They were quite reliable, durable, and extremely sure-footed, although slow. The Native Americans liked them because they were easy to care for and did not like to stray. The saddle on one of the donkeys being led by this Native American woman suggests donkeys were ridden. (Courtesy of the San Diego Museum of Man.)

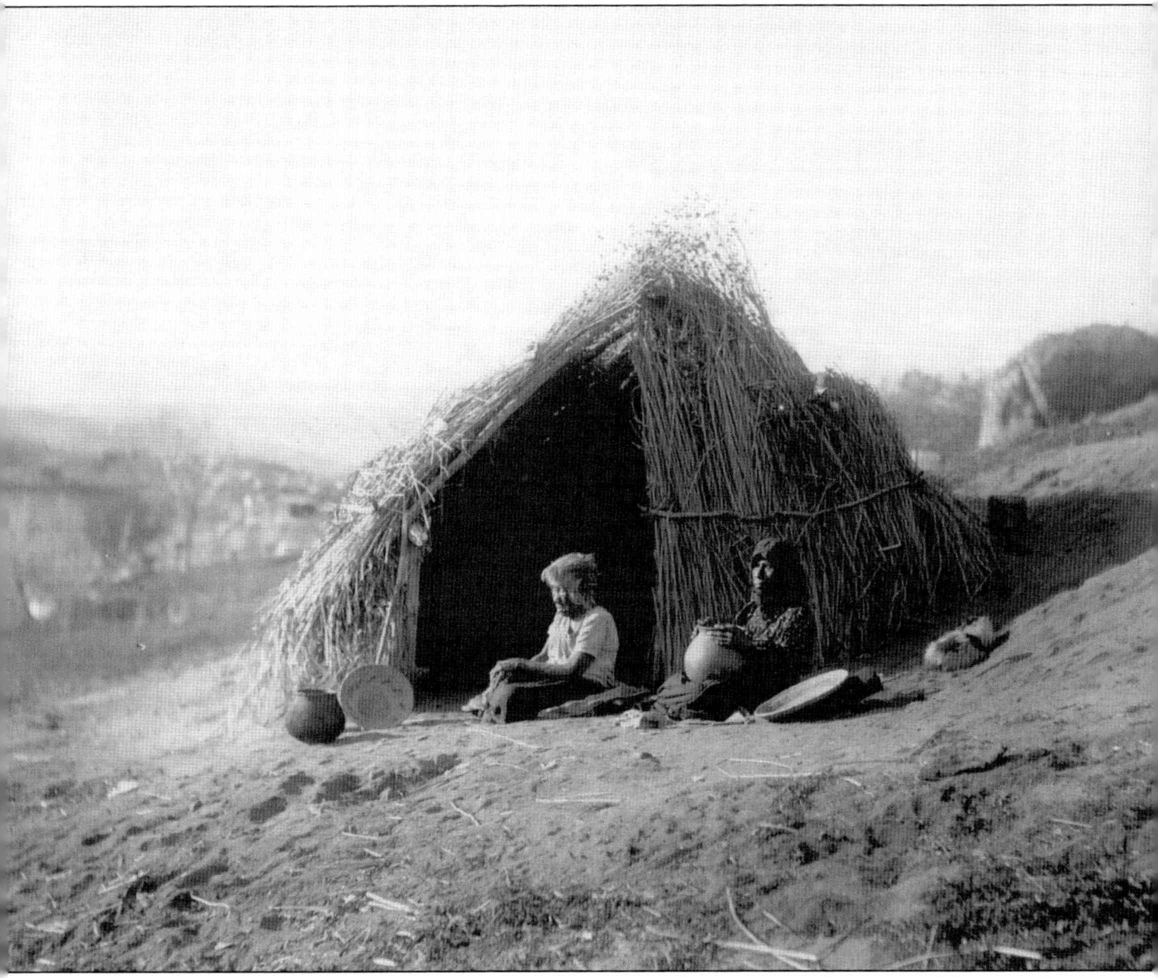

These Cahuilla Mission Indians are engaged in pottery and basket making. These were sophisticated trades, requiring more expertise than routine chores like seed gathering and grinding and the hunting performed by men in the mountains and desert. The pottery and baskets were usually in demand and were great barter items. (Photograph by C. C. Pierce and Company; courtesy of the San Diego Museum of Man.)

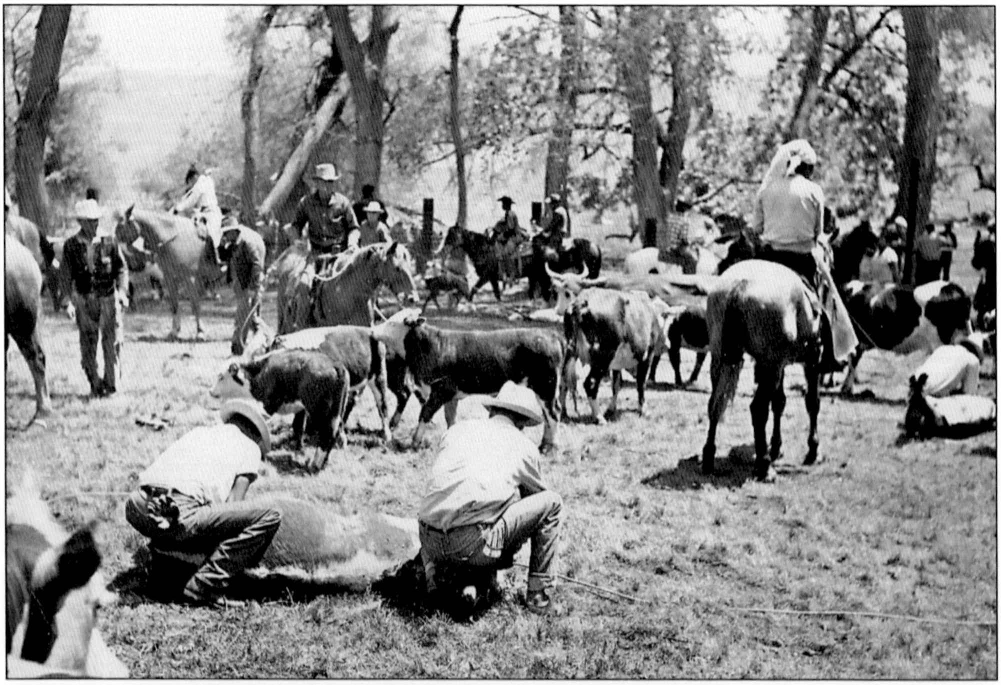

The yearly cattle roundup on the Morongo Reservation was a major job. Some of the farmers around Banning helped the Native Americans corral their cattle so they could be sent to market. This 1940 scene shows how active the roundup actually was after the cattle had been running free on the range for a year. (Courtesy of Marianne Bailiff.)

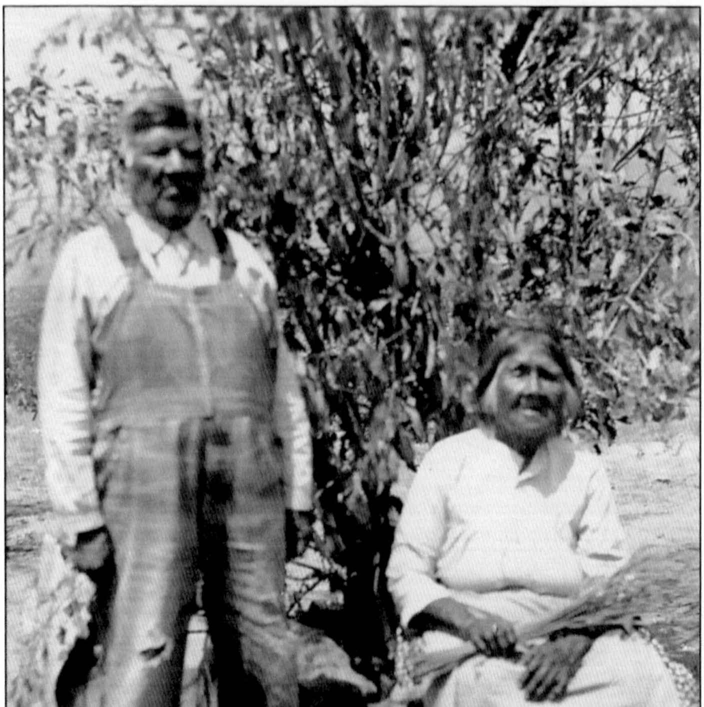

Pictured are Francisco (Pablo) Costo and Louise Costo (Rico), two grandchildren of Juan Antonio Costo, chief of the Mountain Cahuilla Indians. Pablo was said to very closely resemble the old chief. The famous Lugo Californians enlisted the services of Chief Juan Antonio and a group of Native Americans from the San Jacinto Mountains to protect their holdings. He was known to be very loyal to them. (Courtesy of Katherine Siva Saubel.)

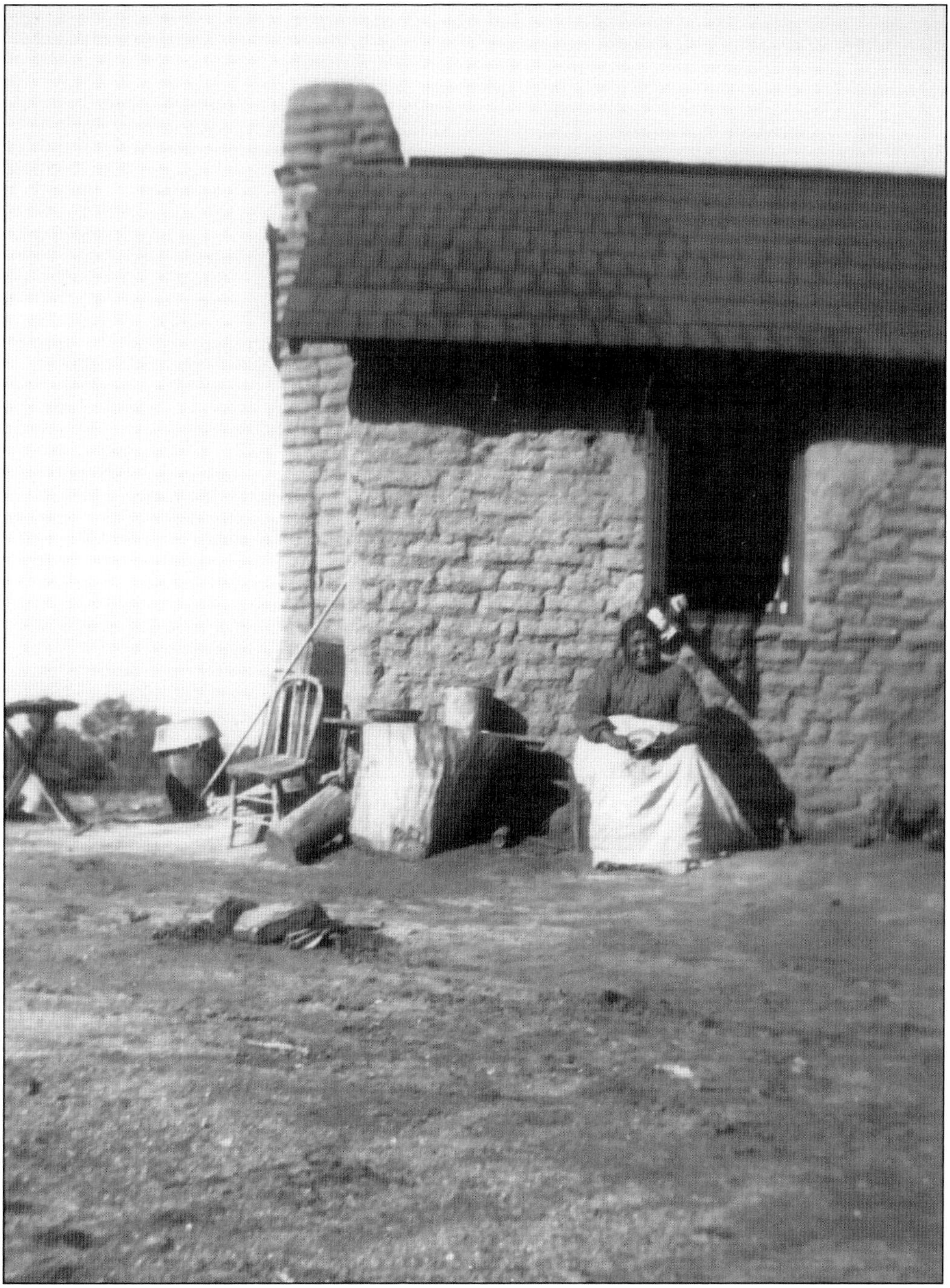

This Native American woman weaves a basket beside her house, which is representative of the more refined form of home construction in later years, when the art of adobe making was incorporated. Basket weaving was an important art form and was essential to almost every Native American household. This basket incorporates the popular rattlesnake design. (Courtesy of the San Diego Museum of Man.)

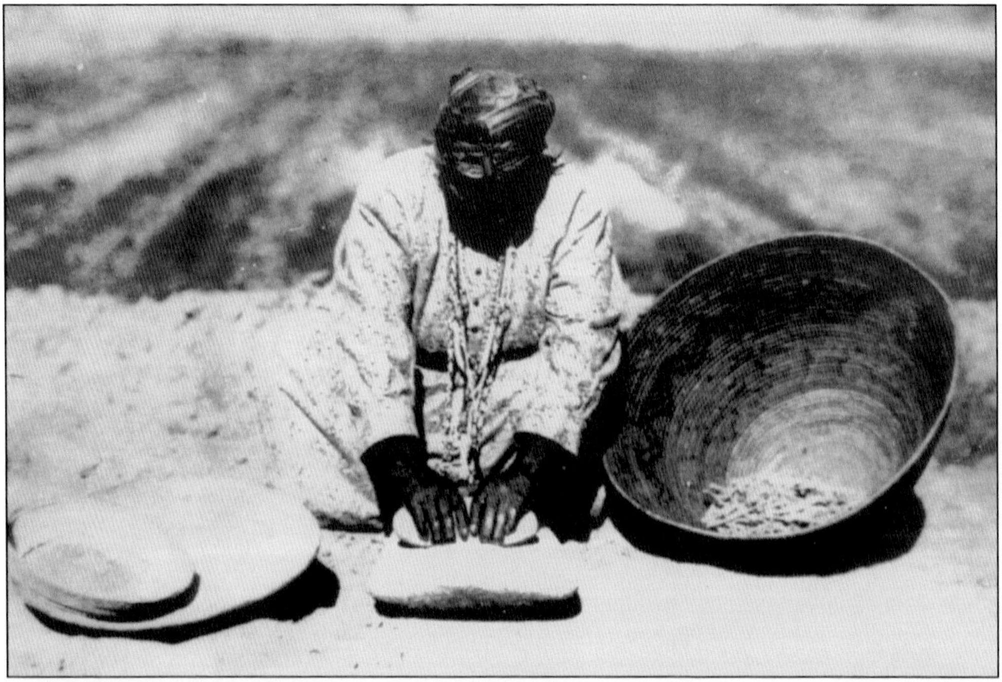

Preparing food was a tedious job, as this task of grinding mesquite beans shows. As many as 11 Cahuilla Indian communities existed in the San Gorgonio Pass area, located on both sides of the pass and some distance to the north and east. Although native food was abundant, it was hard work harvesting and gathering acorns and other staples, which at times had to be foraged from quite a distance. (Courtesy of the Banning Unified School District.)

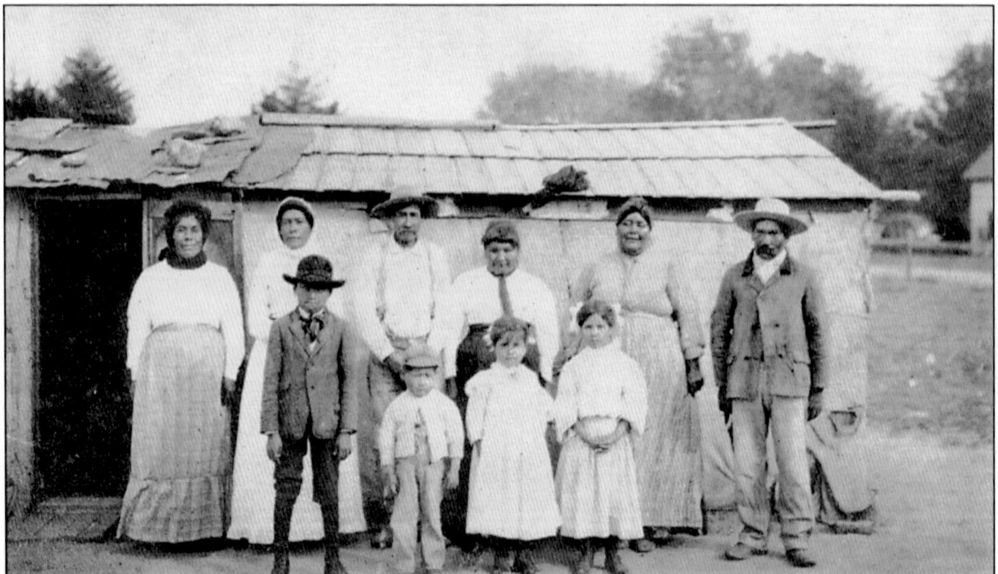

In the early years of Banning's history, the Native Americans tried to adapt to the white man's customs, and this was particularly evident in their modified dress. This family lived in Banning in an abode constructed of material quite uncommon to those normally used for Native American houses. (Courtesy of Steve Lech.)

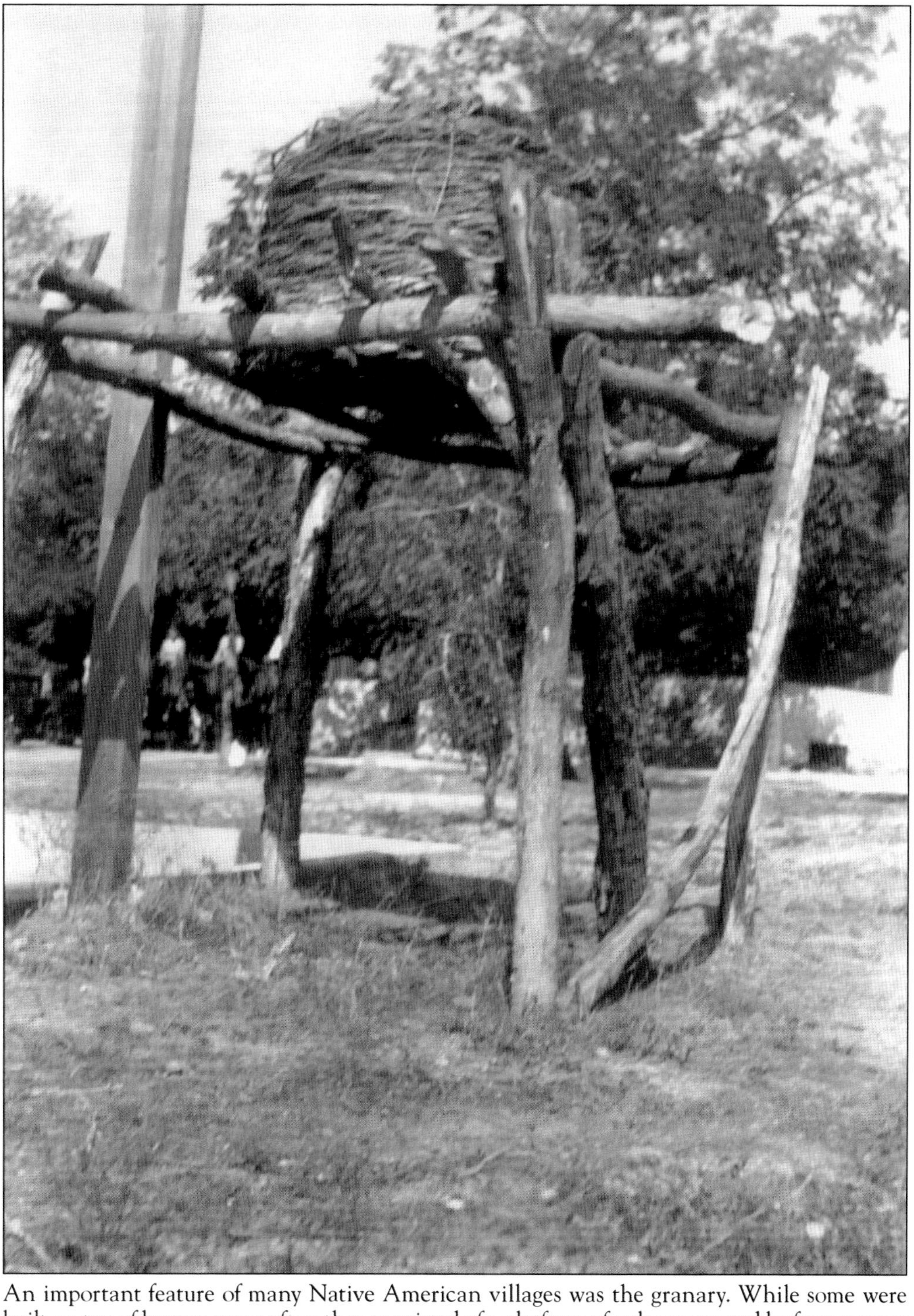

An important feature of many Native American villages was the granary. While some were built on top of houses, more often they consisted of a platform of poles supported by four or more vertical poles set into the ground. Stored here were dry food staples such as acorns, mesquite beans, and a large number of other seed varieties. Seed gathering was an important activity for these communities. (Courtesy of the San Diego Museum of Man, Woodward Collection.)

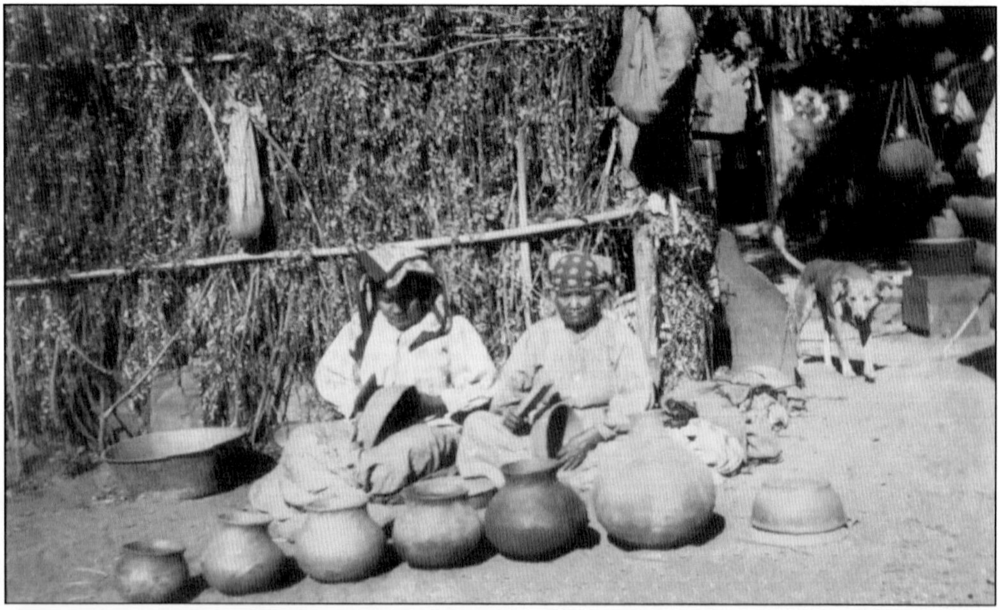

This lineup of pottery items shows the variation in size and type. Sometimes small businesses like this were set up, and the pottery bartered for other needed items. The two pottery makers pictured are in the process of shaping some freshly molded clay bowls to later be put in the sun and dried. (Courtesy of the San Diego Museum of Man.)

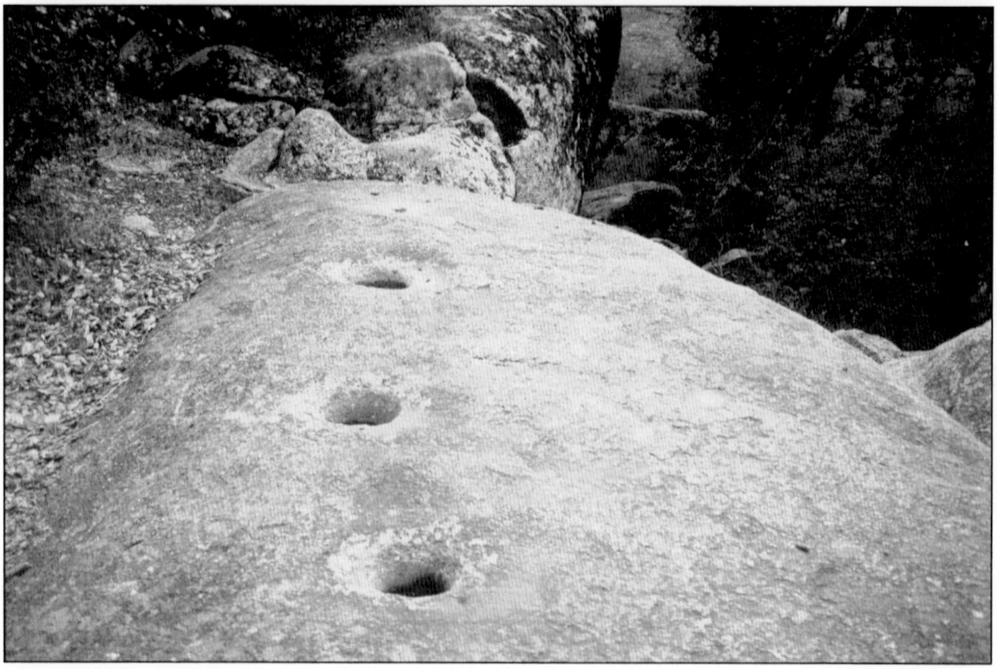

This picture was taken in a wooded area of the San Jacinto Mountains, south of Banning, and shows a large granite rock that was used by Mountain Cahuilla Indians to grind acorns and perhaps other seeds. A large grove of oaks scattered around the area where the grinding rock was located made it an ideal center for grinding. There were numerous mortar holes in the granite, but no rock pestles were found. (Courtesy of the author.)

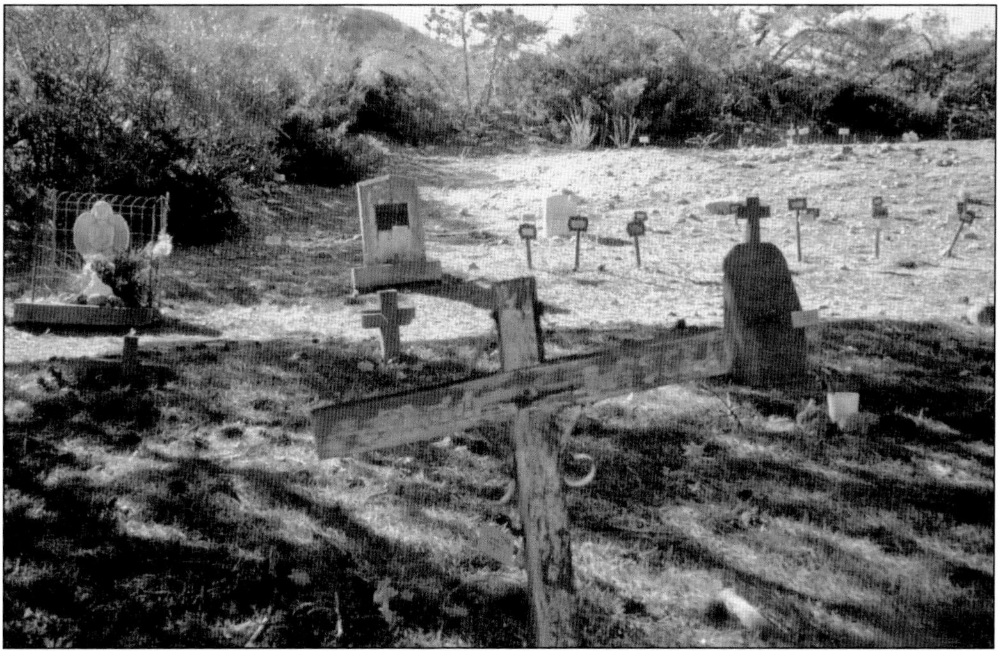

This potter's field is located on the west slope of a hill next to the lower-level cemetery of San Gorgonio Memorial Park. It was appropriated as a burial ground for the destitute and the unknown in the early years of the cemetery's history, and was especially used during the Depression years when many could not afford a burial plot. (Courtesy of the author.)

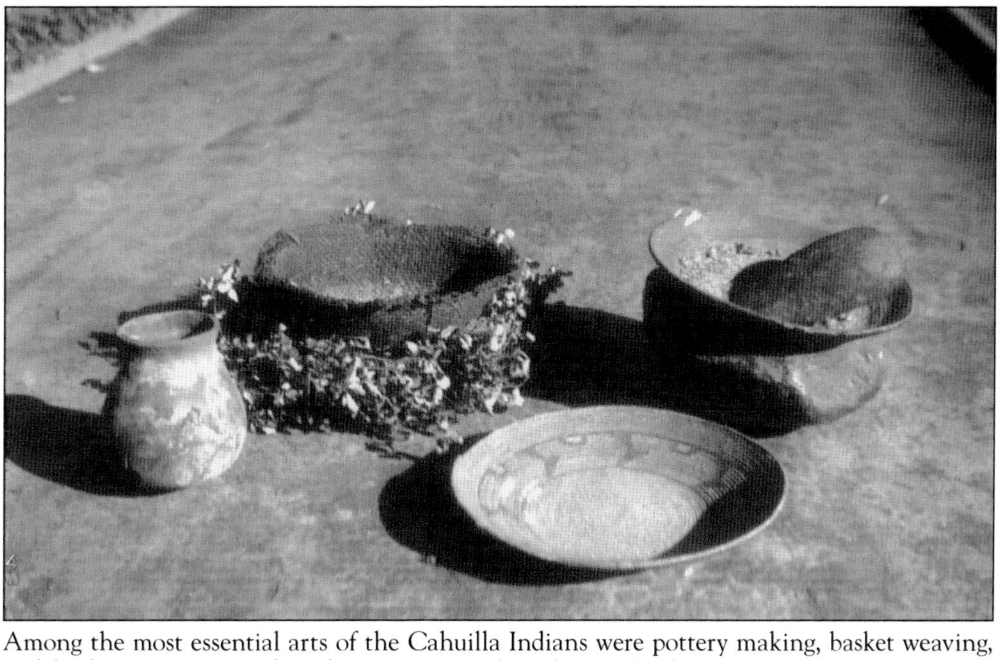

Among the most essential arts of the Cahuilla Indians were pottery making, basket weaving, and food preparation. Laid out here on a smooth surface are baskets, a mortar and pestle, and a pottery jar. Mortar and pestle sets were used in grinding acorns and mesquite beans. Mineralized clay that did not crack when dried in the sun was used for pottery making. (Courtesy of the San Diego Museum of Man.)

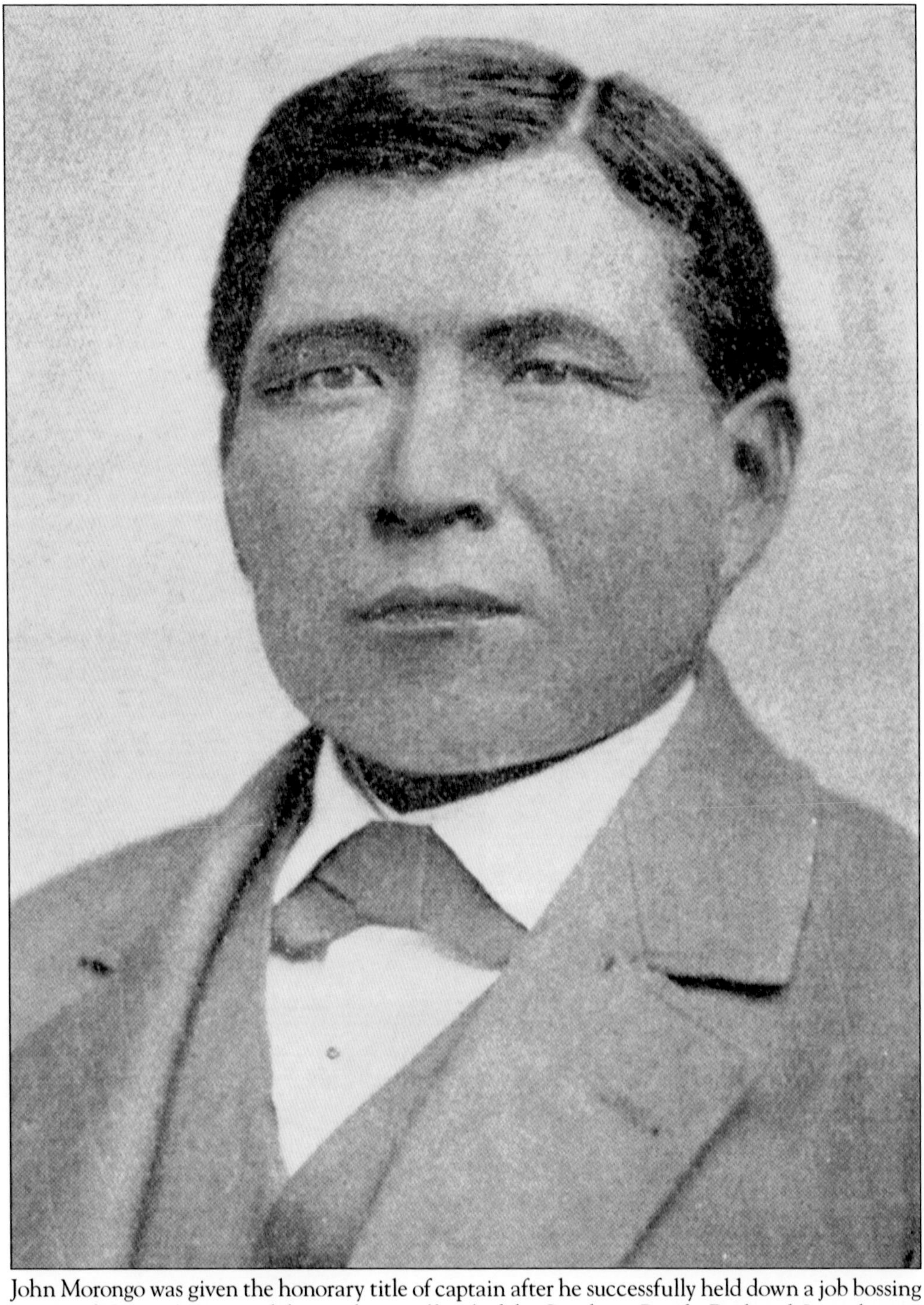

John Morongo was given the honorary title of captain after he successfully held down a job bossing a gang of Native American laborers for an official of the Southern Pacific Railroad. Later he was always referred to by this title. He was appointed interpreter for the Indian Bureau established at Colton and served until the agency was discontinued. He died on the Morongo Reservation in 1898. (Courtesy of Tom Hughes.)

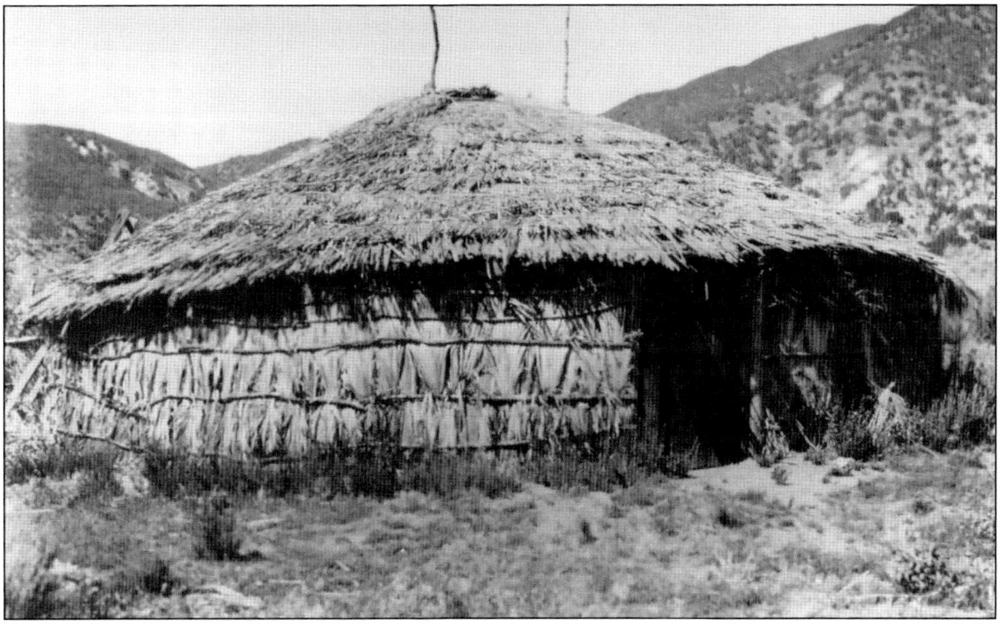

This early ceremonial house once stood on the Morongo Reservation and was used as the site of numerous special events. In the Cahuilla culture, perhaps the most important religious event was an annual, week-long ceremony to commemorate those who had died that year. Prior to the arrival of the Spaniards, most structures, including ceremonial houses, were round. Spanish influence changed that. (Courtesy of Katherine Siva Saubel.)

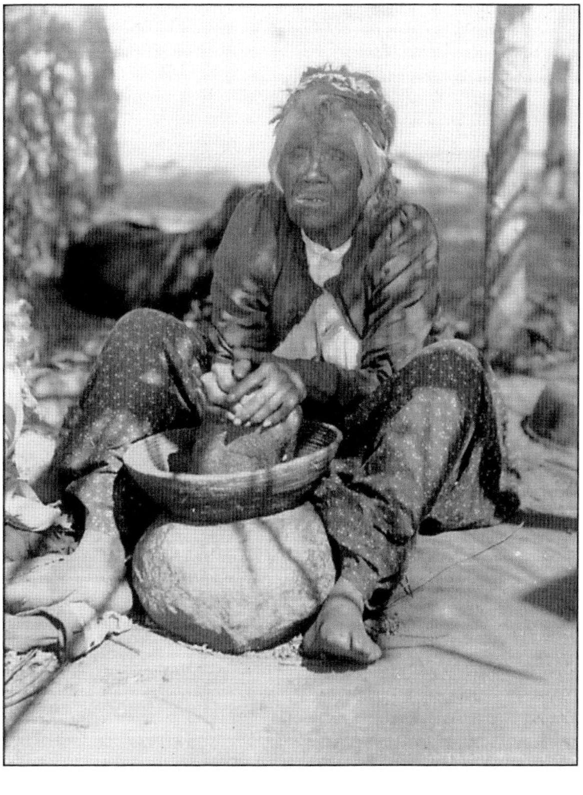

The early inhabitants of the San Gorgonio Pass and Banning area were indigenous peoples who lived quite unaware of the outside world. Here a Native American woman grinds acorns in a stone metate with a basketry hopper. The women's main responsibility was the preparation of the various food products required for survival, while the duty of the men was to hunt and gather food. (Photograh by C. C. Pierce and Company; courtesy of the San Diego Museum of Man.)

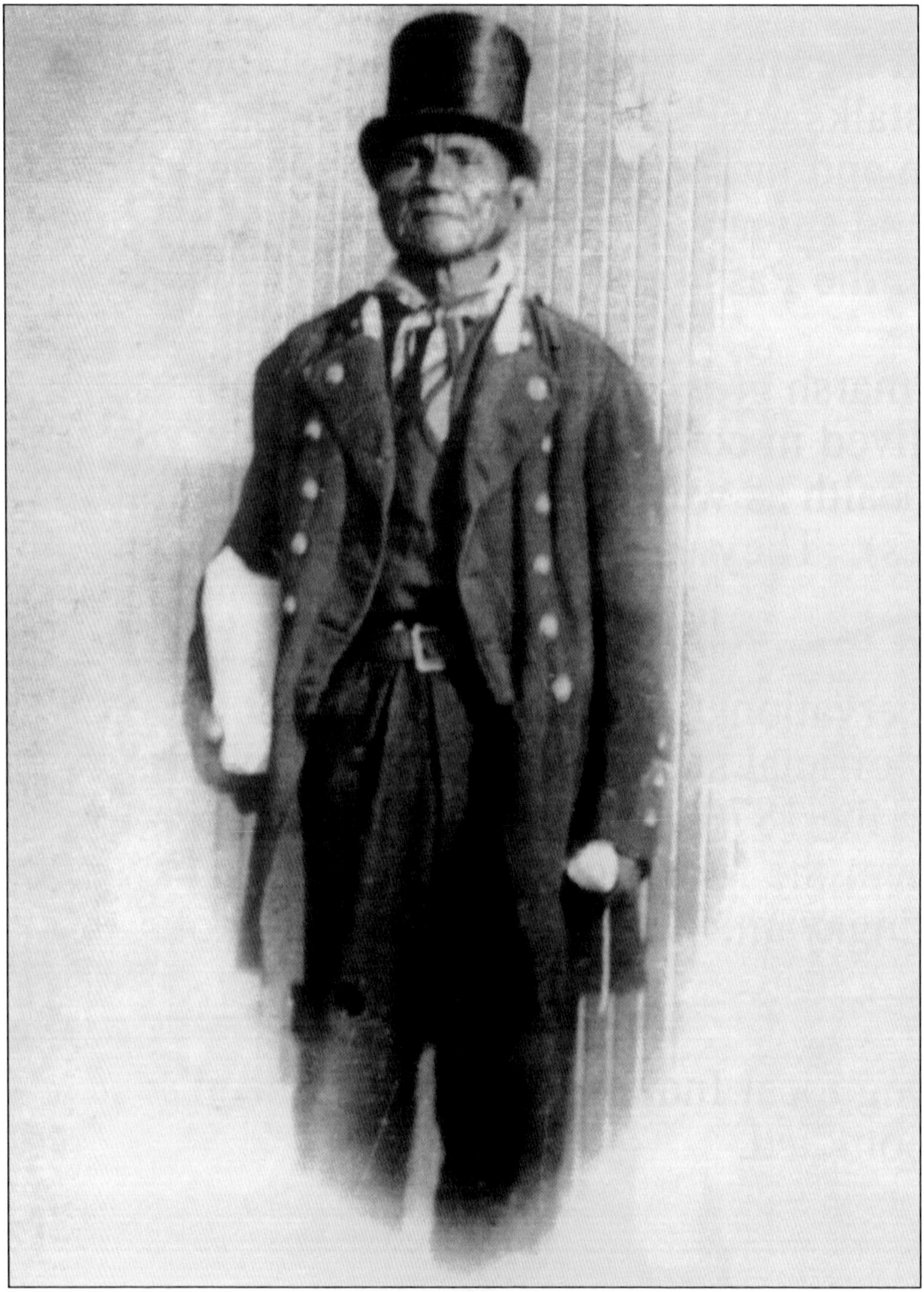

Fig Tree John lived on the edge of the Salton Sink in a hut built from railroad ties. He planted fig trees around his abode, leading to his name. He was well-known in Banning and, on frequent trips, often sat on a bench in front of the Coplin House watching people pass by. He died April 11, 1927, at an age some estimated at being up to 130. He was buried in his regalia-blue army brass-buttoned uniform and high silk hat. (Courtesy of the Banning Unified School District.)

Two

Early Banning Era

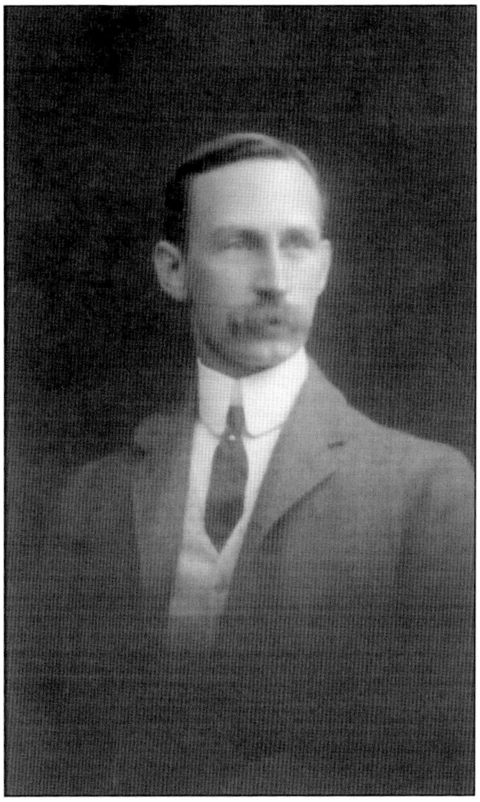

Walter Hathaway was a 44-year resident of Banning, during which time he spent 41 years as a premier merchant. He was born in Milwaukee on January 10, 1861, and was involved in various businesses in Banning, most notably Banning's first lumberyard and Hathaway's Store. He was also Banning's first mayor. Wedded to Sarah Foster, he had no children and died in 1938. (Courtesy of Joan Coombs.)

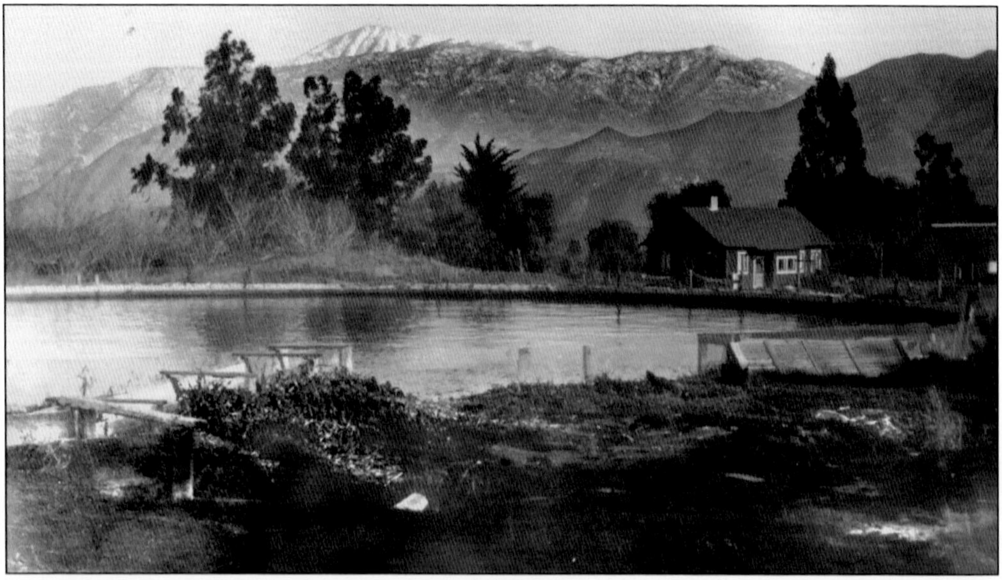

Between 1883 and 1884, the Banning Land and Water Company built two reservoirs beside San Gorgonio Avenue. One was located at the corner of San Gorgonio Avenue and Nicolet Street and the other at the mouth of Water Canyon, pictured here. Both were originally fed water by a water flume, but when the wooden flume blew down in a strong wind, a rock ditch was built along San Gorgonio Avenue between the two reservoirs. (Courtesy of Joan Coombs.)

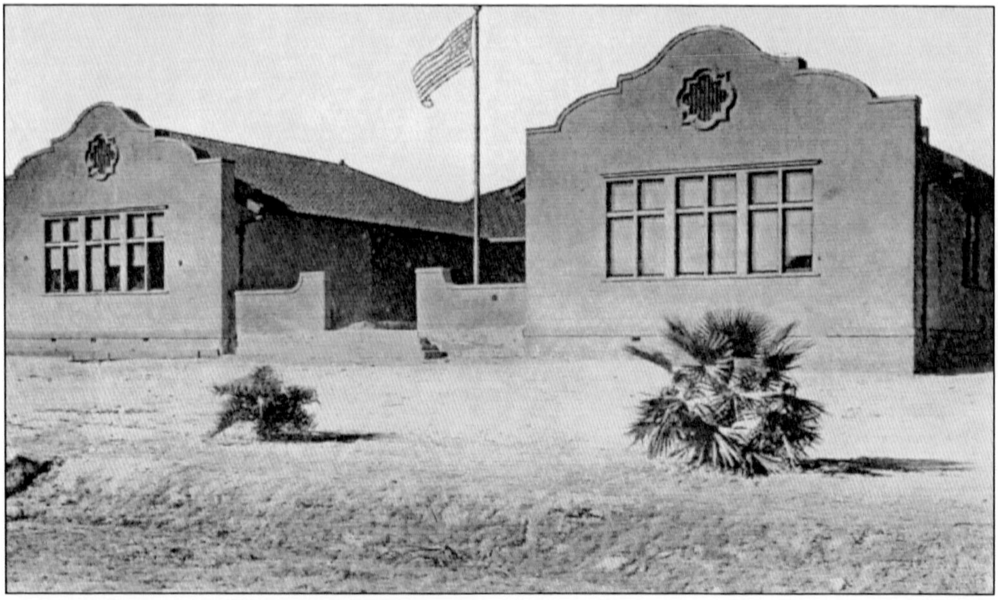

This is how Banning High School appeared in the early years. Prior to its construction, classes were held in a two-story, vine-covered school on north San Gorgonio Avenue that was eventually demolished because it was unsafe. Note the absence of landscaping, which might indicate that the school was relatively new. (Courtesy of the San Gorgonio Pass Historical Society.)

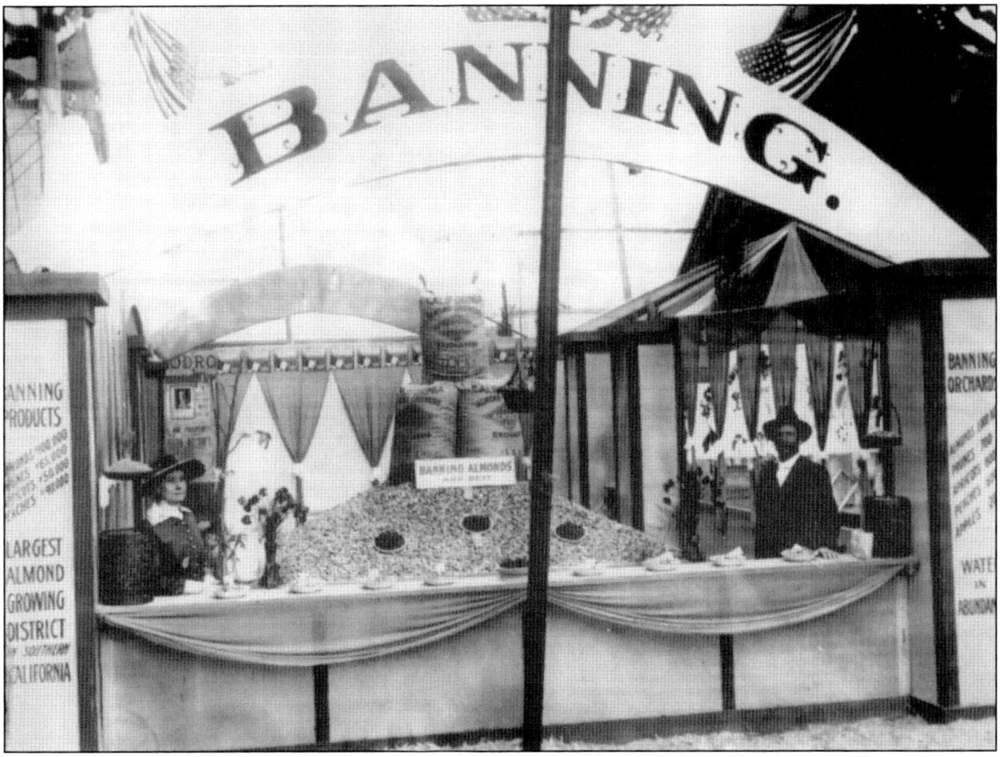

Mr. and Mrs. French Gilman attend the Riverside County Fair about 1910. The display is centered on almonds, with the Blue Diamond logo plainly visible. Banning is advertised on the left as the largest almond-growing district in Southern California, with yearly almond sales of $180,000. On the right, various Banning orchards are mentioned, as well as an abundance of water. (Courtesy of the Banning Unified School District.)

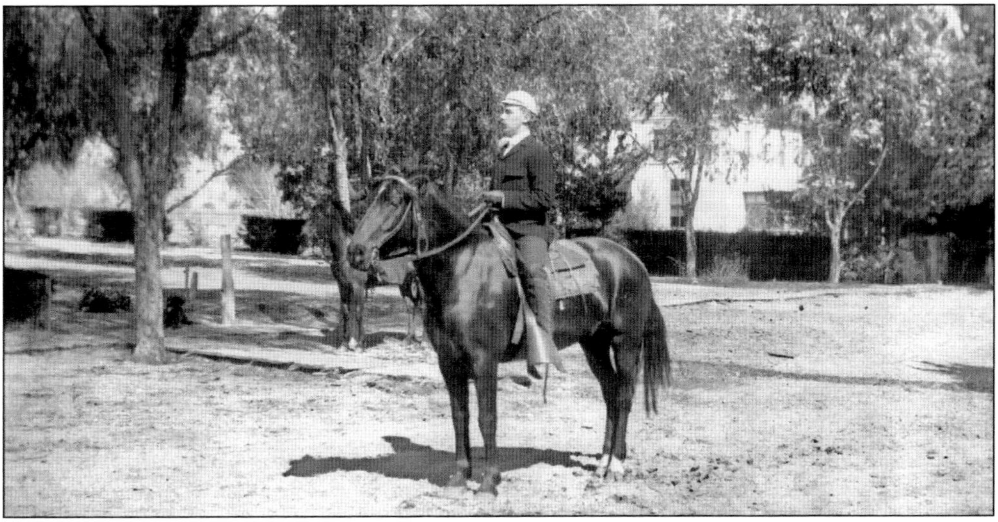

In this early 1890s scene, Banning resident Edward Kant sits on his horse with the Banning Hotel in the background. This was before the era of the automobile, when the streets were not as well defined. In fact, they were usually no more than wide spaces between many of the buildings, and horses and buggies were the chief modes of transportation. (Courtesy of Joan Coombs.)

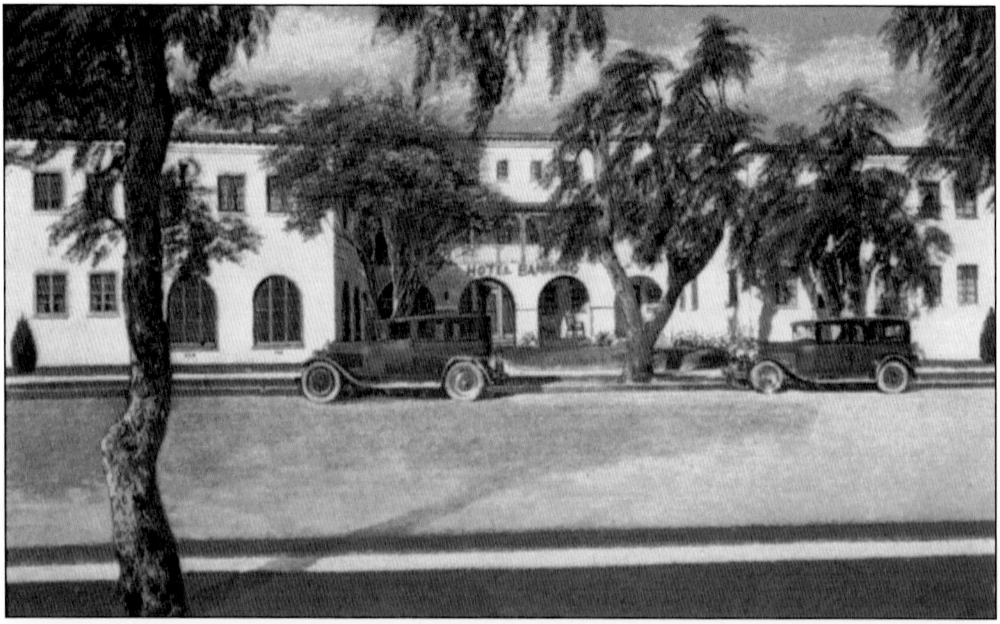

The Hotel Banning was originally described as the New Hotel Banning to differentiate it from another hotel in Banning at that time named The Banning. During this era, it was advertised as "Directly on the highway between the east and west coasts. A real home for the traveler on the desert's edge, beautifully furnished rooms and an excellent cafe, moderate prices, you will be surprised." (Courtesy of the author.)

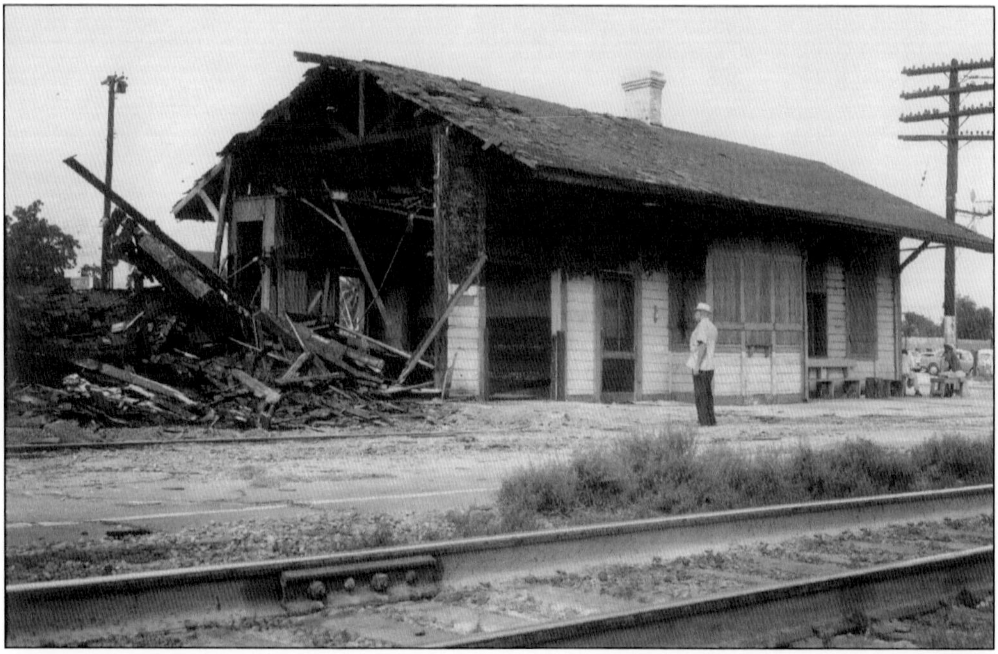

The Banning train station was a great landmark for the town until it was extensively damaged by fire in 1963 and the remaining portion subsequently demolished. Today the only remembrance is a beautiful mural depicting the original train station painted on the side of a building near its original site. (Courtesy of San Gorgonio Pass Historical Society.)

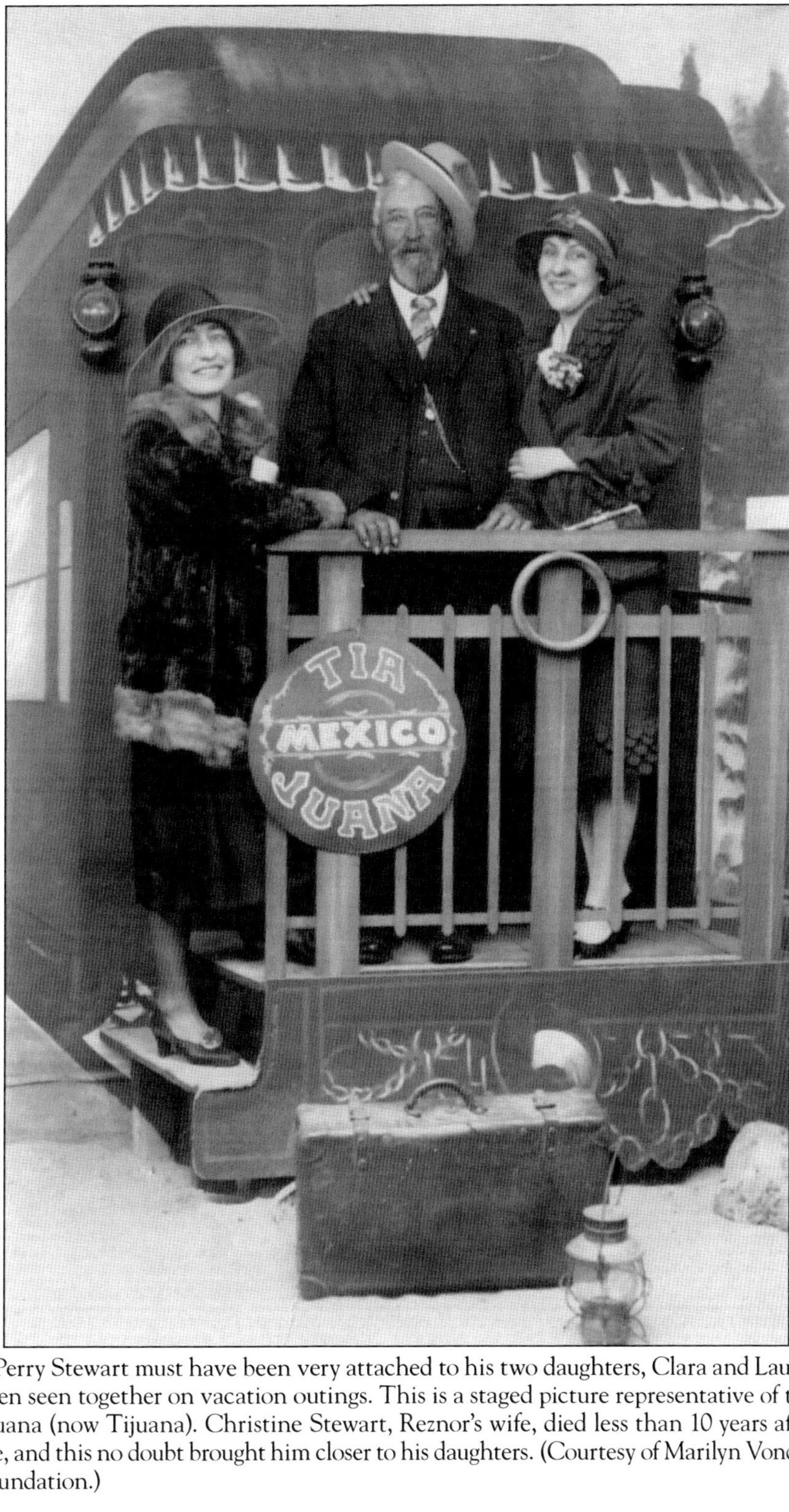

Reznor Perry Stewart must have been very attached to his two daughters, Clara and Laura. They were often seen together on vacation outings. This is a staged picture representative of their trip to Tia Juana (now Tijuana). Christine Stewart, Reznor's wife, died less than 10 years after their marriage, and this no doubt brought him closer to his daughters. (Courtesy of Marilyn Vonderheide, LMS Foundation.)

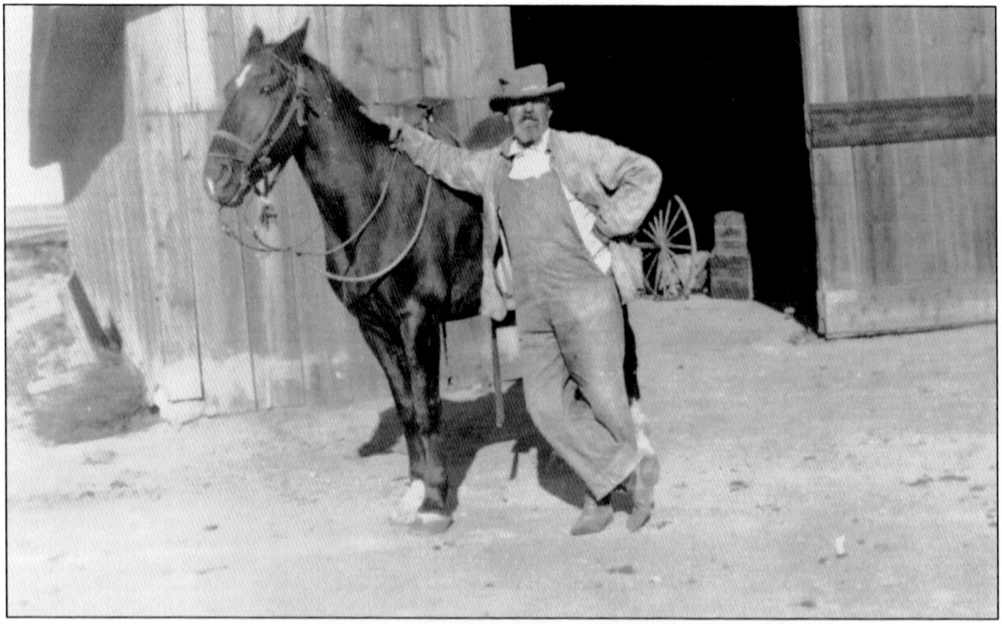

Reznor Perry Stewart owned and operated one of Banning's largest farms. Behind him is the barn he built sometime after he arrived from Yolo County. In August 1883, he took up a homestead south of Banning and today's Interstate 10, extending a number of miles west. He previously farmed on the bench above Banning. He was a hard-working farmer and became quite successful with his venture. (Courtesy of Marilyn Vonderheide, LMS Foundation.)

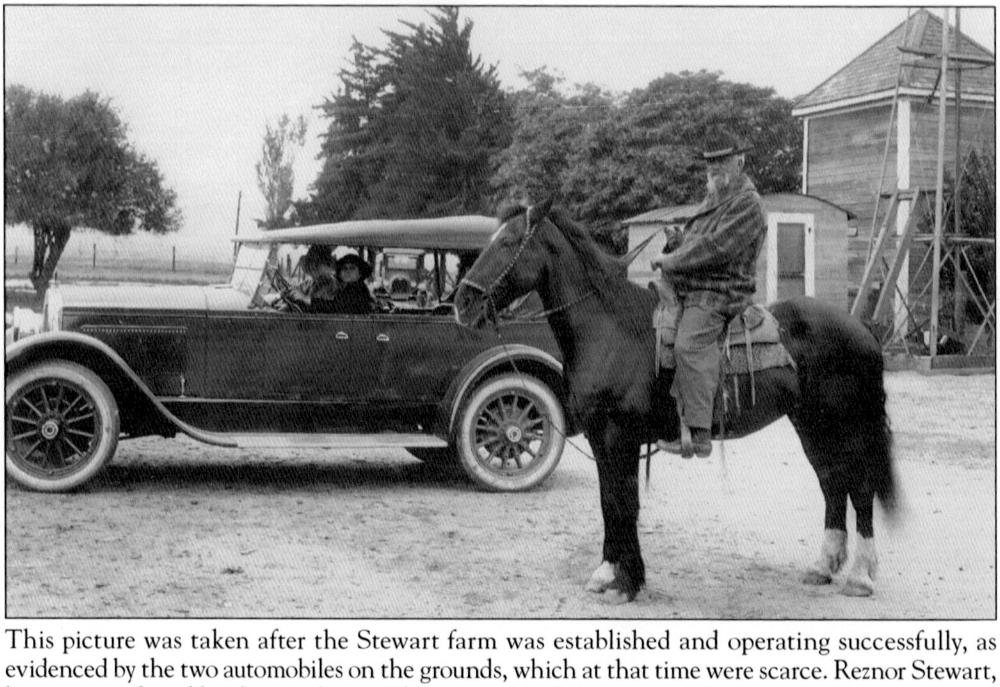

This picture was taken after the Stewart farm was established and operating successfully, as evidenced by the two automobiles on the grounds, which at that time were scarce. Reznor Stewart, however, preferred his favorite horse. The original little homestead that he had taken up in 1883 blossomed when he accumulated over 2,00 acres by buying from the railroad. (Courtesy of Marilyn Vonderheide, LMS Foundation.)

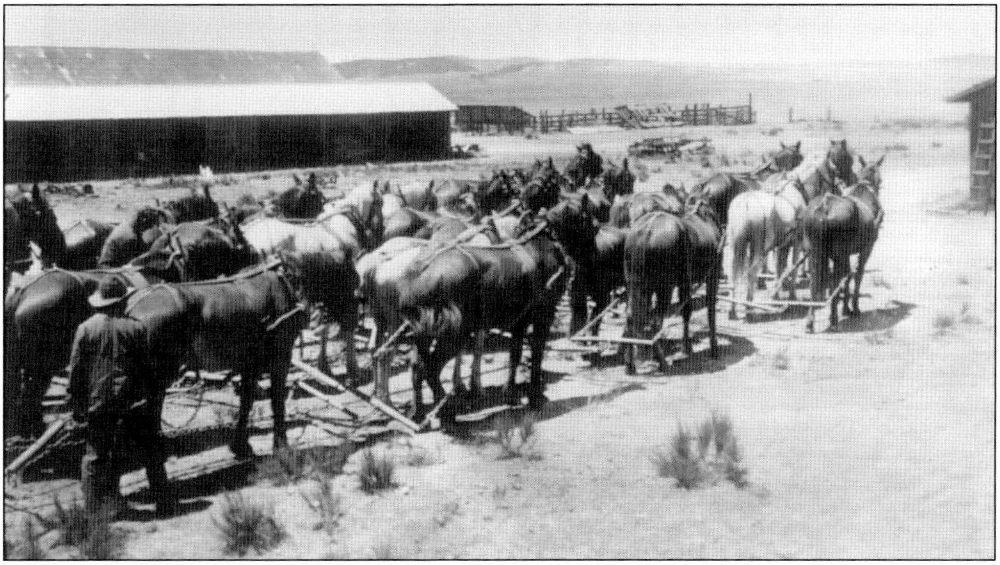

These horse teams are harnessed and ready for work in the field. There was always a rush to get the ground prepared and seeded before the rains came, for this was dry farming. A number of teams were sent out at once and were able to prepare many acres per day. (Courtesy of Marilyn Vonderheide, LMS Foundation.)

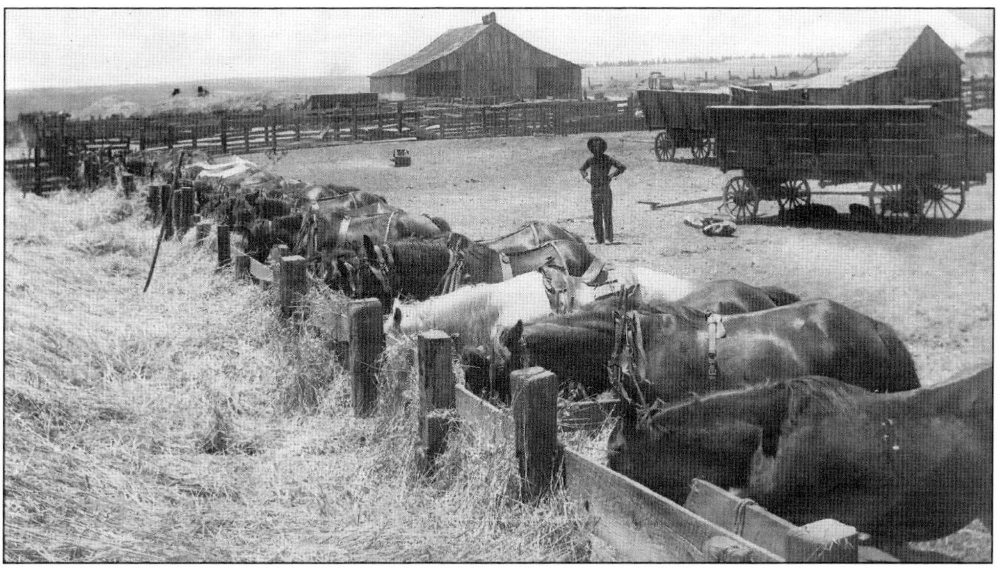

Reznor Stewart brought these two carloads of horses down from Yolo County, California. The large barn in the background was built south of the J. C. Penney store site on the northeast corner of Ramsey and Second Streets in Banning shortly after Reznor took up homesteading there. It did not take him long to set his hand to the plow and begin to develop this farm. (Courtesy of Marilyn Vonderheide, LMS Foundation.)

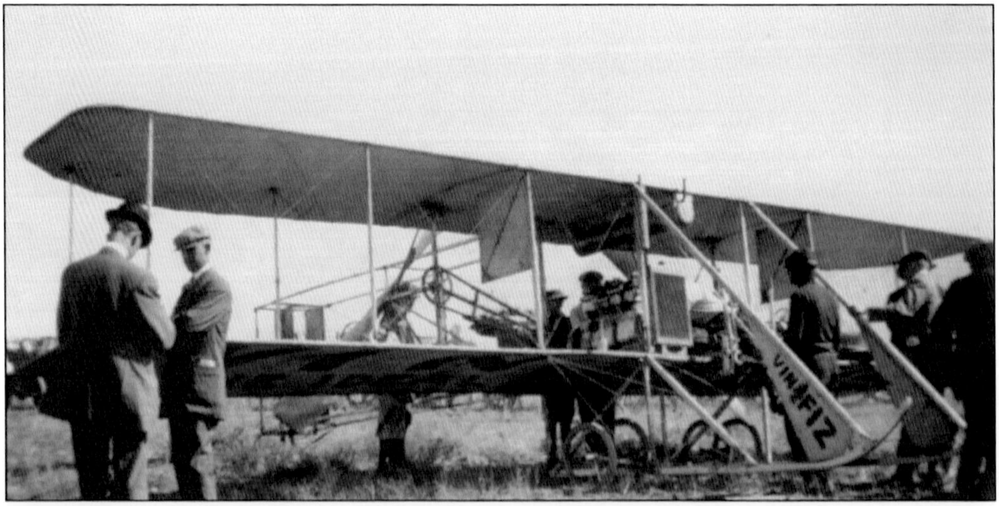

Pilot Calbraith Rogers's plane, an improved Wright Brothers Model B, is pictured here shortly after it was removed from the field on Stewart's ranch, where it landed for repair. Rogers's plane is also shown below after it was forced to land due to engine problems. It has been reported that Rogers received $5 for every mile traveled on his flight from New York for his endorsement of the popular drink Vin Fez. The other incentive for undertaking the adventure was $50,000 in prize money offered by William Randolph Hearst to anyone who could fly across the continent in less than 30 days. Rogers plane can now be seen in the Smithsonian Air and Space Museum in Washington, D.C. (Courtesy of Marilyn Vonderheide, LMS Foundation.)

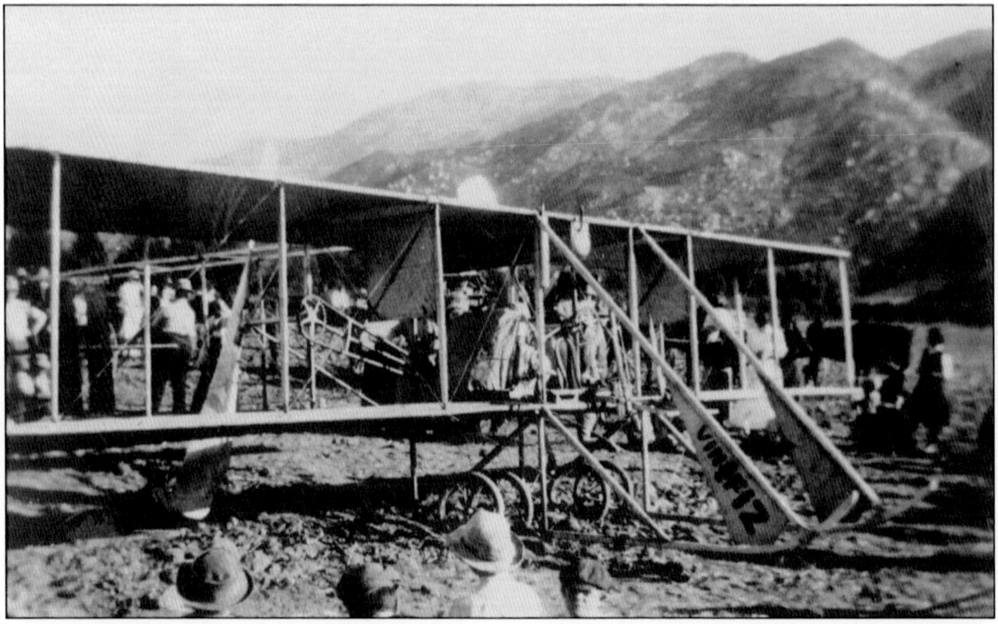

Rogers, who flew from the East Coast, was one of two aviators who were competing for Hearst's prize money. The other was Robert Fowler, who flew a similar plane from the West Coast. They both landed in Banning in 1911, about two weeks apart and on the same ranch. Fowler landed first. Rogers exceeded the time limit after leaving Long Island and making numerous stops along the way. Vin Fiz, a popular grape drink, was advertised in large letters on the airplane's bottom wings. (Courtesy of Marilyn Vonderheide, LMS Foundation.)

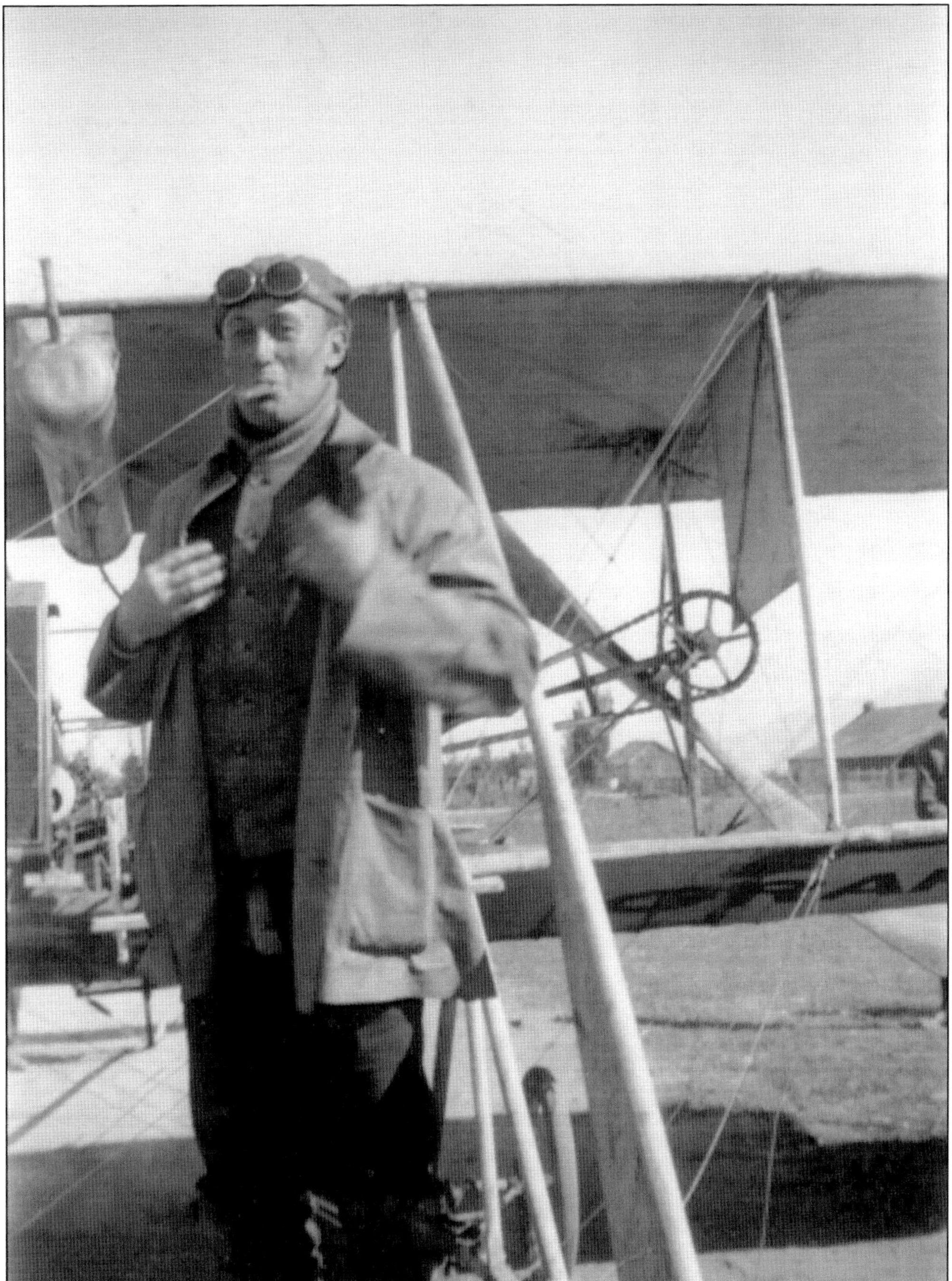

Robert Fowler poses in front of his Model B Wright Brothers plane at the Stewart ranch. By the expression on his face, it appears that the plane has been repaired, and he is ready to continue his flight. During his several days stay at the ranch, he became good friends with the Stewart family, as is evidenced by his cordial writings to the Stewart sisters after he reached El Paso, Texas. Like Rogers, he did not make the transcontinental flight in 30 days and therefore did not receive the prize money. (Courtesy of Marilyn Vonderheide, LMS Foundation.)

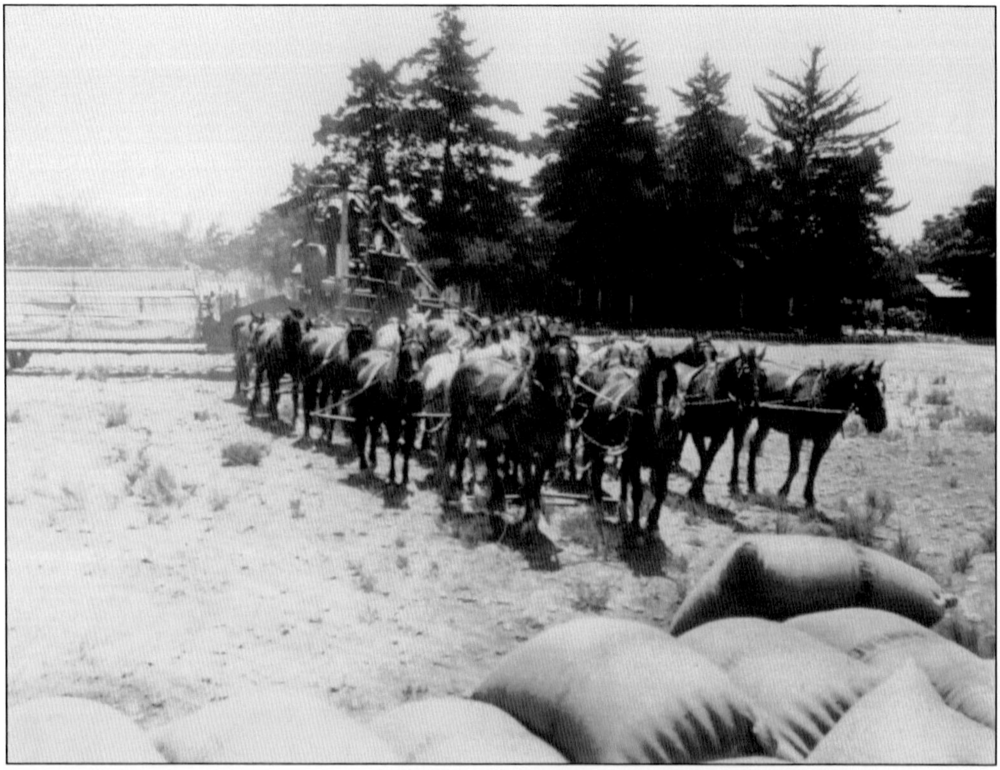

A load of sacked barley grain is brought back to the Stewart barn followed by the cutting machine being pulled by a 20-horse team. The day's work was not over yet; the horses all had to be unhitched, fed and watered, and put up for the night. Harvest time was long and tedious, but barley farming during this time was very lucrative. (Courtesy of Marilyn Vonderheide, LMS Foundation.)

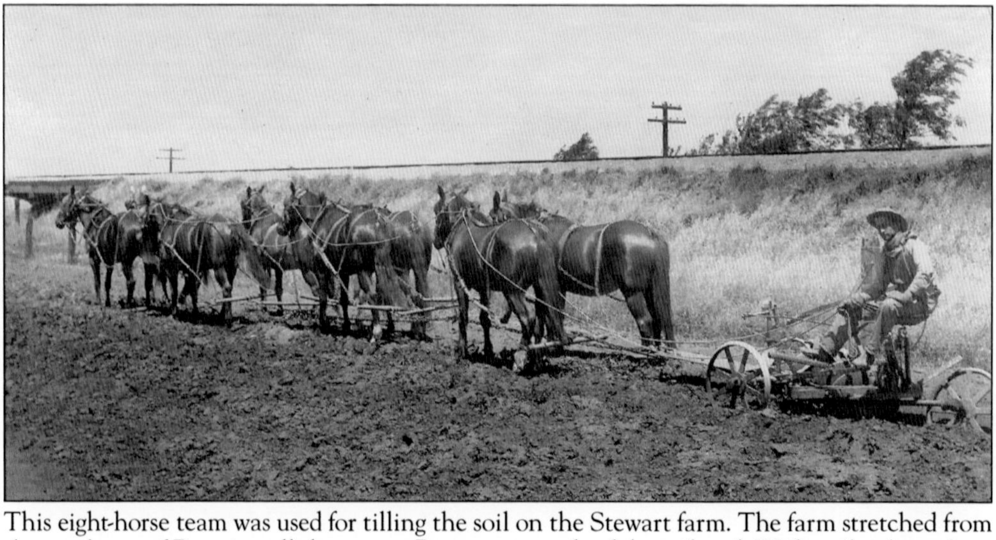

This eight-horse team was used for tilling the soil on the Stewart farm. The farm stretched from the southeast of Banning all the way to Beaumont south of the railroad. With such a large farm to tend, the teams were kept quite active preparing the ground for the next crop. Barley was a desired commodity and one that was grown almost exclusively. (Courtesy of Marilyn Vonderheide, LMS Foundation.)

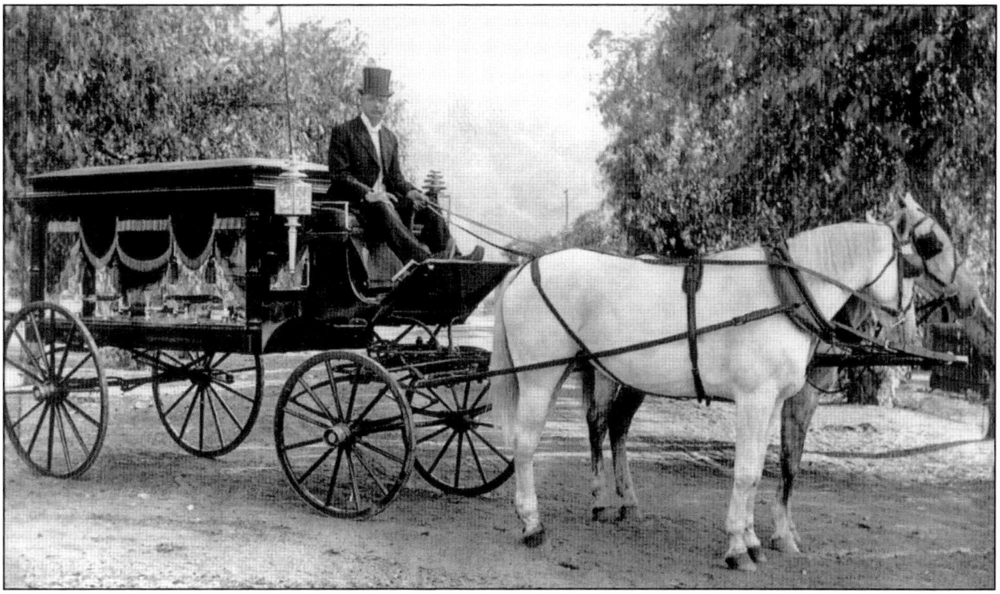

Undertaker Frank J. Wiefels, wearing a top hat, drives his wagon hearse. He was born on January 15, 1860, in Krefeld, Germany, and served in the Philippines in the hospital corps during the Spanish-American War. In 1908, he opened the first and, for years, the only undertaking parlor in the San Gorgonio Pass in Banning. Initially he did his own embalming. (Courtesy of Michael Wiefels.)

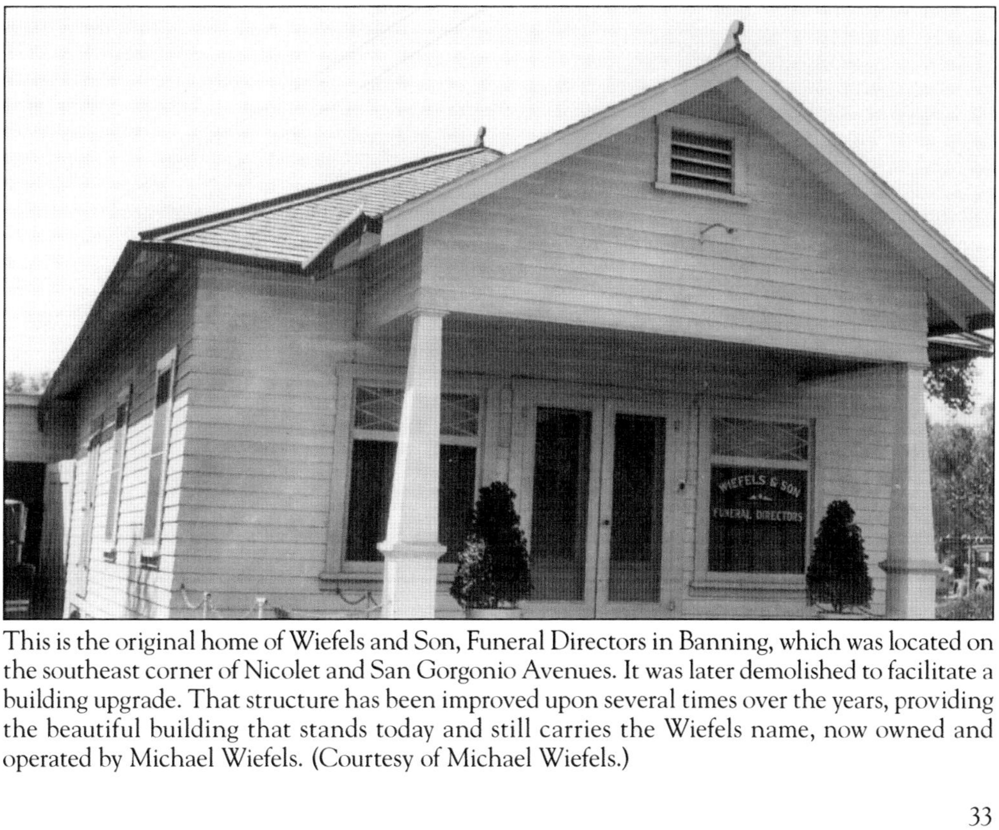

This is the original home of Wiefels and Son, Funeral Directors in Banning, which was located on the southeast corner of Nicolet and San Gorgonio Avenues. It was later demolished to facilitate a building upgrade. That structure has been improved upon several times over the years, providing the beautiful building that stands today and still carries the Wiefels name, now owned and operated by Michael Wiefels. (Courtesy of Michael Wiefels.)

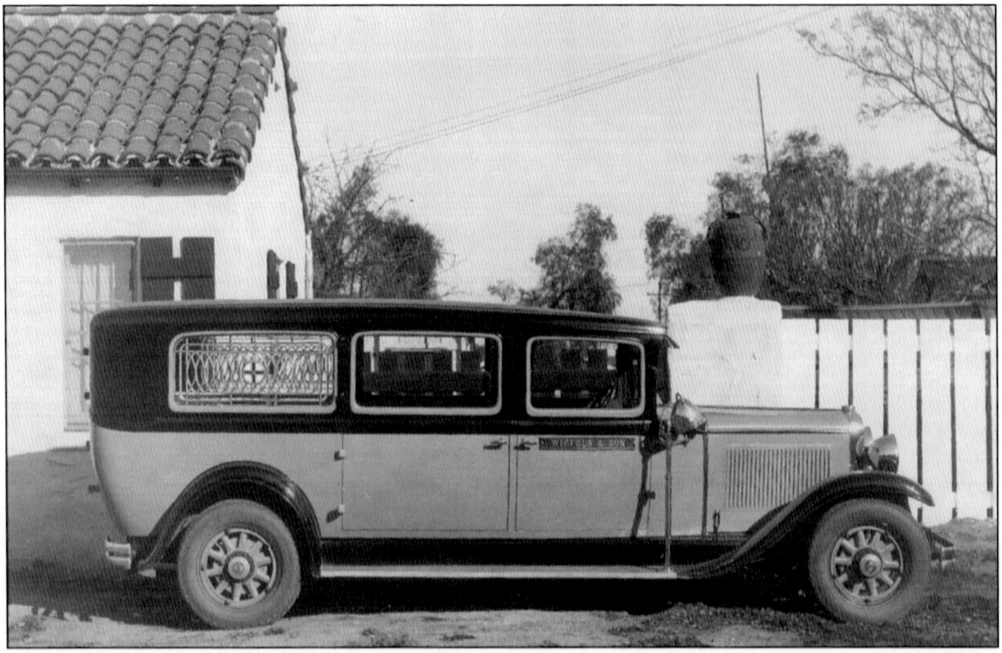

This beautiful vintage hearse once served the Wiefels and Son Memorial Chapel on the southeast corner of Nicolet and San Gorgonio Avenues. A vehicle of showroom quality with wood-spoke wheels, two-tone paint, and a side-mounted floodlight on the running board, it was no doubt an acquisition that the Wiefels offered with pride to their clientele. (Courtesy of Michael Wiefels.)

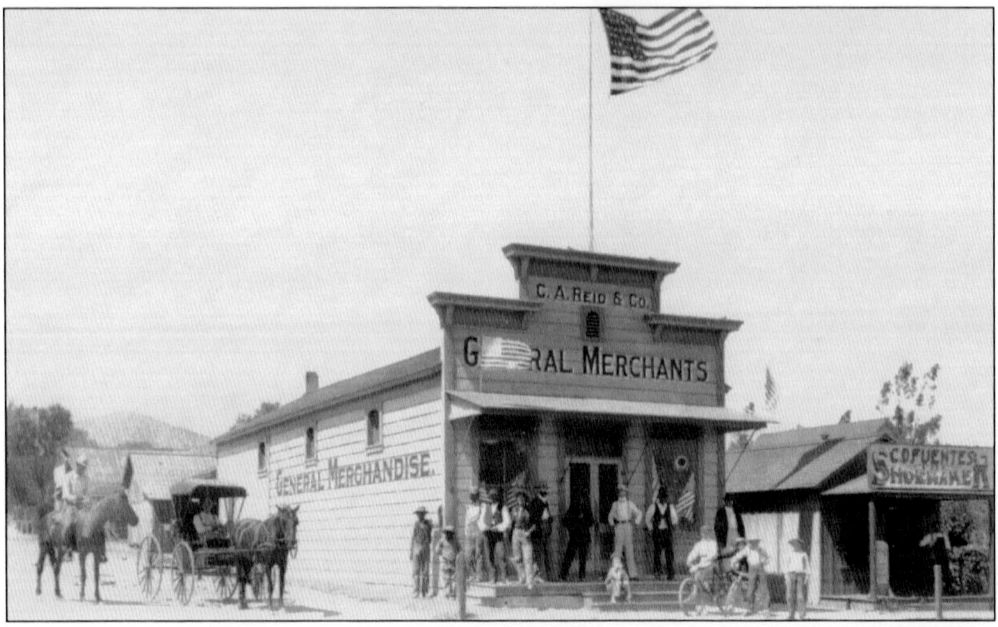

The U.S. flag proudly waves atop the C. A. Reid and Company General Merchandise store on the northeast corner of San Gorgonio Avenue and Livingston Street in the late 1800s. Soon after coming to Banning, Reid went to work in Hathaway and Company's store, eventually becoming sole owner and later moving into what became known as the Reid Building, which still stands today. Note C. D. Fuentes's shoe shop next door. (Courtesy of Steve Lech.)

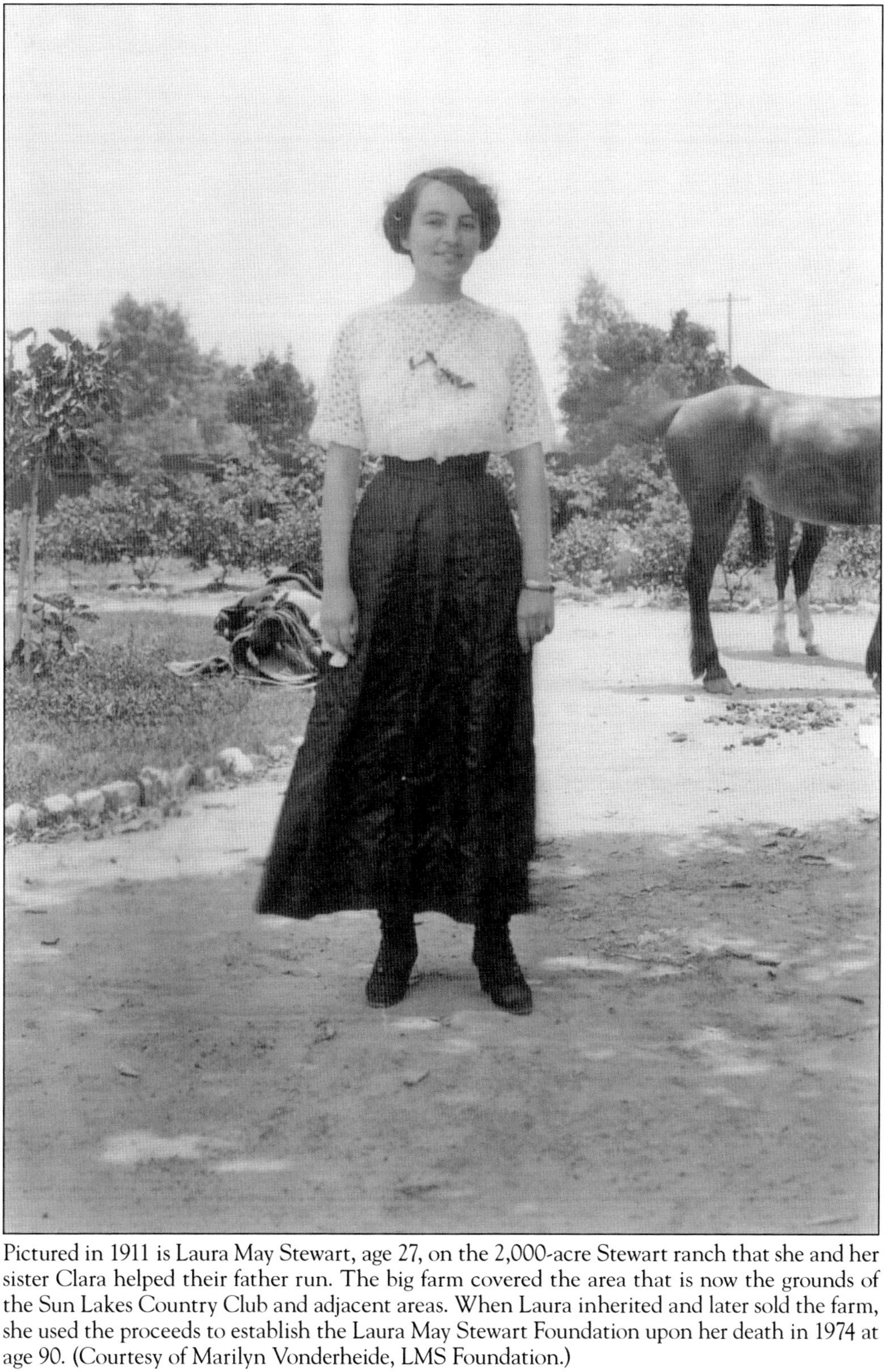

Pictured in 1911 is Laura May Stewart, age 27, on the 2,000-acre Stewart ranch that she and her sister Clara helped their father run. The big farm covered the area that is now the grounds of the Sun Lakes Country Club and adjacent areas. When Laura inherited and later sold the farm, she used the proceeds to establish the Laura May Stewart Foundation upon her death in 1974 at age 90. (Courtesy of Marilyn Vonderheide, LMS Foundation.)

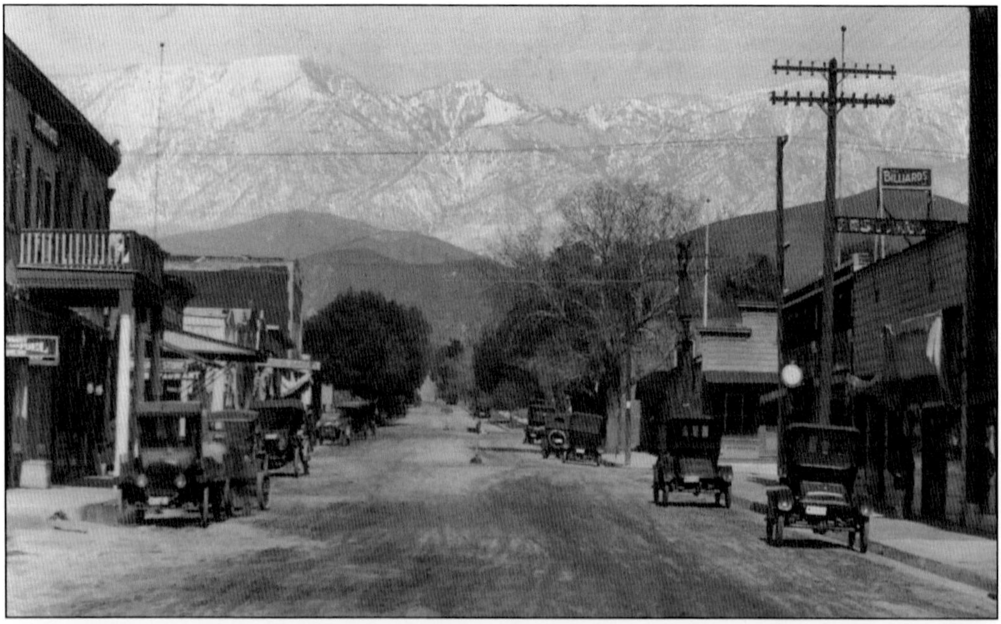

This old Banning street scene looks up San Gorgonio Avenue north of today's Interstate 10, which runs from east to west. The old Alta Vista Hotel south of here was demolished because of the freeway. The second building to the north and at the right of the picture was later known as the C. A. Reid Building, facing Livingston Street and extant today. (Courtesy of the San Gorgonio Pass Historical Society.)

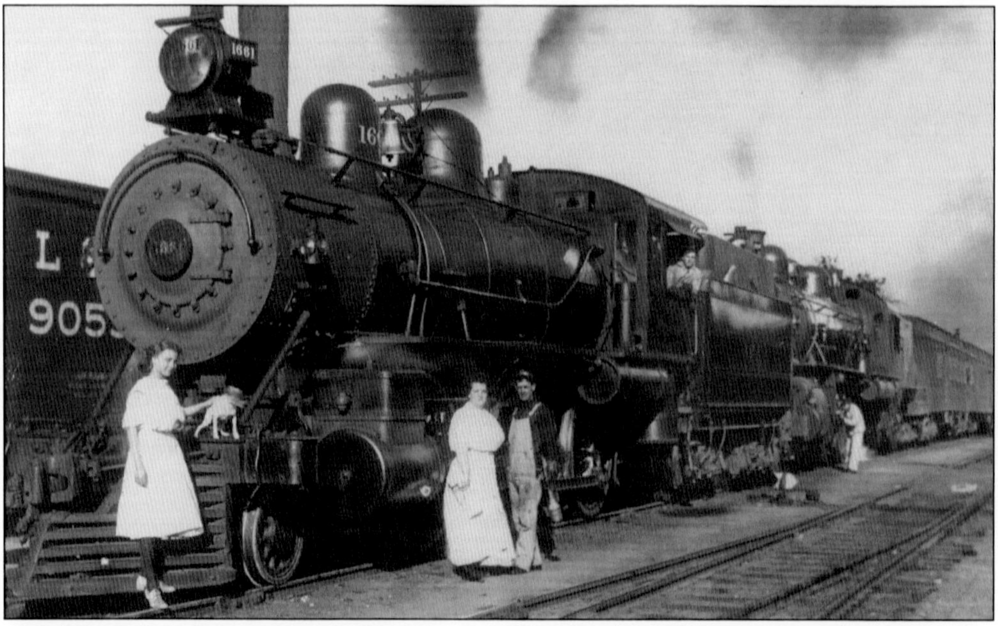

Train No. 1661 makes a stop at the Banning station. Several people have taken advantage of the stop to pose beside the big locomotive for a photograph. The train roared through the pass, often making its route from east to west, and was relied upon by many San Gorgonio Pass citizens of Banning and Beaumont for travel to select vacation destinations. Note the engineer, who is also aware of the photograph being taken. (Courtesy of Nara Haskell.)

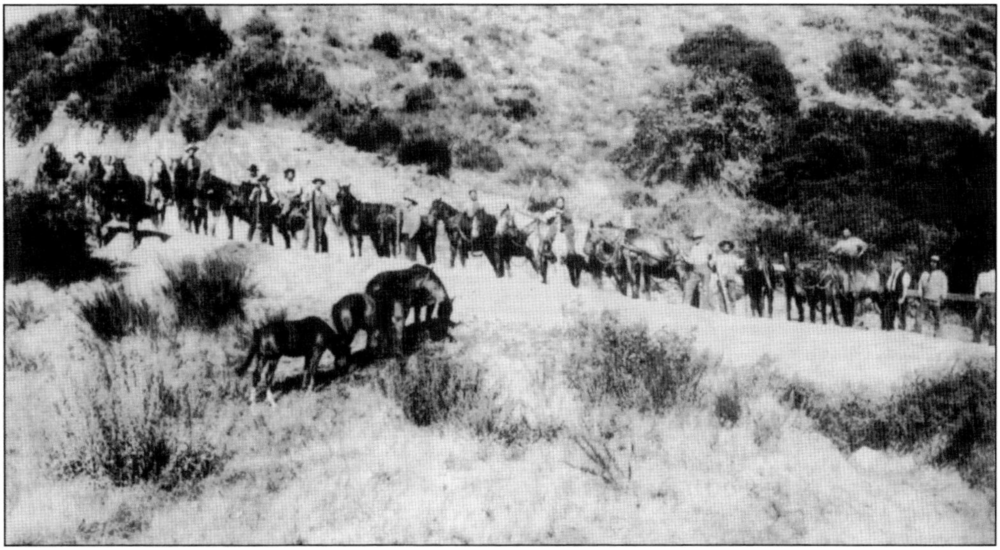

This lineup of reapers has their scythes sharpened and ready to harvest the grain from nearby barley fields. Before the introduction of mechanized equipment, barley was harvested by this method. It was tedious work and required numerous laborers to perform. Additionally, much time was spent getting horses and equipment ready and sharpening tools before the field was ever reached. (Courtesy of the Banning Unified School District.)

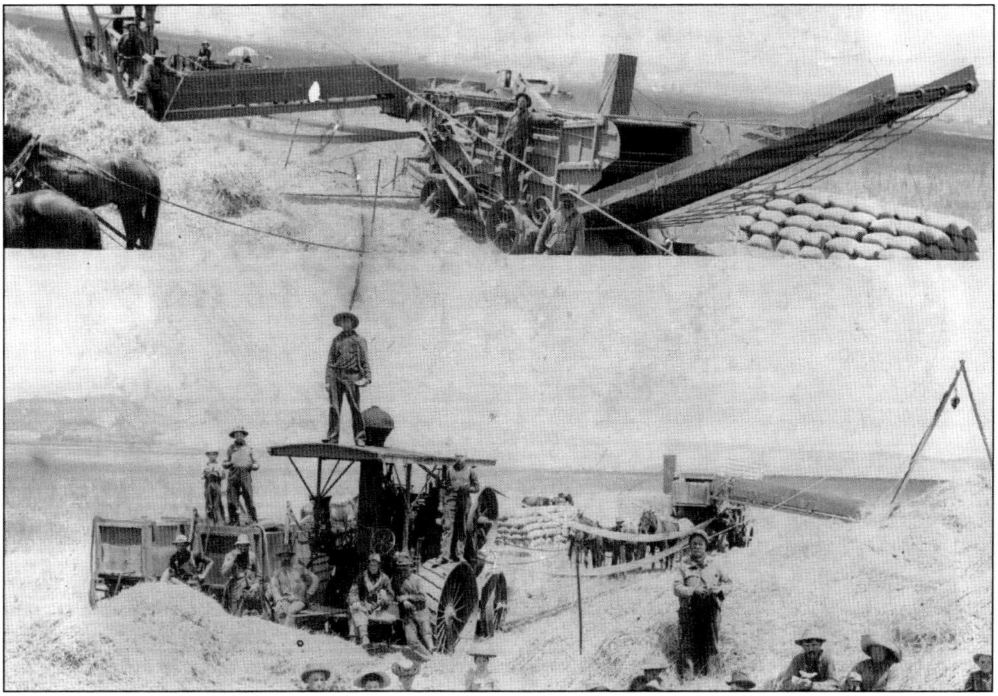

This composite picture has been put together to show the complex belt system required for the threshing operation. In the upper picture, the long belt leading from the threshing machine is feeding other small belt systems that operate the overall process of threshing. Viewing this setup may perhaps explain why it was so toilsome to move the equipment too often. (Courtesy of Marilyn Vonderheide, LMS Foundation.)

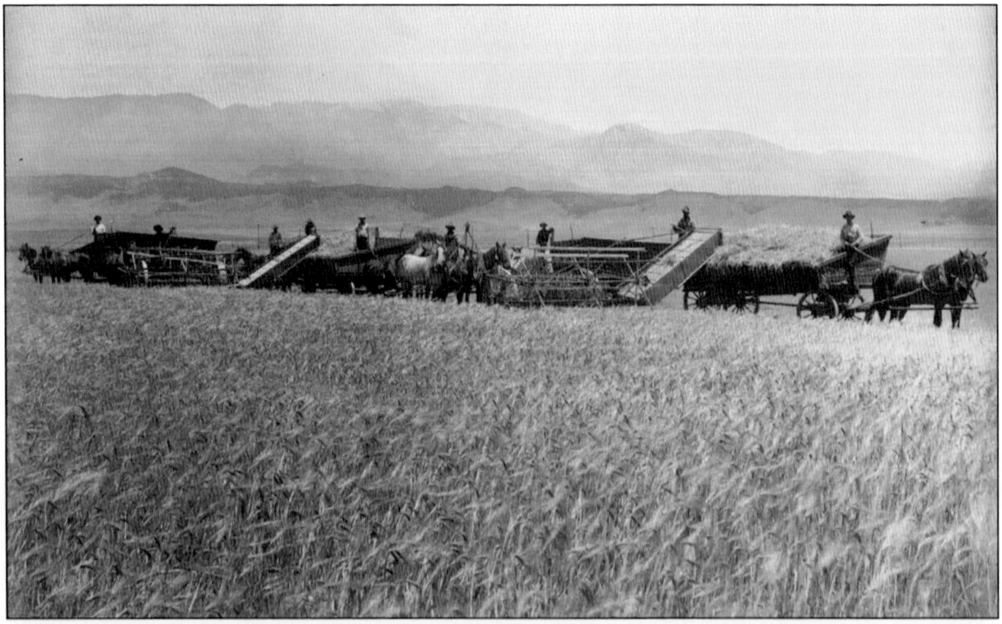

This excellent stand of barley on the Stewart ranch is being cut and loaded onto carts to be taken to the threshing machine. The threshing machine and outfit were not moved too often because of the great effort in doing so. Therefore, when each cart was loaded with barley straw and grain, it was then hauled some distance to the threshing area, though this also required much effort. (Courtesy of Marilyn Vonderheide, LMS Foundation.)

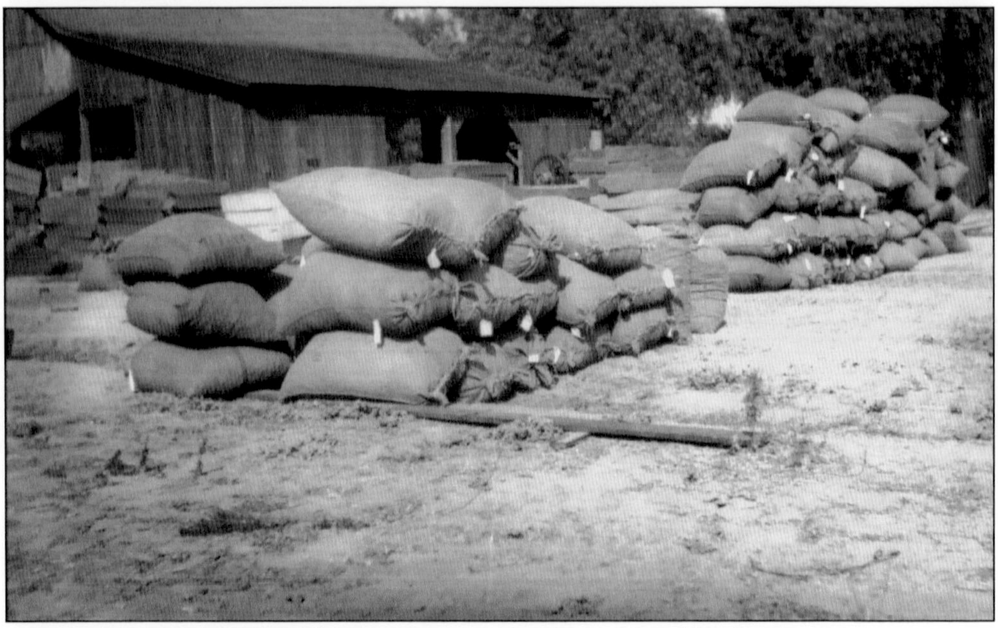

During the years that almonds were grown in Banning, scenes like this were quite common. This almond huller and dry yard at Livingston and Third Streets is surrounded by numerous large sacks of almonds, tagged and ready for shipment by train to various parts of the country. Workers were kept extremely busy during the almond harvest and processing season in Banning. (Courtesy of Joan Coombs.)

Dr. King was one of Banning's early pioneers. Born February 9, 1853, in Pittsburgh, Pennsylvania, he arrived in Banning in the latter part of September 1883. Before he came west, he was led to believe that he would not live more than six months or a year because, after 10 years of practicing medicine, he had contracted tuberculosis. In fact, he lived much longer and was instrumental in founding the Banning Hospital and Sanatorium. (Courtesy of Tom Hughes.)

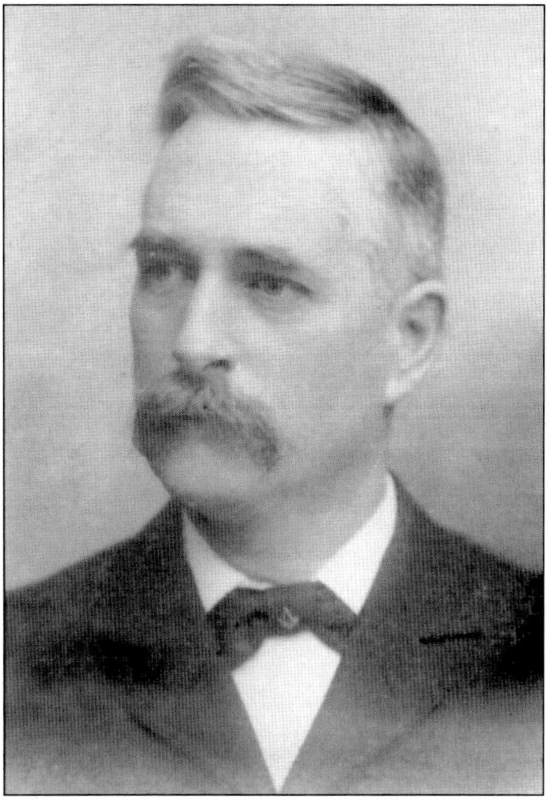

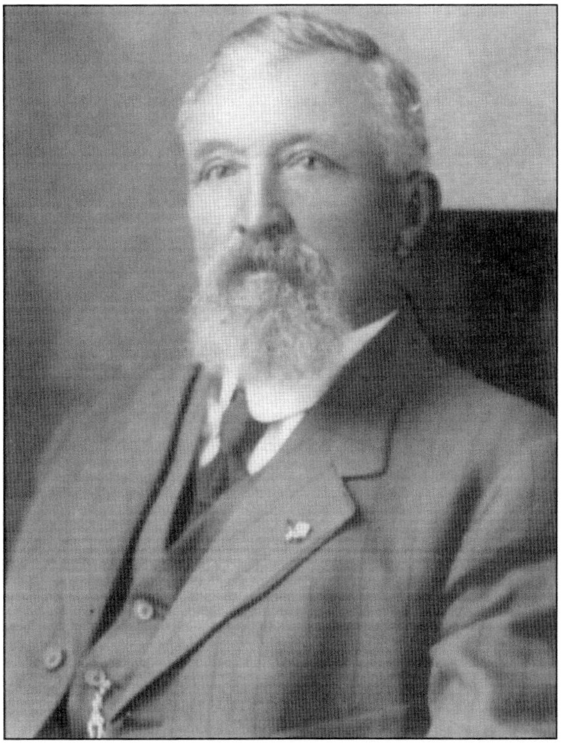

Reznor Perry Stewart came to Banning in 1878 when it was little more than a name. On December 30, 1880, in San Bernardino, he wedded Mary Christian, stepdaughter of C. F. Jost. Three boys and two girls were born to them—all in Banning. Mary Stewart died August 30, 1890, and Reznor Stewart on November 12, 1933, at the age of 88. (Courtesy of Tom Hughes.)

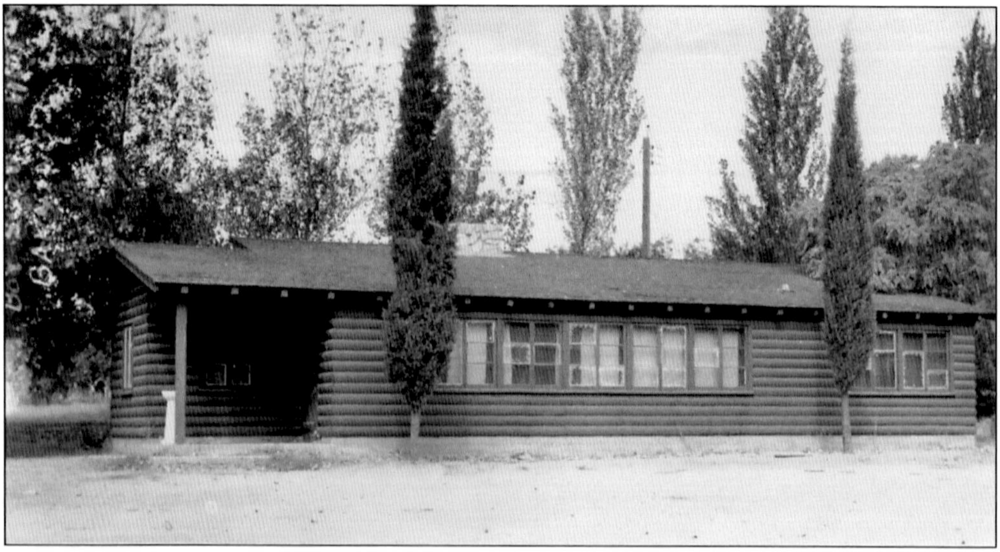

This early boy scout hall in Banning still stands. On October 4, 1920, the Riverside County Boy Scouts was organized. Throughout the years, several different boy scout troops were established, including ones for Mexicans and Native American boys from the Morongo Reservation. Sea Scout Troop 102 maintained a 24-foot whale boat and a 15-foot sailboat at Salton Sea. (Courtesy of Steve Lech.)

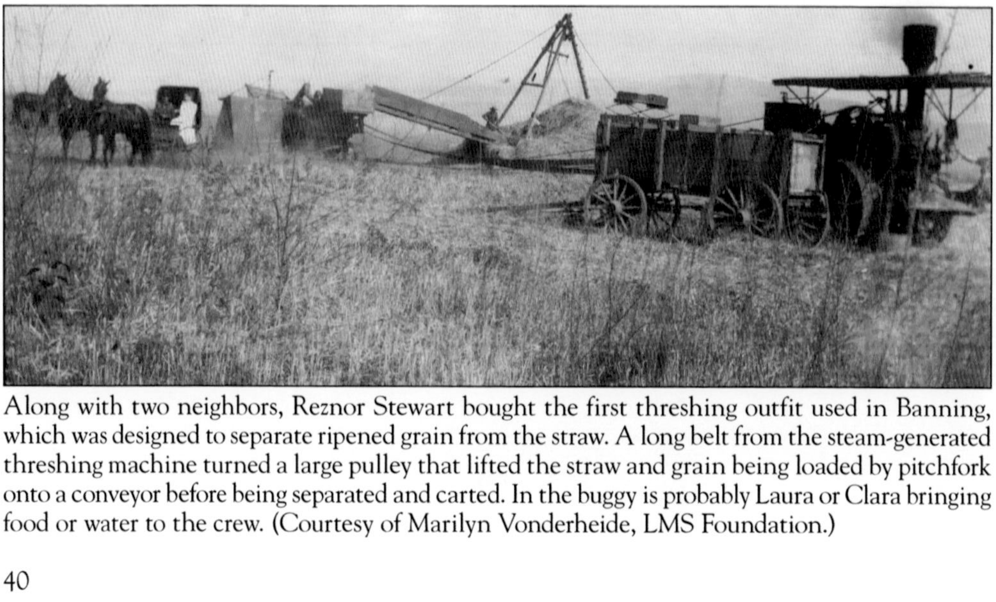

Along with two neighbors, Reznor Stewart bought the first threshing outfit used in Banning, which was designed to separate ripened grain from the straw. A long belt from the steam-generated threshing machine turned a large pulley that lifted the straw and grain being loaded by pitchfork onto a conveyor before being separated and carted. In the buggy is probably Laura or Clara bringing food or water to the crew. (Courtesy of Marilyn Vonderheide, LMS Foundation.)

On July 16, 1892, the Methodist Episcopal church was incorporated. A brick foundation was started in September on San Gorgonio Avenue north of Ramsey Street. The first service in the new Methodist church building was held on November 20, 1892. Prior to this time, the Banning congregation met at the Union church and in the town hall. The Methodist church is pictured here in 1903. (Courtesy of Joan Coombs.)

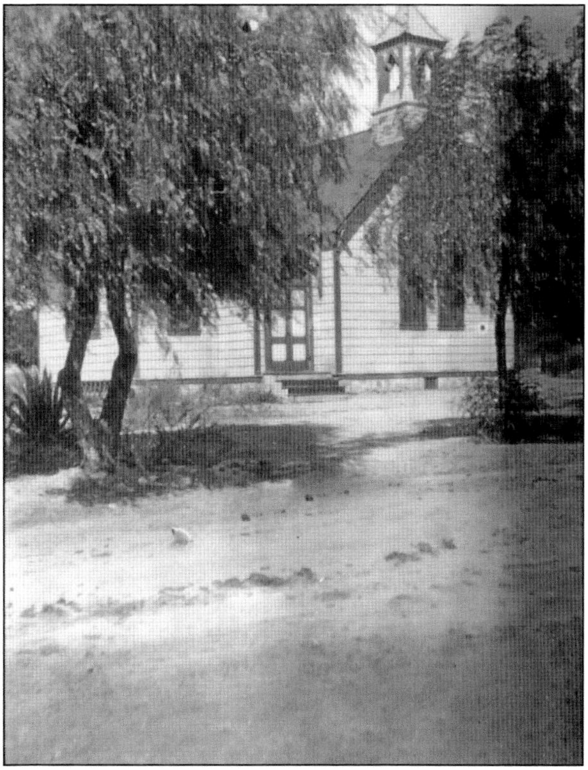

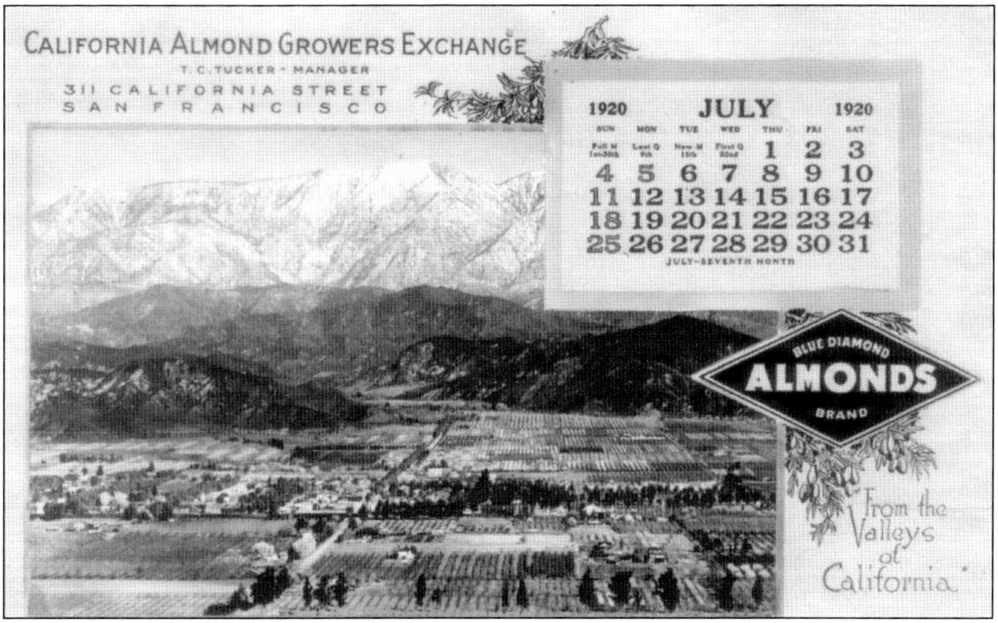

In the 1920s, almond growing reached it peak in Banning. The town's invested share of the state's total $30 million was $70,000. It was estimated at this time that there were over a thousand acres planted in almonds. Many growers were members of the California Almond Growers Exchange, a cooperative organization begun in 1910. Shown here is the Blue Diamond almonds brand logo, which originated in Banning. (Courtesy of Joan Coombs.)

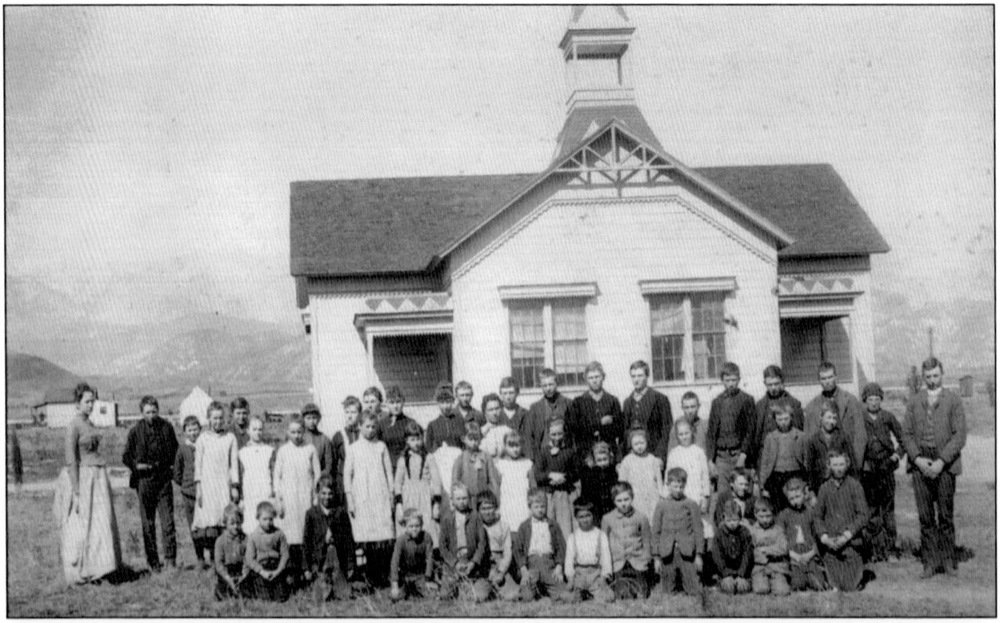

This two-room school was built in 1885 at the Murray Street wash and was therefore named the Murray School. This pretentious structure was financed by the first bonds issued by the San Gorgonio district. C. O. Barker opened the school on September 7, with six girls and six boys. The two-room school, to which another room was added later for a kindergarten, served the needs of Banning children for 18 years. (Courtesy of Joan Coombs.)

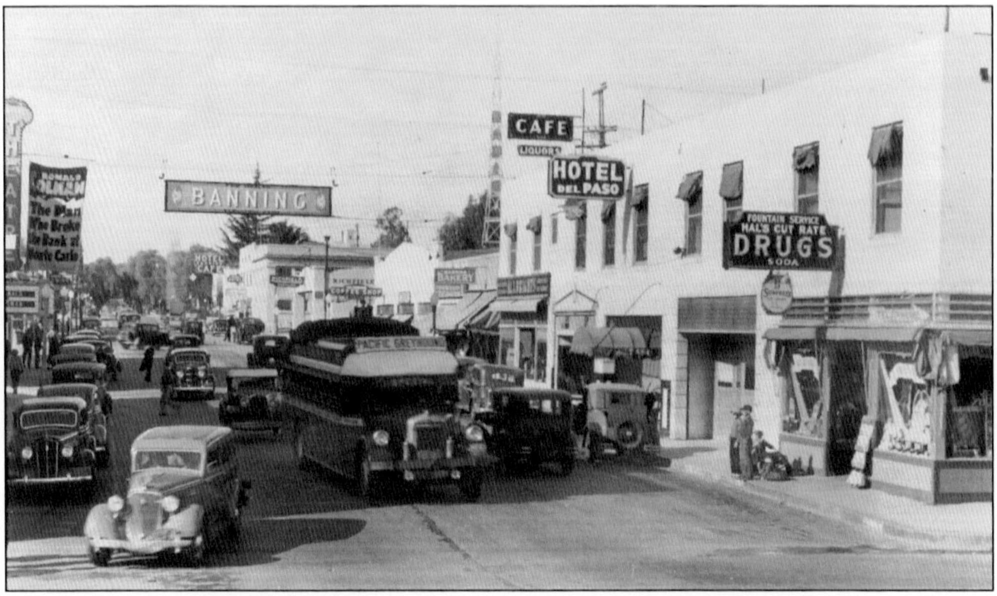

Based upon the vintage of some of the cars, this photograph was probably taken in the mid-1930s. It is interesting to note a number of features in this picture, especially the old Pacific Greyhound bus, the Banning sign hanging over the street, the Banning Theatre sign at the left of the picture (later to become the Fox Theater), and the Ronald Colman sign at the left portraying *The Man Who Broke the Bank at Monte Carlo*. (Courtesy of Steve Lech.)

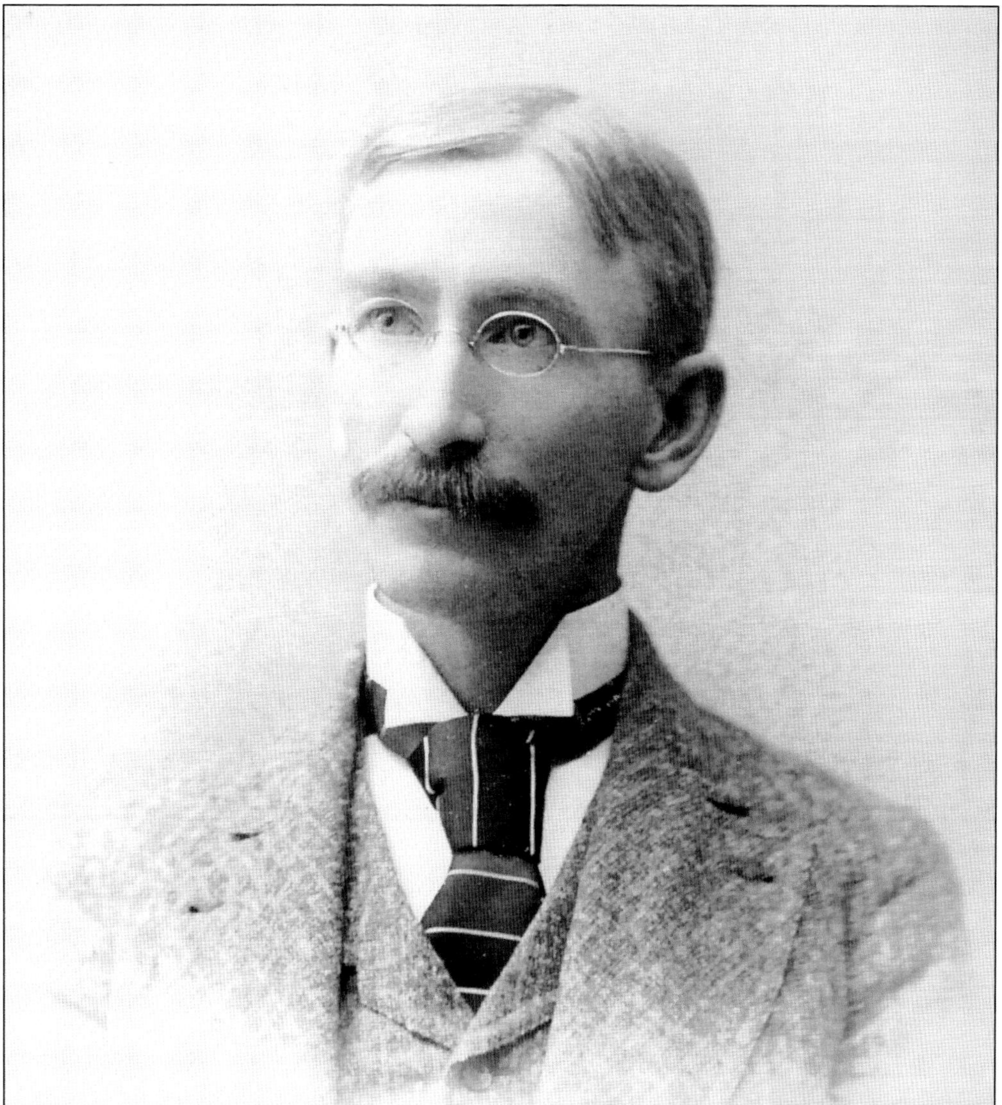

Louis Munson was born in Indiana in 1859, and Banning's history would be incomplete without him, for no one did more to advertise Banning to the reading world. His enthusiasm was of a contagious kind, and he lured many an ailing mortal to Banning, promising it would be their "fountain of health." On August 18, 1888, he put out the first issue of *The Banning Herald*. (Courtesy of Tom Hughes.)

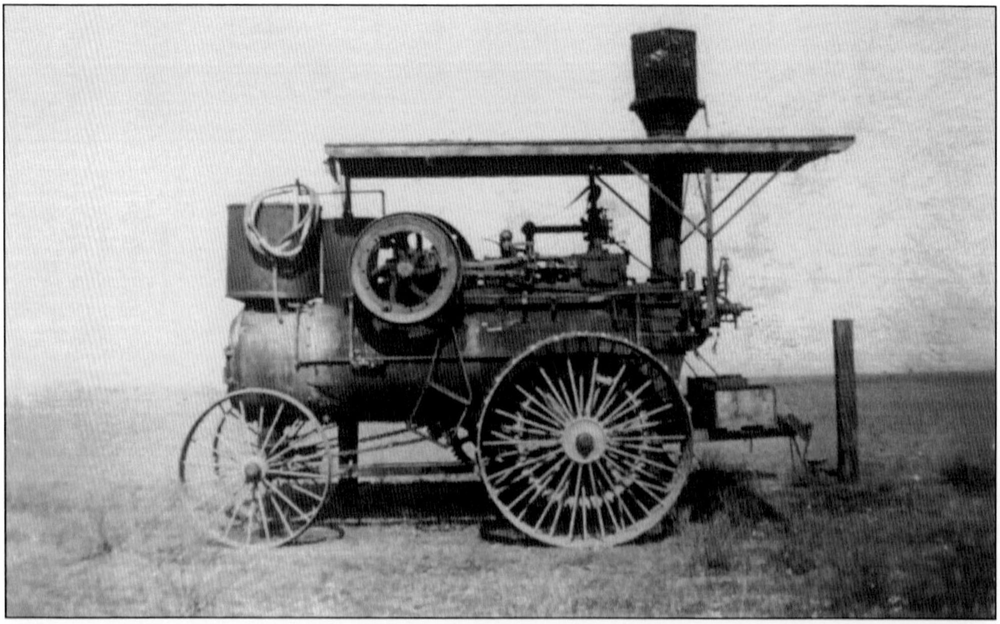

This was the first threshing machine ever used in the San Gorgonio Pass area and in Banning. Purchased by Reznor Stewart and two of his neighbors, it was desperately needed in order to harvest barley grown on a large scale. After its purchase, the barley yield at the Stewart farm alone would reach 10,000 sacks of grain and 200 tons of hay a year. (Courtesy of Marilyn Vonderheide, LMS Foundation.)

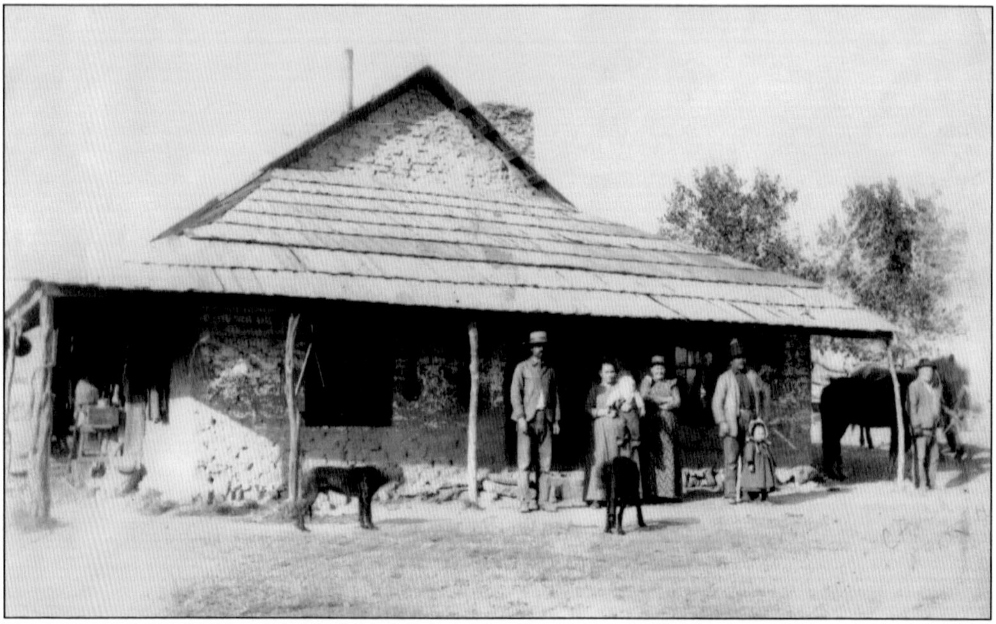

The Chuck Warren ranch home was located northeast of Banning and was constructed of adobe. Warren was among the early freighters who hauled over desert and mountain roads before the railways came. He was a familiar figure in Banning, for this was the nearest market for supplies. He raised cattle, ranging them far over the desert and into the mountains. (Courtesy of Joan Coombs.)

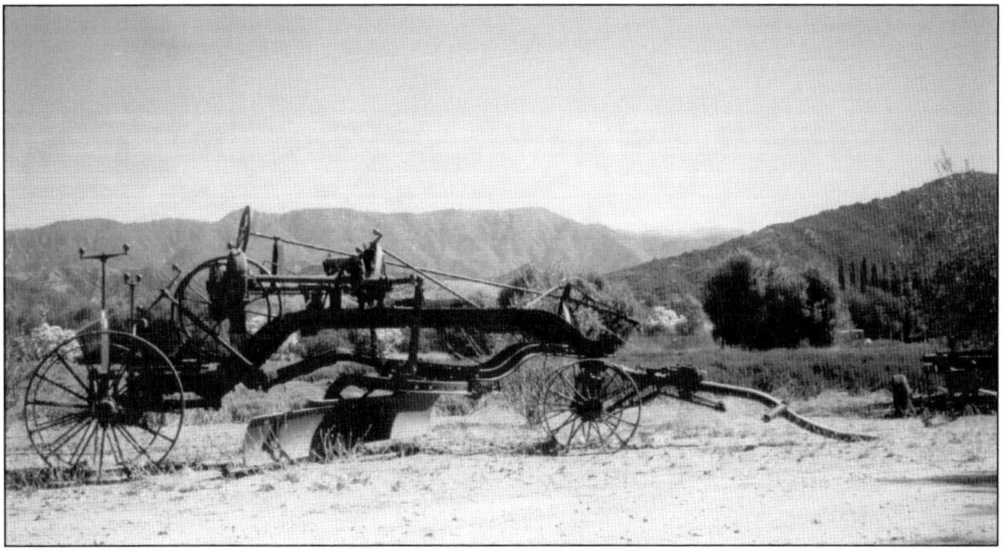

This grader may have been used on some of the early roads around Banning. Road construction at this time was a tedious task because roads were graded with horse-drawn graders. In 1908, a struggle began for the completion of the Banning–Idyllwild road, which had earlier stalled due to a stalemate caused by the difficulty in constructing roads during this era. (Courtesy of the author.)

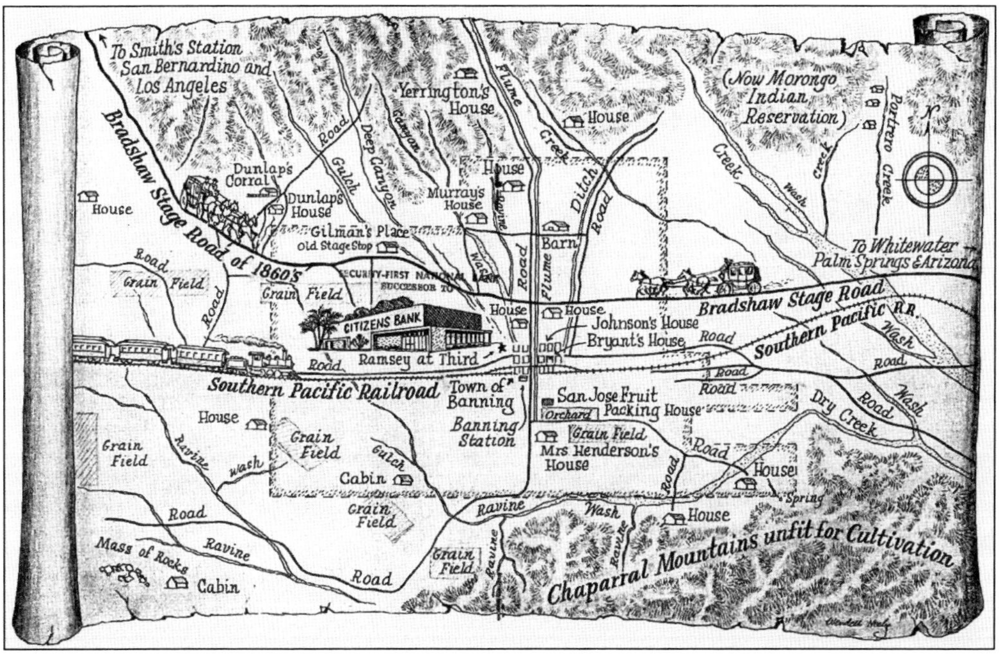

This map shows how Banning looked in 1886, with the exception of the inserted bank building and present city limits (dotted lines), which have been indicated to help relate the land of many years ago to the present. The location of the houses, roads, grain fields, orchards, and canyons is authentic and taken from an 1886 map of Townsite No. 3, Range No. 1 East, San Bernardino Meridian. The only route not shown on the original map, which has been added here, is the old Bradshaw Stage Road of the 1860s. (Courtesy of the author.)

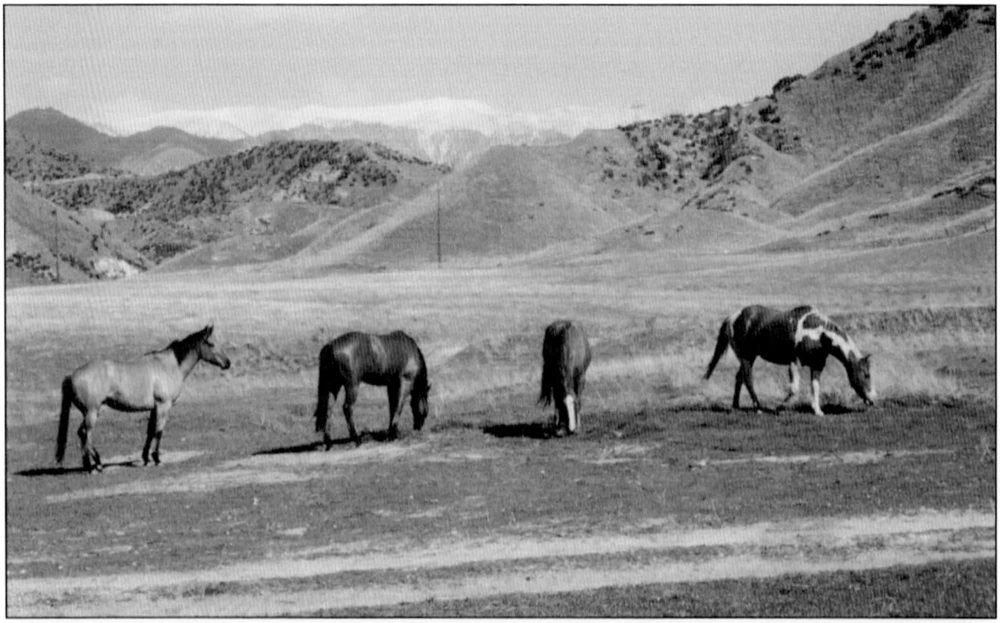

Four of the beautiful horses owned by Brian Lugo are shown here, just after he put them out to range on a plain in Banning, below the snow-capped San Gorgonio Mountain. Brian Lugo's family tree goes back to Antonio Maria Lugo, one of the largest landowners in California's Mexican rancho days. He operated a 35,000-acre cattle ranch, ultimately selling out to Mormon settlers in 1851. (Courtesy of the author.)

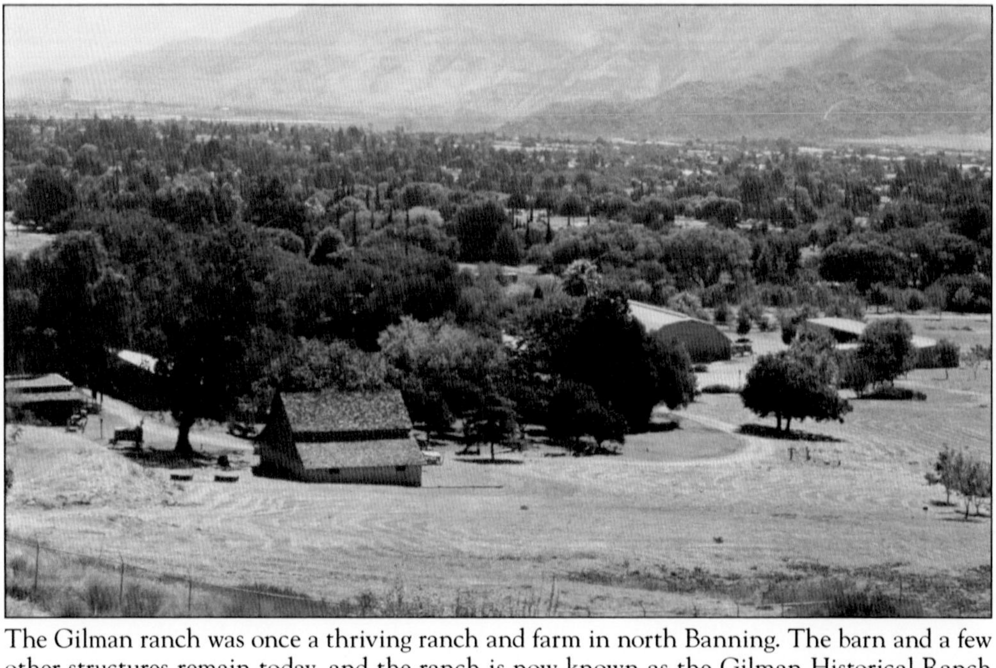

The Gilman ranch was once a thriving ranch and farm in north Banning. The barn and a few other structures remain today, and the ranch is now known as the Gilman Historical Ranch and Wagon Museum, where a large building has been constructed to house the museum's wagon collection. The foundation of an adobe can still be seen on the grounds where once a stagecoach stop existed. (Courtesy of the author.)

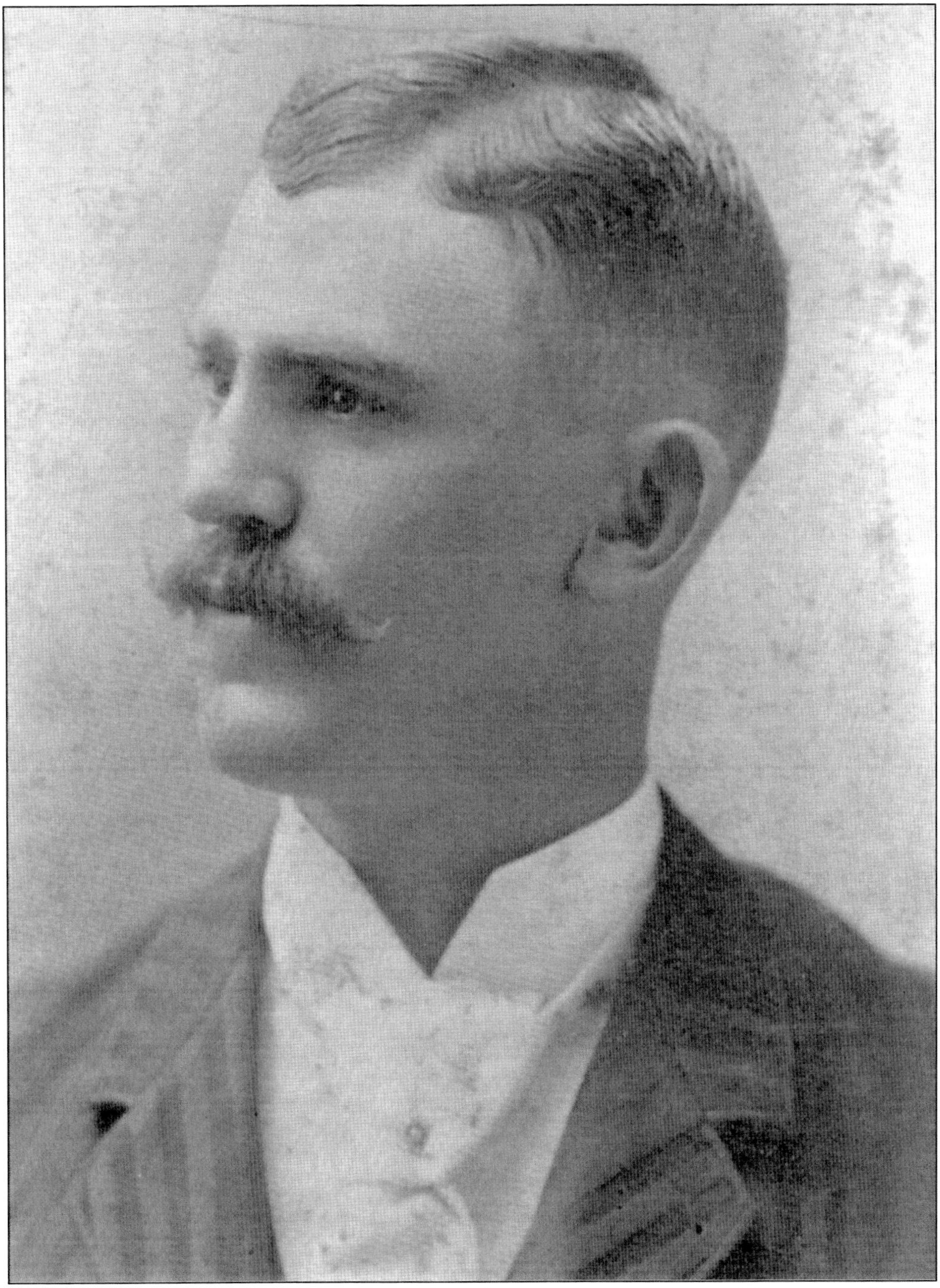

Hugh Carpenter (pictured) and Hamilton (an early Banning pioneer) were fellow constables and business partners, each situated in one of two adjoining counties separated by a line running through the center of Banning. Legend holds that Carpenter got a bounty on every vagrant taken to San Diego from his San Diego County. He was dubbed the "Millionaire Constable of Banning," but only perhaps because Hamilton's vagrants from San Bernardino County were thrown into the pot. (Courtesy of Tom Hughes.)

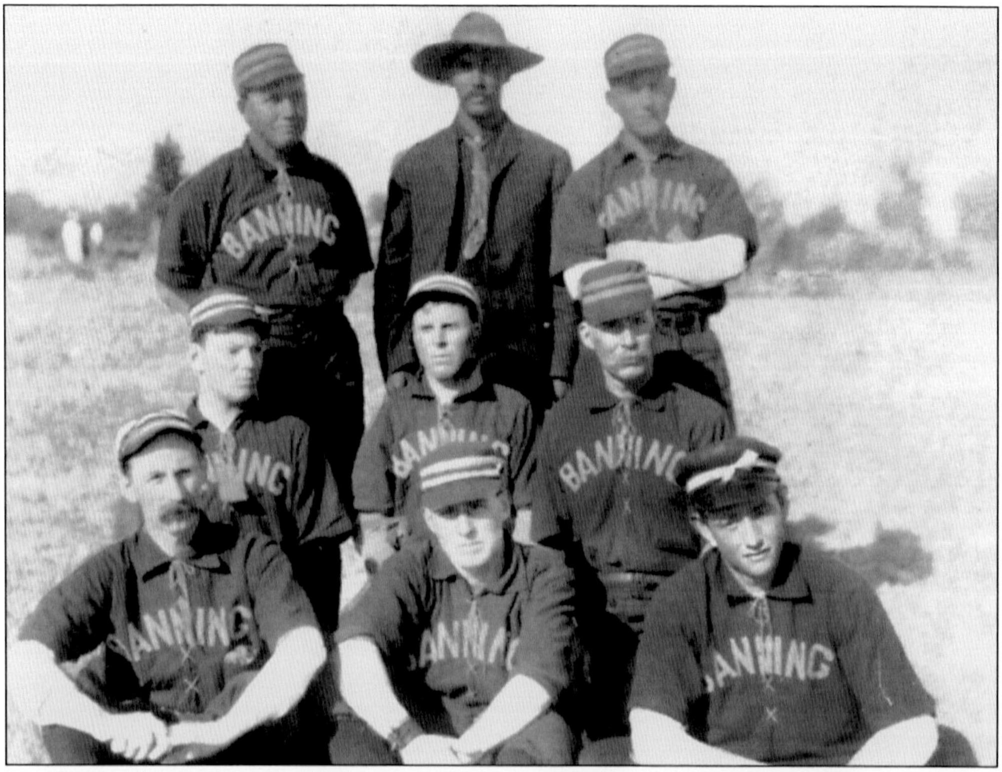

Members of the Banning baseball team in the late 1890s, from left to right, are (first row) Walter Hathaway, Duffy Smallwood, and Frank Waite; (second row) Enos Reid, Bud Williams, and Frank Dudley; (third row) Eddie Johnston, Will Mathews, and Harry Holcomb. Baseball was popular during this era and Banning often played communities in the outlying areas, with the games attracting many spectators. (Courtesy of Steve Lech.)

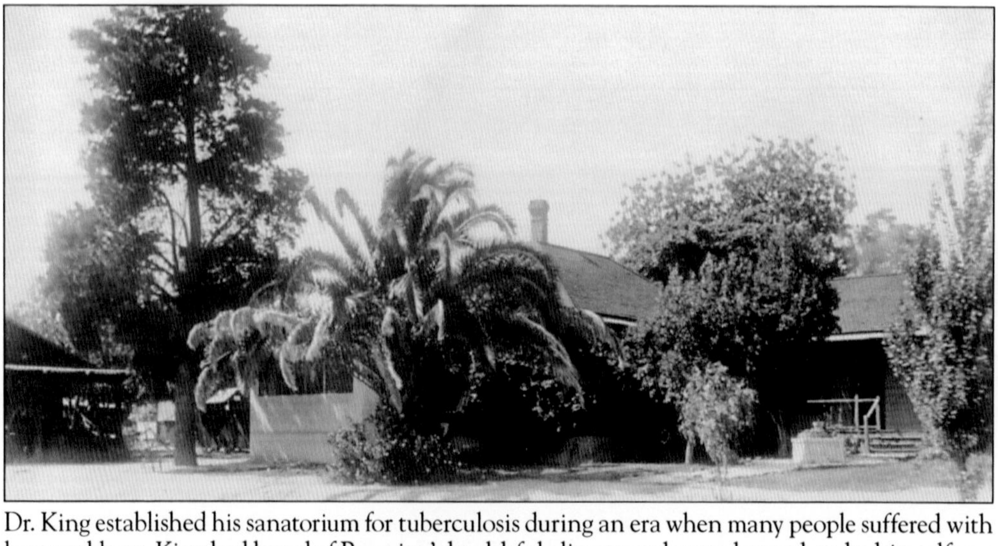

Dr. King established his sanatorium for tuberculosis during an era when many people suffered with lung problems. King had heard of Banning's healthful climate and came here when he himself was under the assumption that he would not live more than six months to a year. The sanatorium he established was one of Banning's first and was quite successful. (Courtesy of Steve Lech.)

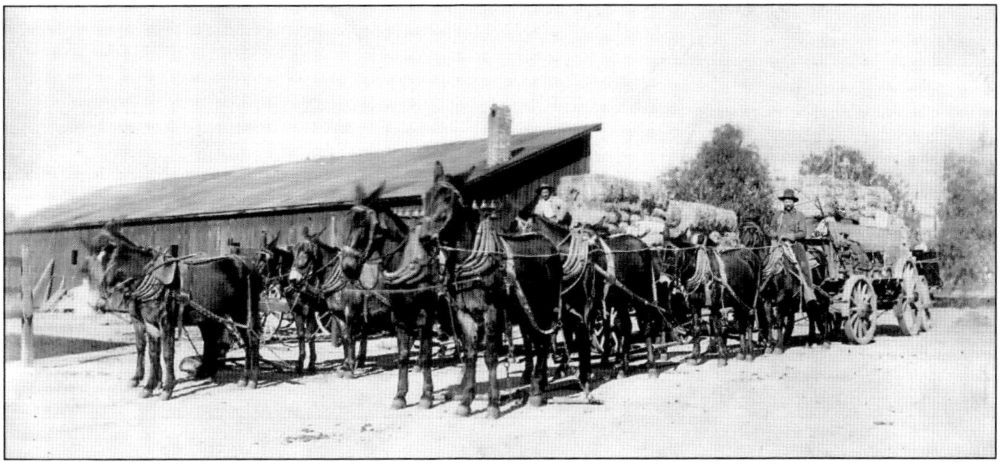

Prior to the Southern Pacific Railroad coming through the San Gorgonio Pass and the installation of a train station in Banning, freight hauling by horse was quite active in Banning, especially during the Civil War when freight hauling was in great demand and extended as far as Yuma, Arizona. When gold was discovered on the Colorado River near La Paz, more freight hauling was promoted. Note the heavily loaded pair of six-horse teams. (Courtesy of Joan Coombs.)

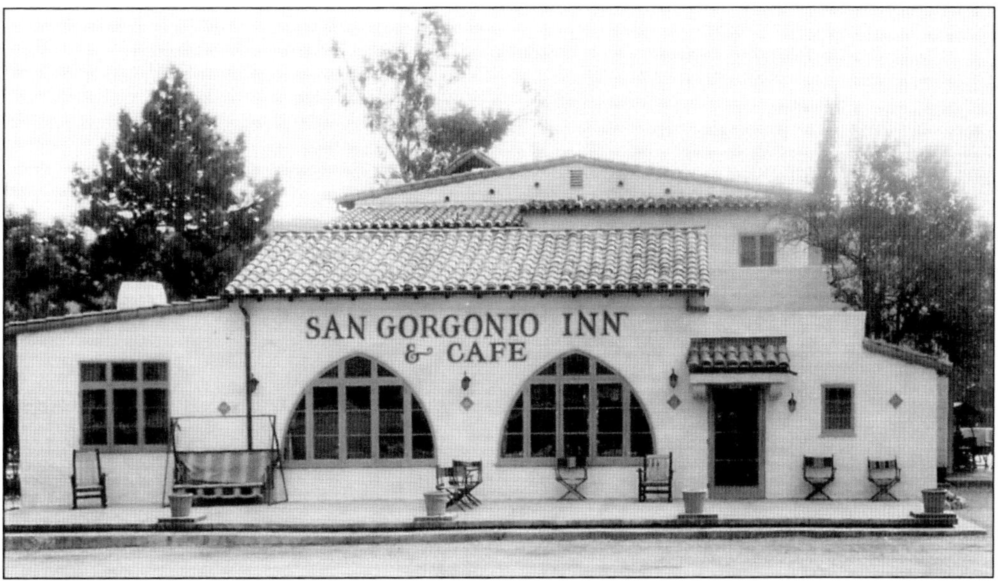

The San Gorgonio Inn still stands today but has been remodeled and enlarged, thereby diminishing the beauty of the original structure, captured in this early photograph. The inn has metamorphosed through the years from the original Bryant House to The Banning and, in 1923, was renamed the San Gorgonio Inn. It is Banning's oldest restaurant and is a popular eatery. (Courtesy of Steve Lech.)

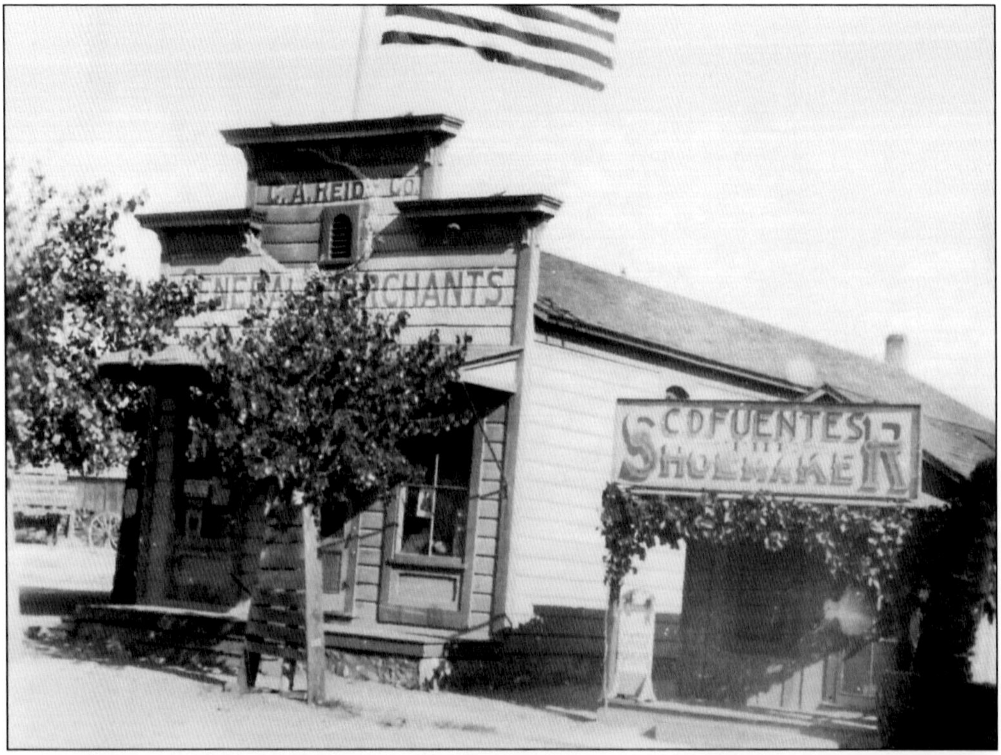

As Banning grew, other businesses were established around the Reid Building. One such business was started on its east side. A story is told that the water flume coming down from Water Canyon passed beside these buildings and a drinking dipper was hung on the side of one of them so that anyone who wanted a drink could just reach out and scoop one up. (Courtesy of Joan Coombs.)

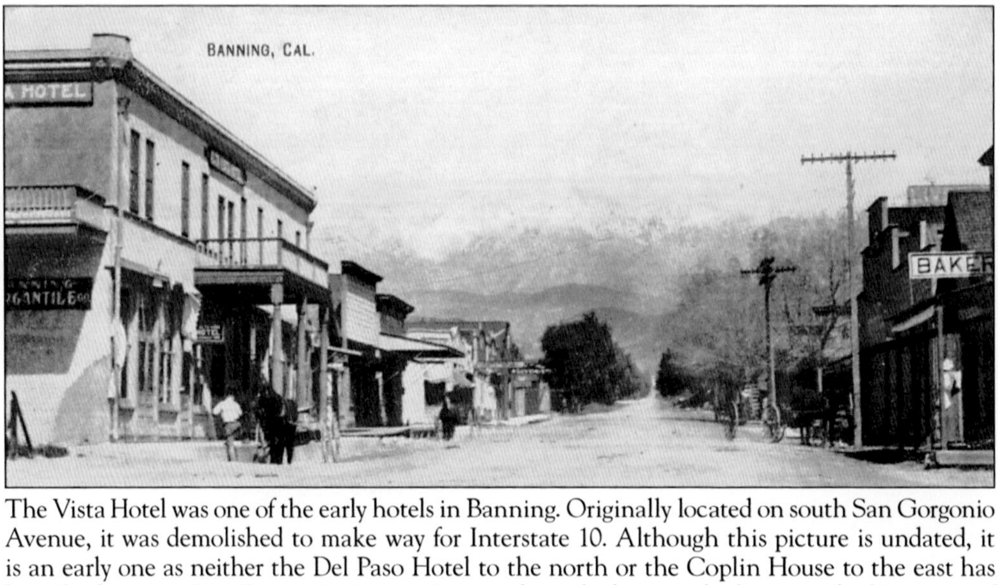

The Vista Hotel was one of the early hotels in Banning. Originally located on south San Gorgonio Avenue, it was demolished to make way for Interstate 10. Although this picture is undated, it is an early one as neither the Del Paso Hotel to the north or the Coplin House to the east has been built as yet. San Gorgonio Avenue is seen through the trees looking north. (Courtesy of Steve Lech.)

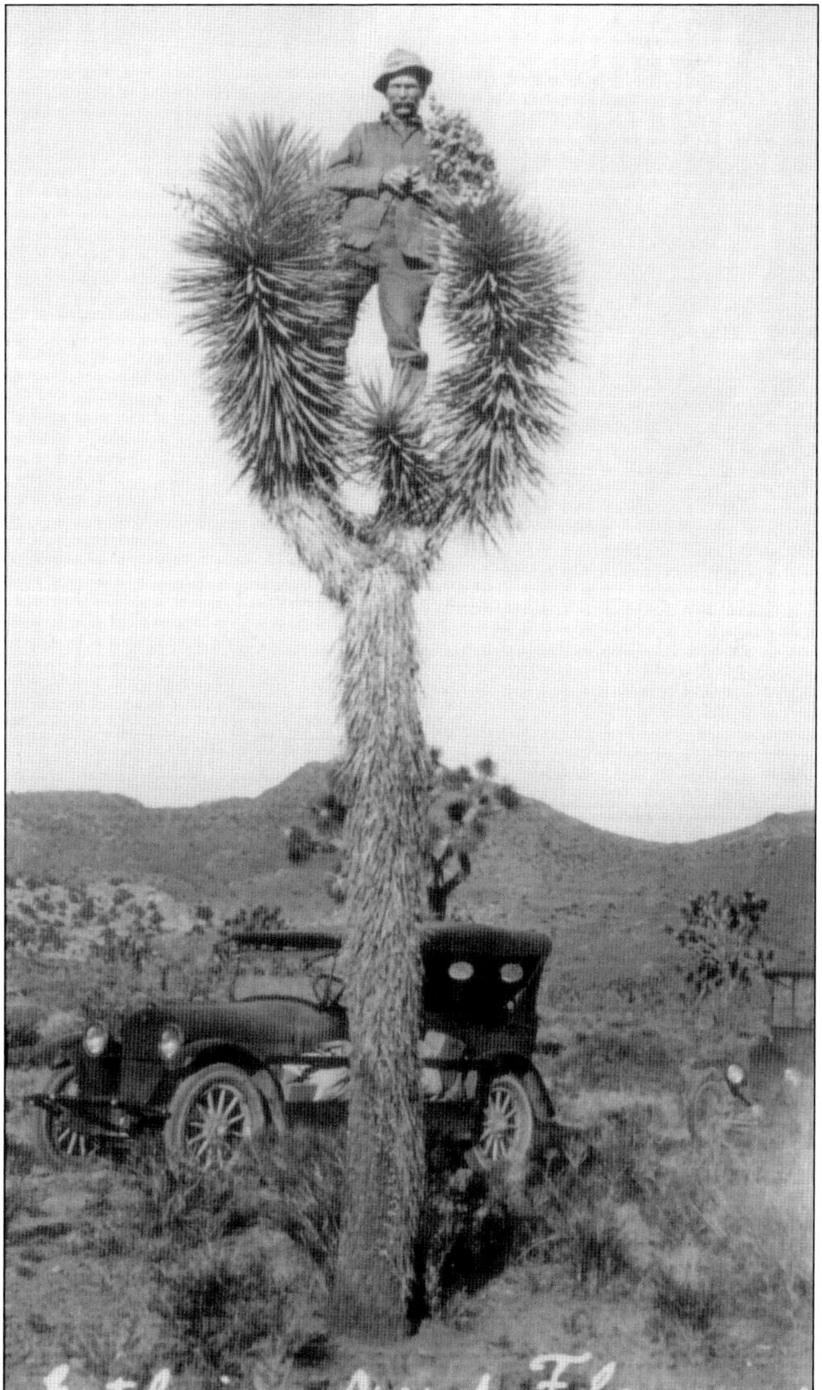

Horticulturalist French Gilman stands high atop a yucca plant in the desert surrounding Banning. He is Jim Gilman's eldest son and became quite popular in the field of horticulture. How he ascended to the branch of this tall plant is unknown, as no ladder or ropes are present to account for the climb. The two cars perhaps indicate that it was a team effort. (Courtesy of Joan Coombs.)

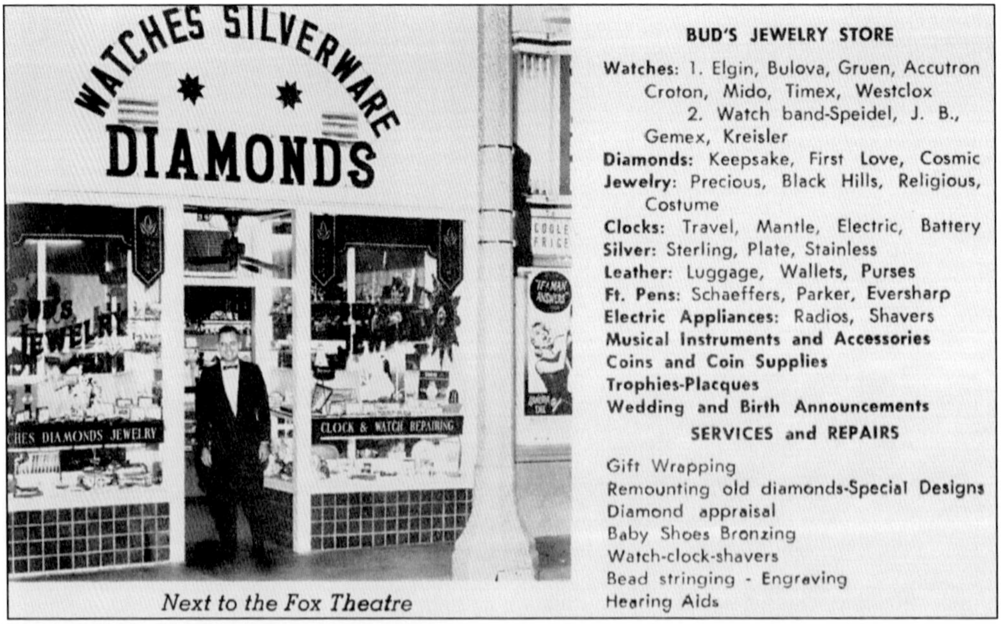

Bud Mathewson came to Banning in 1956 and opened his store next to the Fox Theater. He had previously completed studies at the Van Slyke School of Horology in Oakland. Since then he has run unsuccessfully for Congress a number of times. He later relocated his business to a larger building on Ramsey Street and filled it with rare historical treasures. He films many of Banning's events for the local TV station. (Courtesy of Steve Lech.)

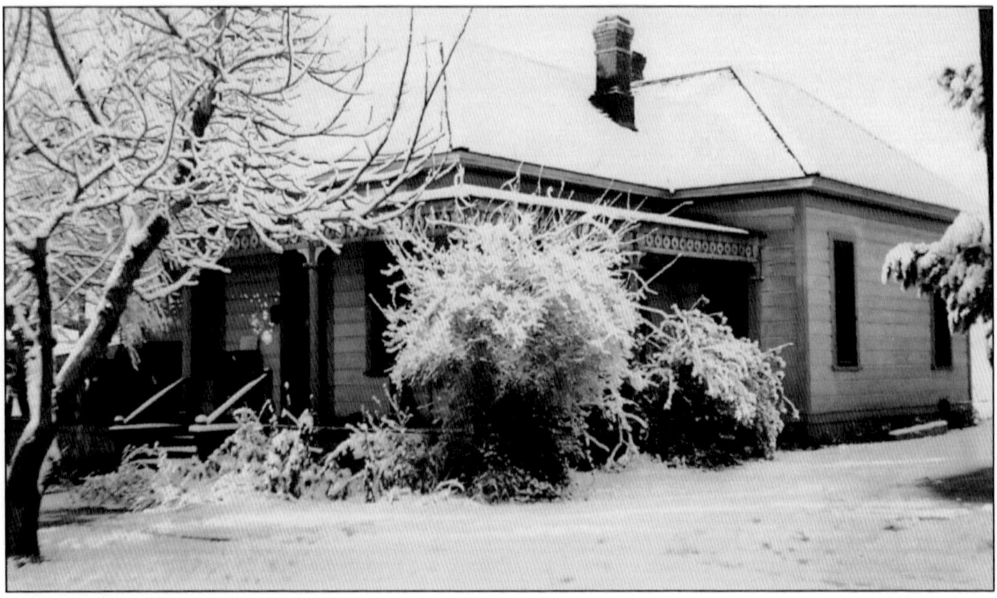

Christopher Jost, whose residence is seen here, was an early pioneer to Banning. At age 30, he left his native town of Guysboro, Nova Scotia, reaching San Francisco and then San Pedro by boat. He came with a $2,600 stock of general merchandise, and arrived in Banning on March 6, 1877. He hauled his freight by team to Water Canyon where he operated one of Banning's first stores, later moving it near the tracks. (Courtesy of Joan Coombs.)

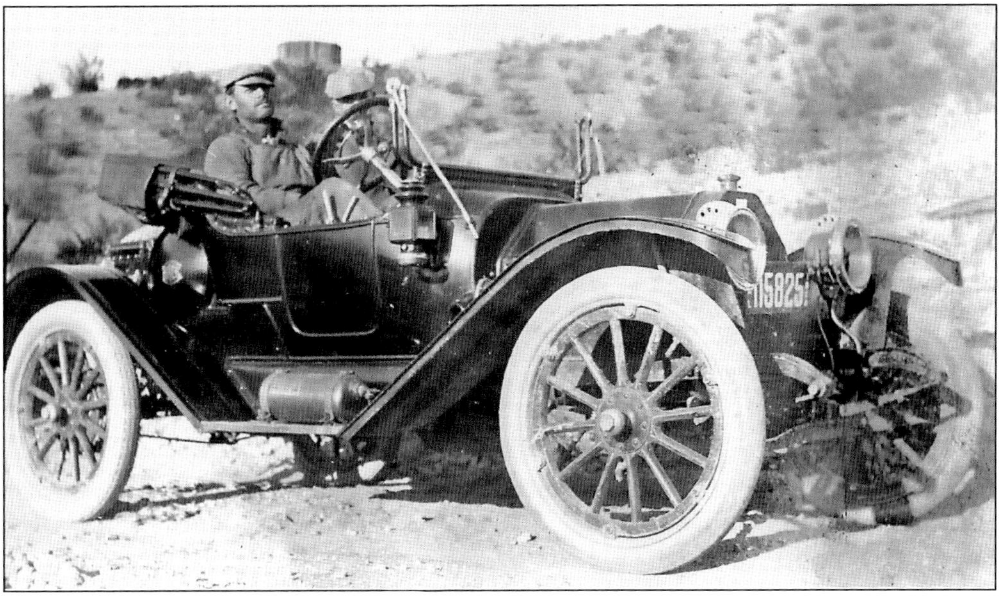

By 1910, cars like this were becoming popular in Banning. An auto census at the time disclosed seven Fords, two Mitchells, and one each of a Maxwell, Oakland, Tarantula, Blue Racer, EMF, Buick, Reo, and Cadillac. Considerable comment was caused around this time by a report that an automobile had made the round trip to 29 Palms without mishap. (Courtesy of Marianne Bailiff.)

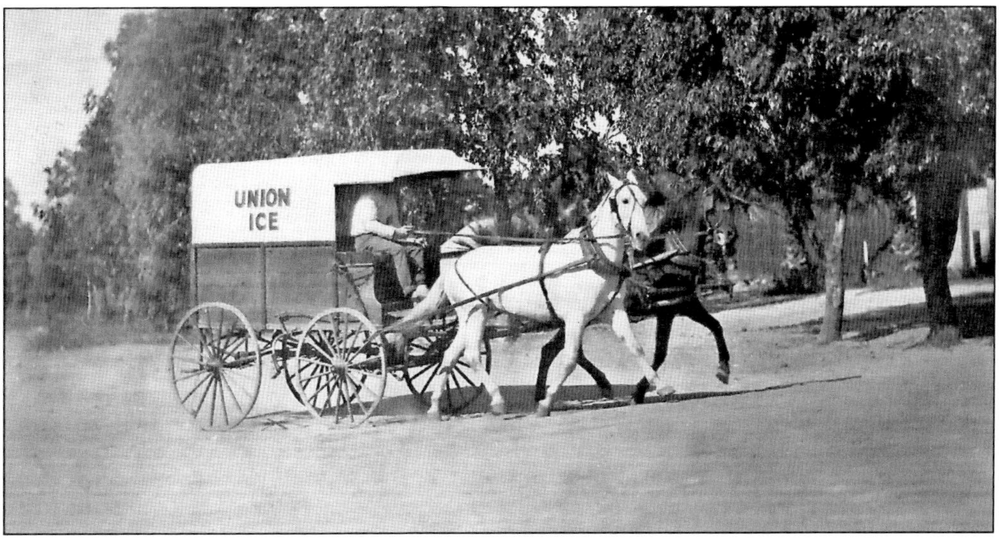

In 1900, the first commercial ice plant was opened in Banning by a Mr. Kolb. Mr. and Mrs. Kolb came to Banning in 1895. Kolb also operated two six-horse freighting outfits to the desert for some 15 years, after which he and Mrs. Kolb conducted the Coplin House. Banning's Union Ice Company also had an agency and outlet in Beaumont. Pictured is the delivery wagon of the Union Ice Company traveling its route. (Courtesy of Marianne Bailiff.)

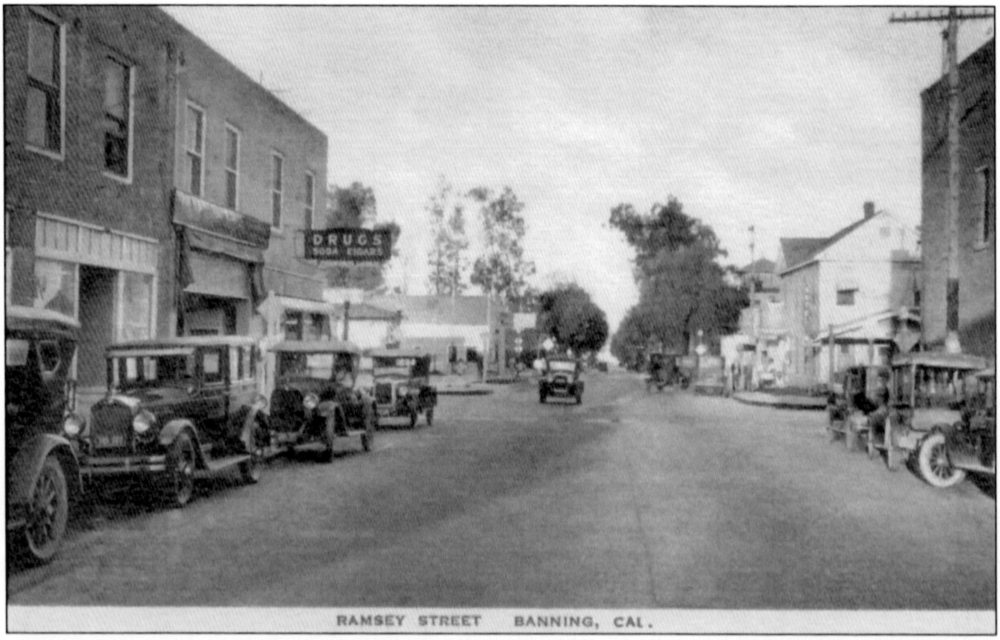

This photograph can perhaps be dated by the parade of old cars in this view looking east on Ramsey Street, crossing the intersection of San Gorgonio Avenue. The Del Paso Hotel, which was destroyed by fire, is on the left where today a parking lot is situated. The Coplin House, which was then a hotel, stands out well on the southeast corner of Ramsey Street and San Gorgonio Avenue, on the right of this image. (Courtesy of Steve Lech.)

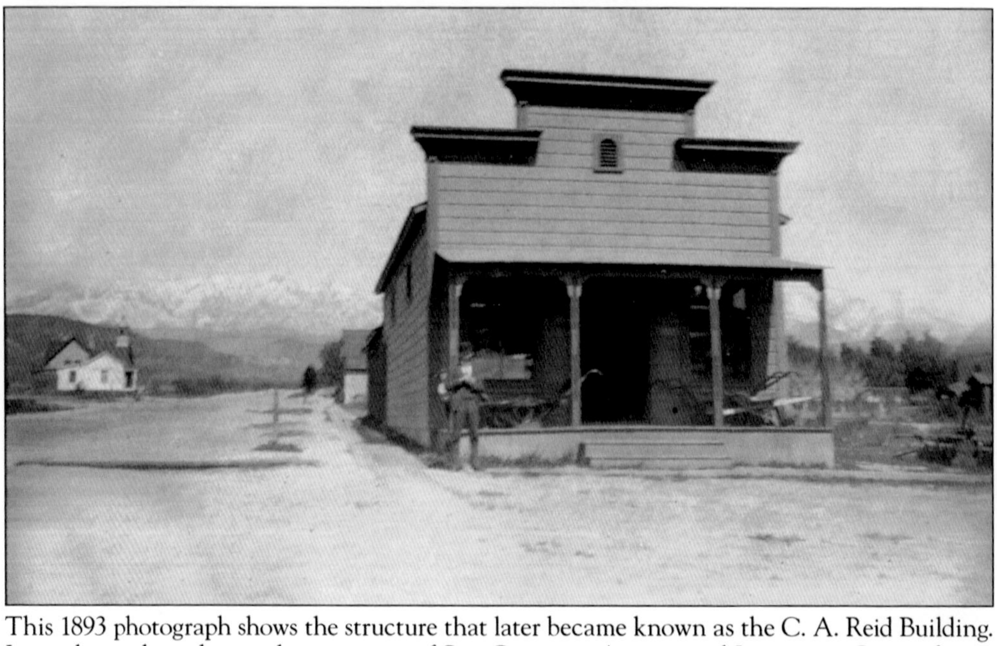

This 1893 photograph shows the structure that later became known as the C. A. Reid Building. It was located on the northeast corner of San Gorgonio Avenue and Livingston Street, facing Livingston. Extant today, it is believed by some to be the oldest remaining building in Banning. The small structure to the left is the town's first Methodist church, which faces San Gorgonio Avenue. (Courtesy of Joan Coombs.)

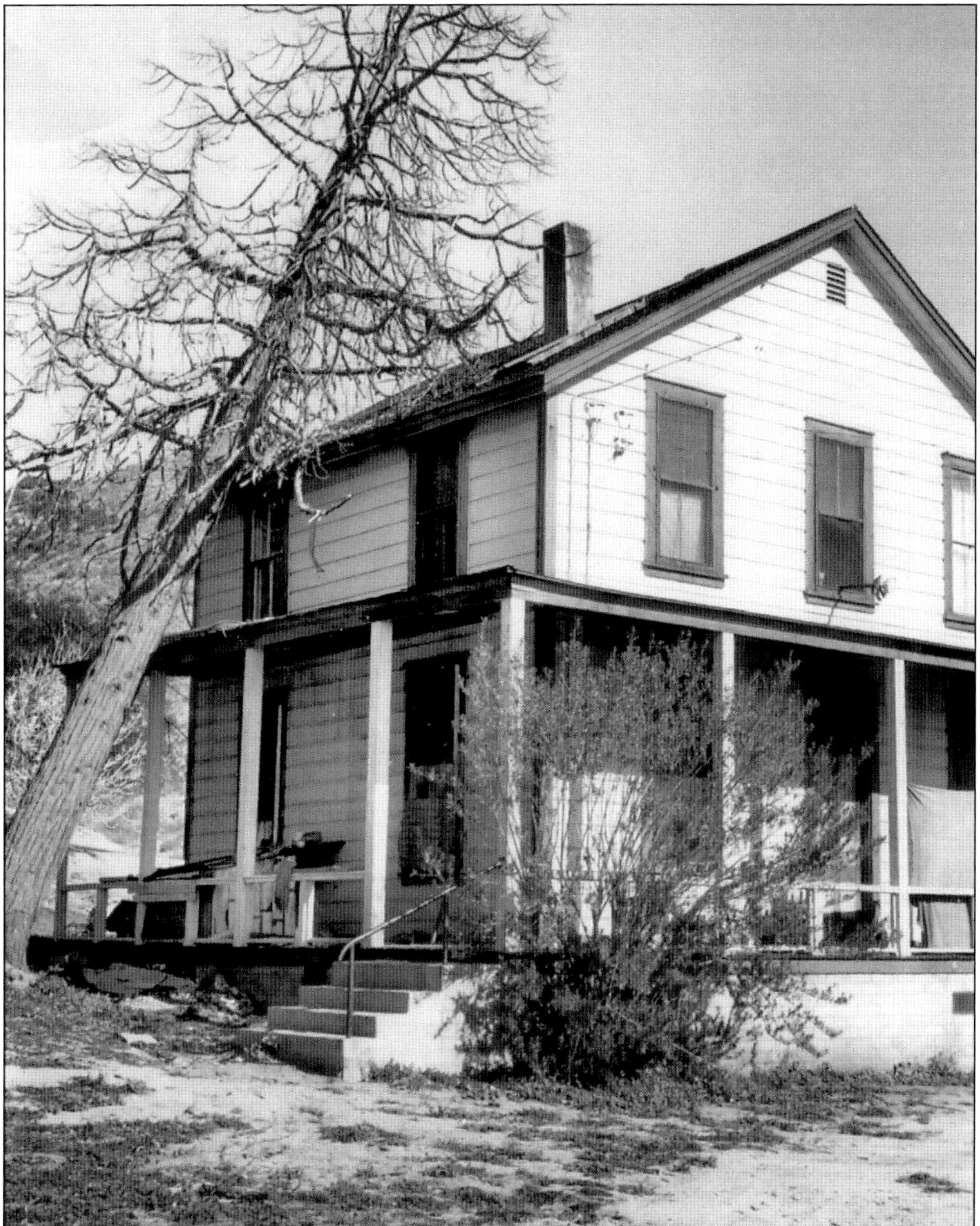

Dr. Wellwood Murray was one of Banning's early leaders. His 80 acres spread west from Eighth Street and north of Gilman Street, and his house, which is shown here, was built in 1896. The property was sold to the Catholic Indian Bureau and St. Boniface Indian School was built here between 1889 and 1890. The priest lived in Dr. Murray's house, which was later razed. Murray moved to Palm Springs and opened the Palm Springs Hotel. (Courtesy of Joan Coombs.)

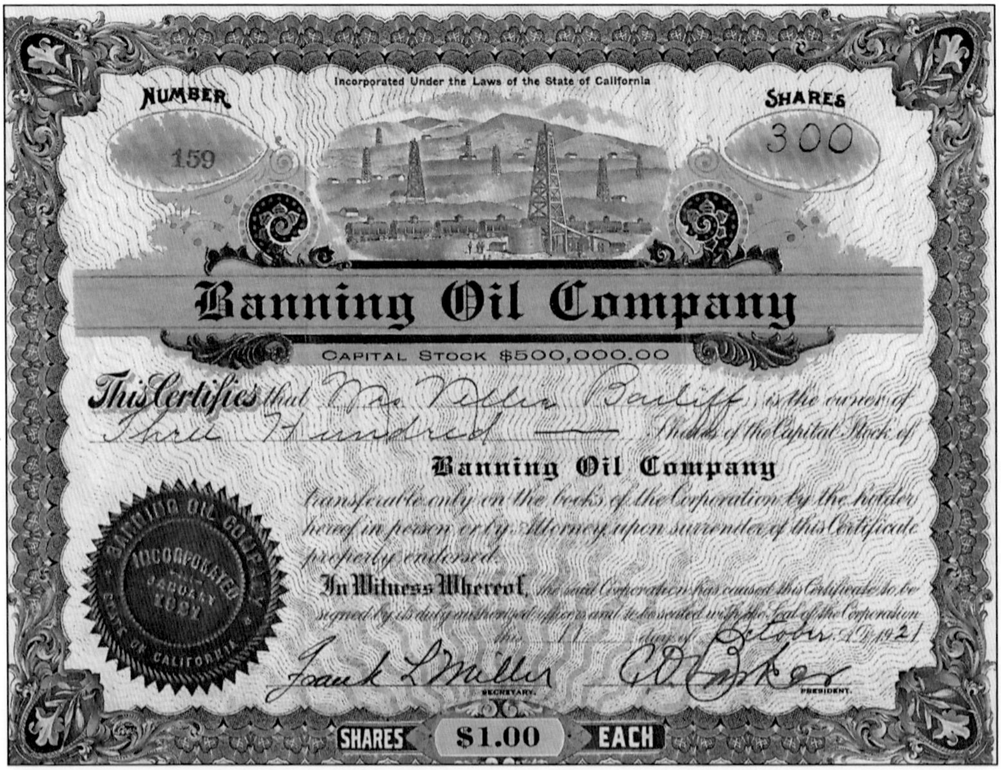

By 1920, oil drilling was active and quite popular in California. The drill-for-oil fever struck the Banning area in the spring of that year, with three companies sinking wells in the San Gorgonio Pass. None of them proved successful. Soon after, the Banning Oil Company was formed under the presidency of C. O. Barker, as shown on this stock certificate. It too did not bring in a gusher and died away. (Courtesy of Marianne Bailiff.)

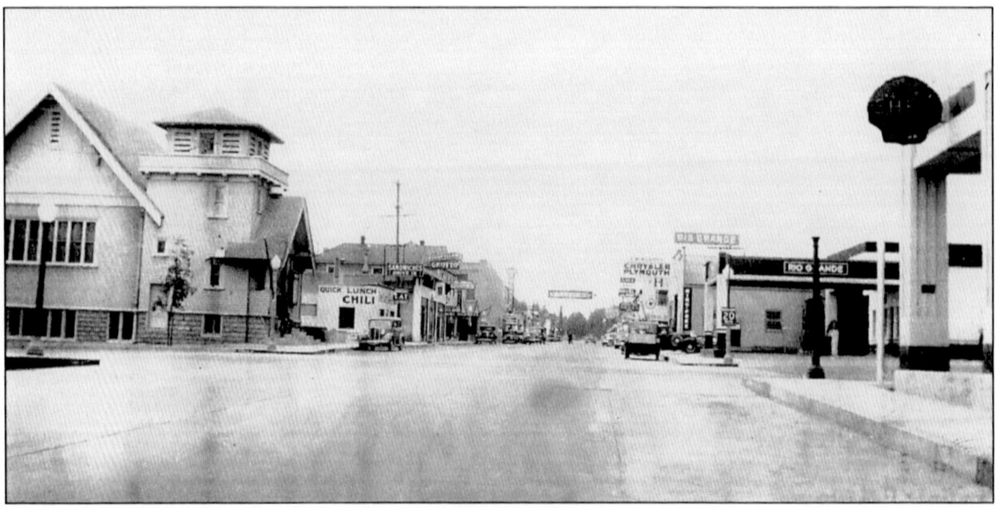

This scene looks east on Ramsey Street, with the Banning Theater sign near the center of the photograph and the Banning sign overhanging the street. The large building in the foreground to the left of the photograph on the north side of Ramsey Street is the Baptist church, which was built in 1910 and dedicated December 3, 1911. (Courtesy of Marianne Bailiff.)

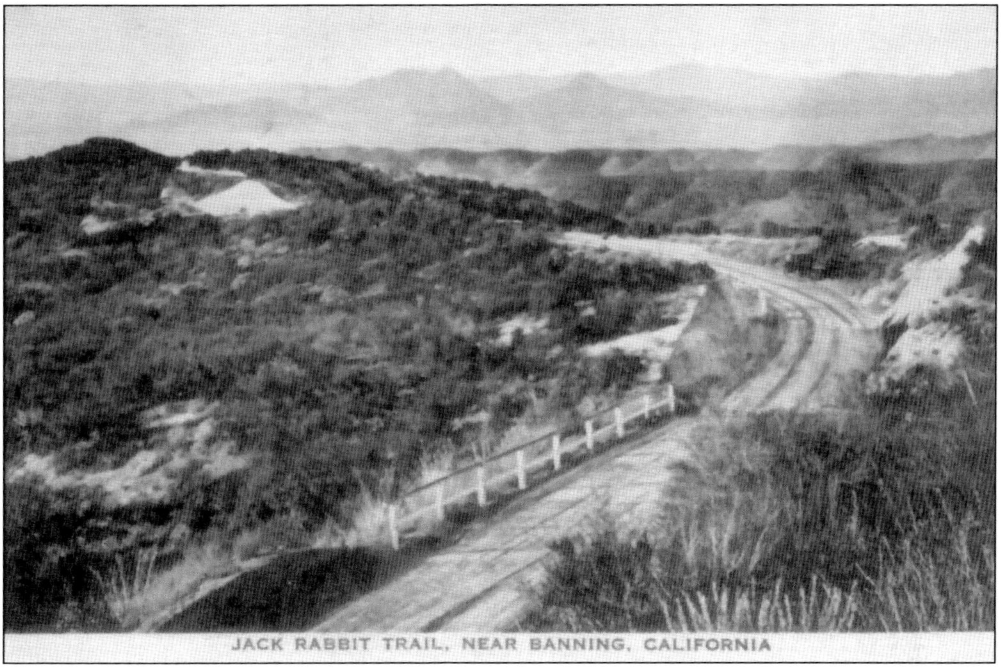

Jack Rabbit Trail is a remote road originally used to travel from Banning to Riverside. It never supported heavy traffic as can be seen on today's Highway 60, which was later constructed through the canyon traversing the "bad lands" leading to Riverside. Today Jack Rabbit Trail is considered unsafe and has been closed to vehicular traffic. (Courtesy of Steve Lech.)

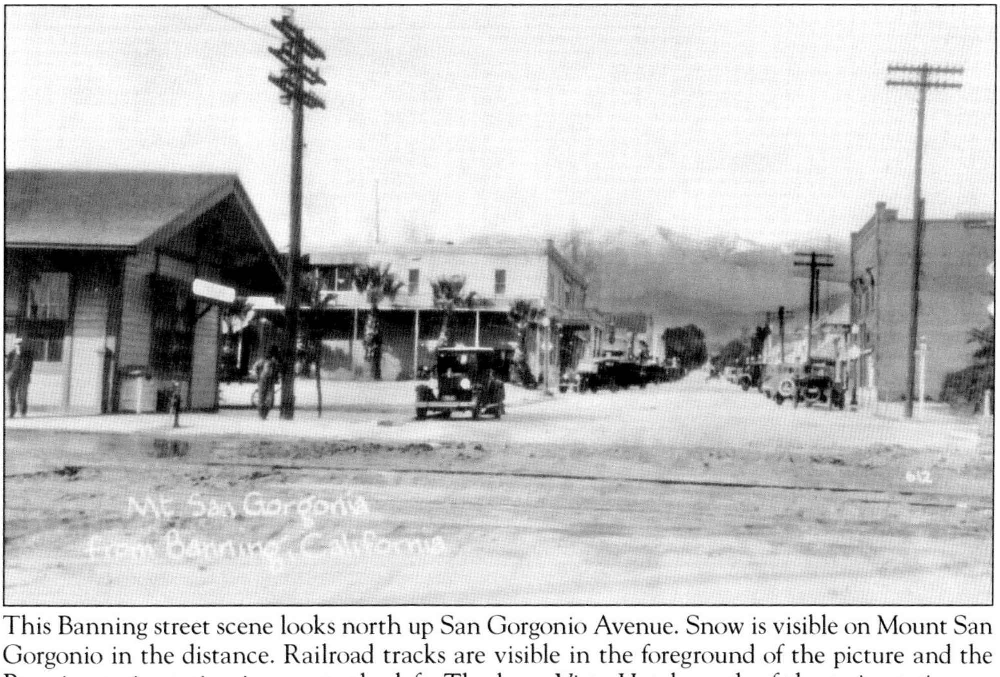

This Banning street scene looks north up San Gorgonio Avenue. Snow is visible on Mount San Gorgonio in the distance. Railroad tracks are visible in the foreground of the picture and the Banning train station is seen to the left. The large Vista Hotel, south of the train station on South San Gorgonio Avenue, was demolished when the freeway came through. (Courtesy of Steve Lech.)

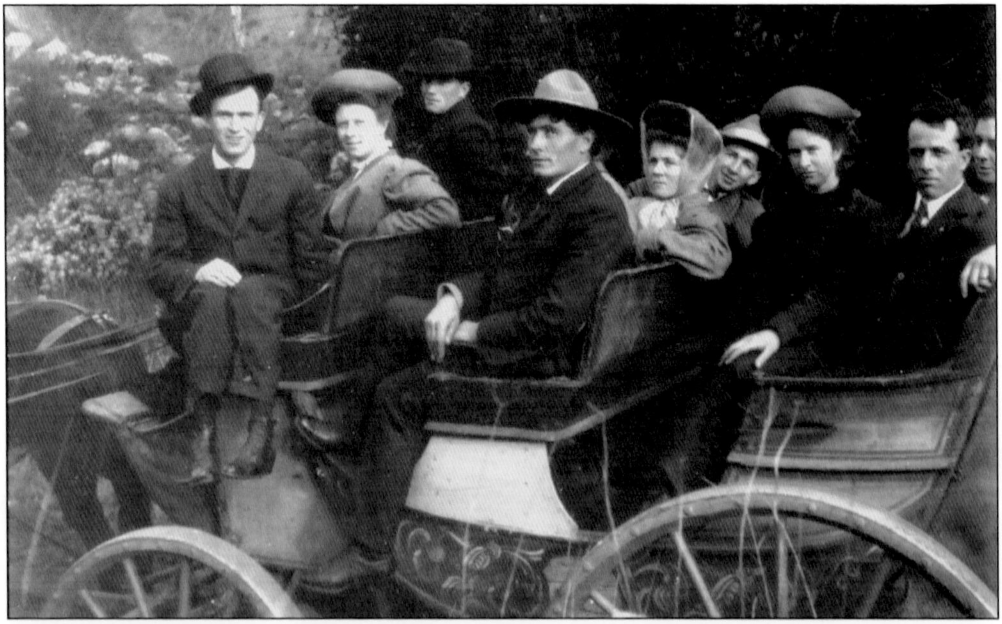

Several members of the well-known Gilman family and some of their friends are shown here with their buggy hooked up and ready to proceed down the hill from their ranch into Banning. Banning night life during this era was quite active and they could possibly have been going to an evening at the opera house or perhaps to dinner at one of several well visited hotels or restaurants. (Courtesy of Joan Coombs.)

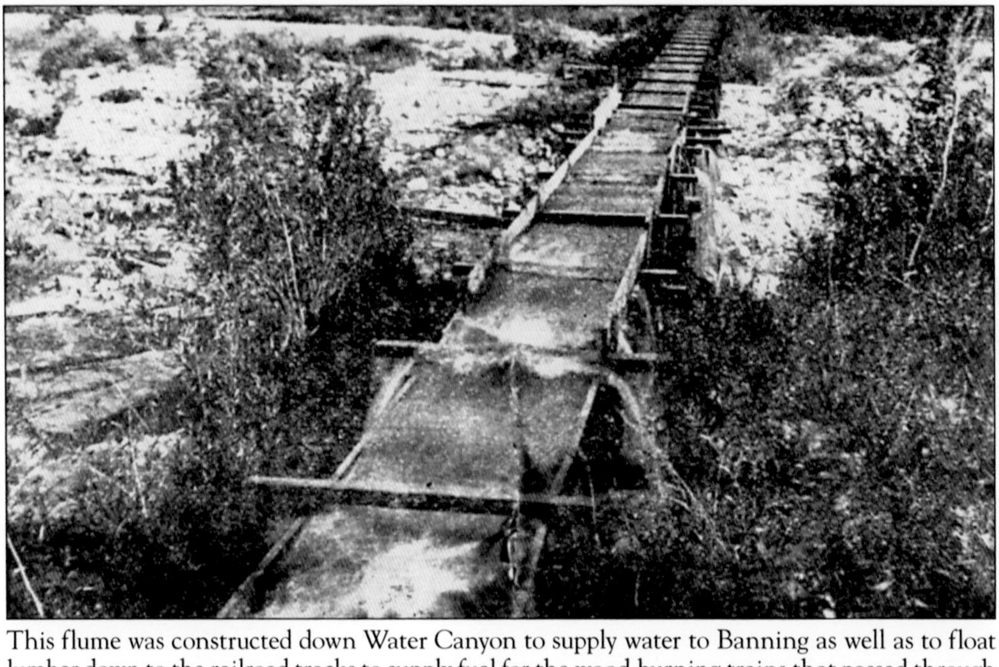

This flume was constructed down Water Canyon to supply water to Banning as well as to float lumber down to the railroad tracks to supply fuel for the wood-burning trains that passed through town. The flume is shown here crossing the creek, where it has been partly washed out. The flume's lumber venture was abandoned around 1880, but the settlers kept it in partial repair because it provided the water supply for the community. (Courtesy of Joan Coombs.)

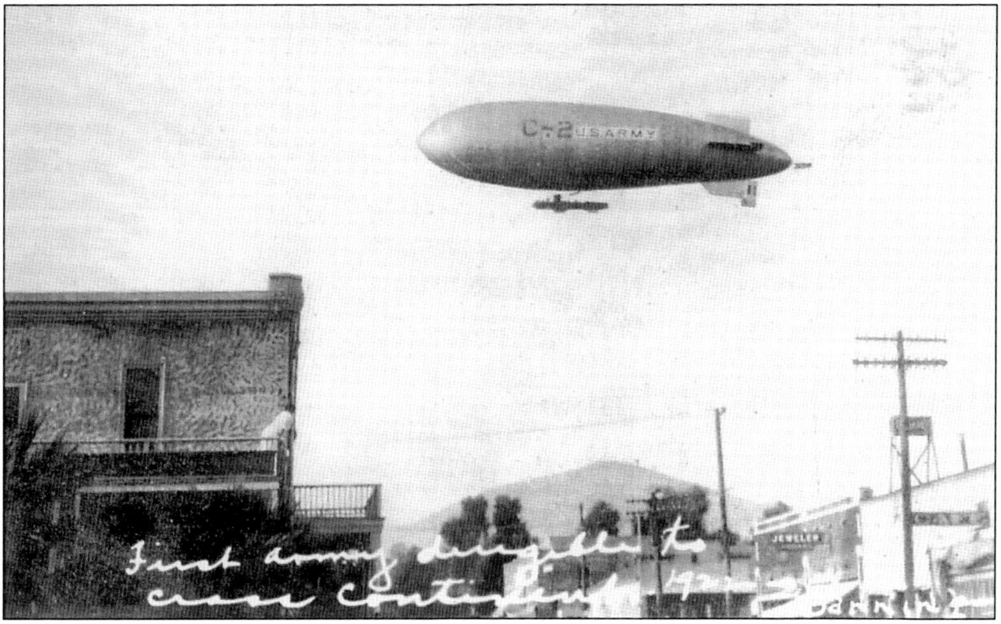

The U.S. Army's C-2 dirigible was the first one to cross the continental United States. Like the planes of Fowler and Rogers, which both landed in Banning about two weeks apart a number of years before this event, it too stirred up much attention as it passed close over the town. (Courtesy of Marianne Bailiff.)

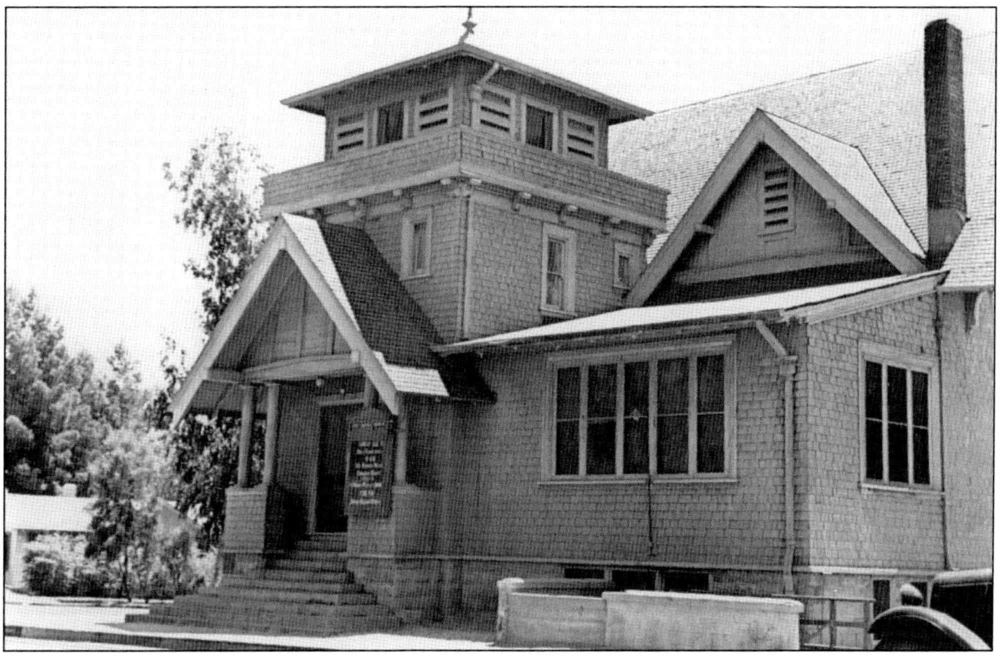

The Baptist church was organized February 18, 1883, in a one-room schoolhouse with no furniture save a few rough desks and benches. It was the first church in the entire pass. Banning was, at this time, a railroad station in a sparsely settled farming community. By 1910, a church was constructed. It was dedicated on December 3, 1911. Its first baptism was held in a reservoir. (Courtesy of Steve Lech.)

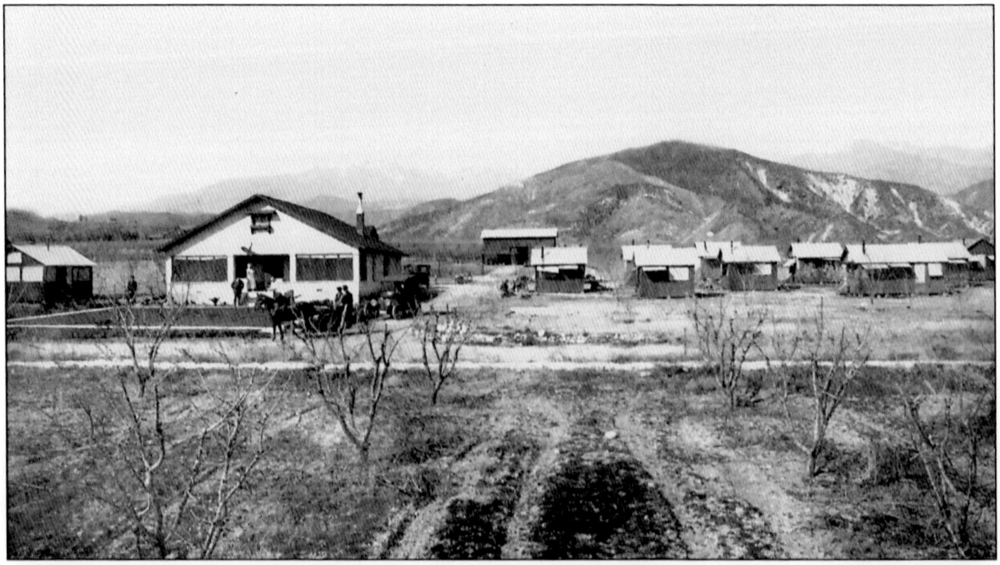

Seen here in 1912 is the Southern Sierras Sanitarium on Theodore Street in Banning. The medical director was L. M. Ryan, and the rate was $80 per month. There were several similar establishments in Banning, as it was a popular place to come for health reasons, especially as a cure for lung ailments. (Courtesy of Marianne Bailiff.)

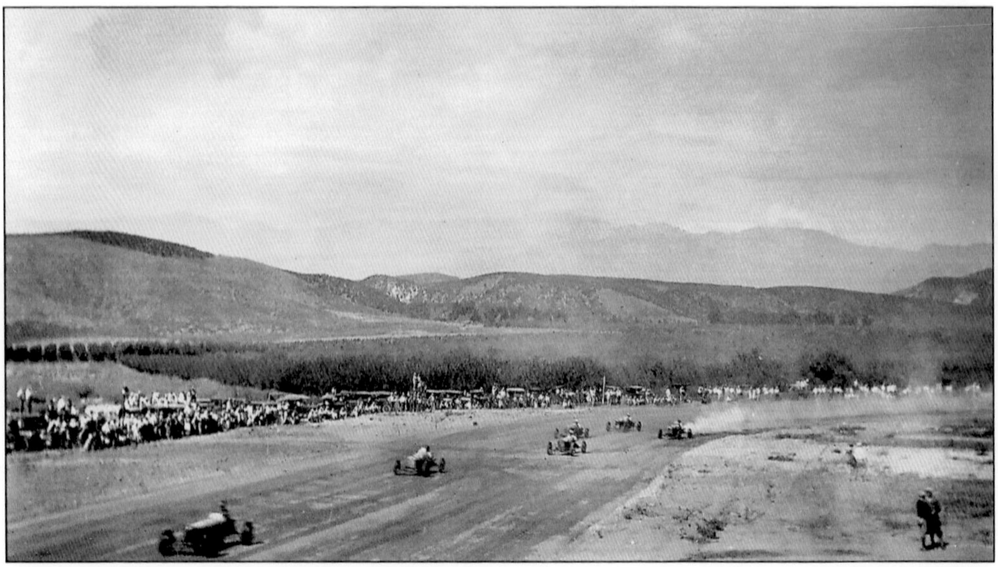

Auto racing was popular in Banning's early years. The first automobile race on the American Legion half-mile speedway in Banning at Ramsey and Sixteenth Streets was held July 4, 1925, and was won by John Brinton, driving a Franklin. On New Year's Day 1926, an unofficial world speed record was made here by Bert Spencer. Of course, it was only a small fraction of the speeds obtained on today's race tracks. (Courtesy of Marianne Bailiff.)

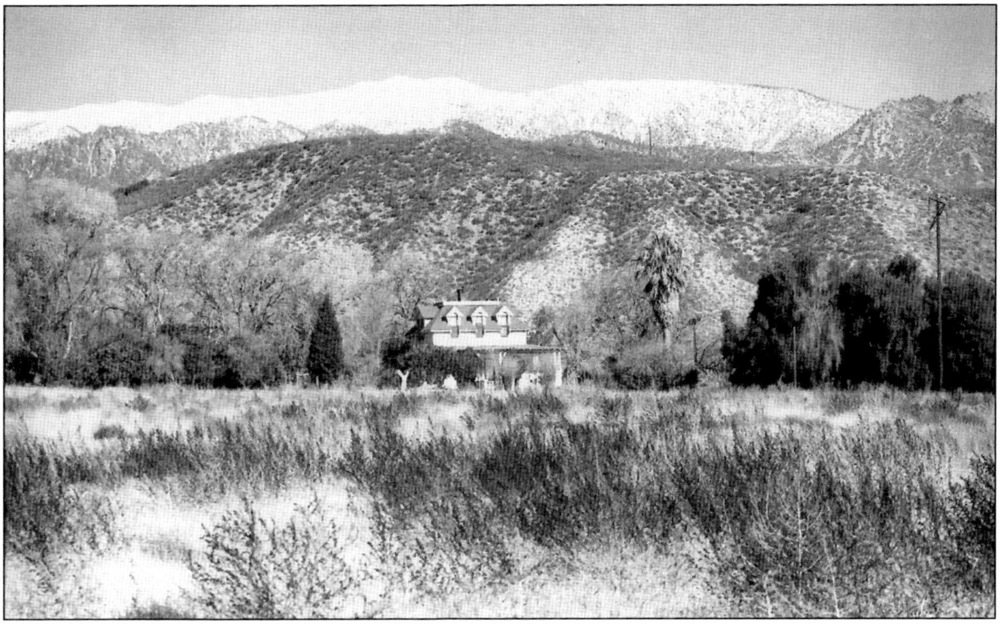

Built in 1879, this tall, beautiful ranch house north of Banning above Wilson Street was the residence of the Gilman family for many years. Destroyed by fire on March 23, 1977, it is currently being rebuilt and will be a great addition to the Gilman Historical Ranch and Wagon Museum, now operated by the San Bernardino County Park Services as a county park. (Courtesy of Marianne Bailiff.)

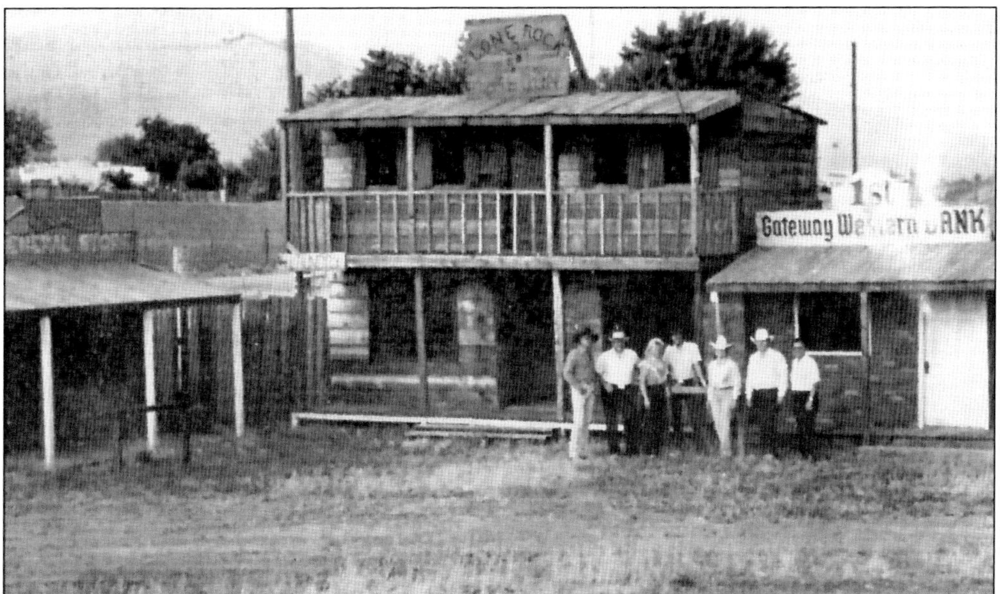

In the early years of Banning's history, a number of popular businesses began to develop. Pictured here are perhaps the first saloon and bank in Banning. It is interesting to note that the Lone Rock Saloon is larger than the Gateway Western Bank. The town's first church services were held in the Lone Rock Saloon prior to construction of any church buildings. (Courtesy of Marianne Bailiff.)

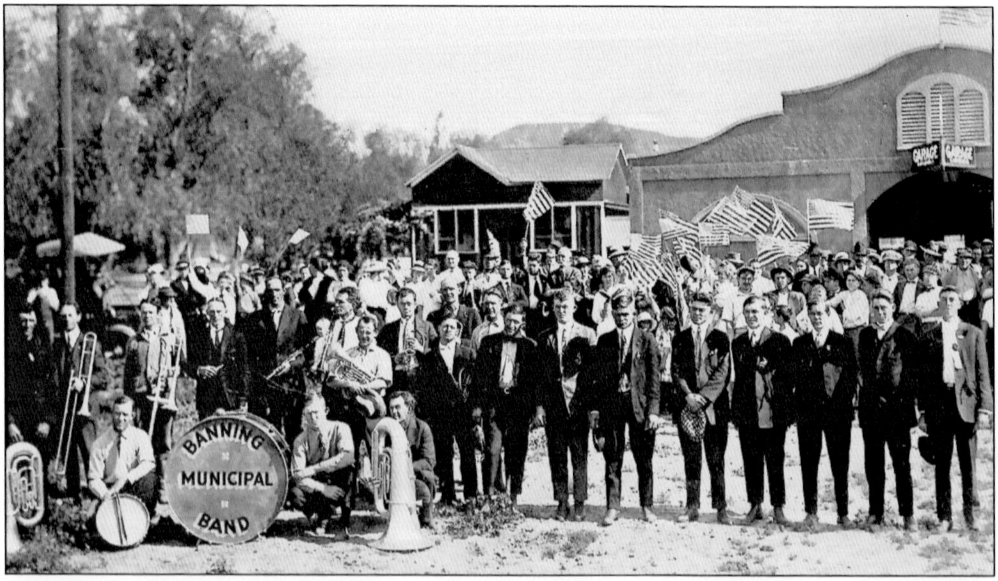

The Banning Municipal Band added much to instill a sense of pride to the town in its early years. It often played during the town's parades, Fourth of July celebrations, and other major events. The date of this photograph is not exactly known, but it is surmised that the band may be playing in celebration of Banning's citizens saying goodbye to those leaving to fight in World War I. (Courtesy of Marianne Bailiff.)

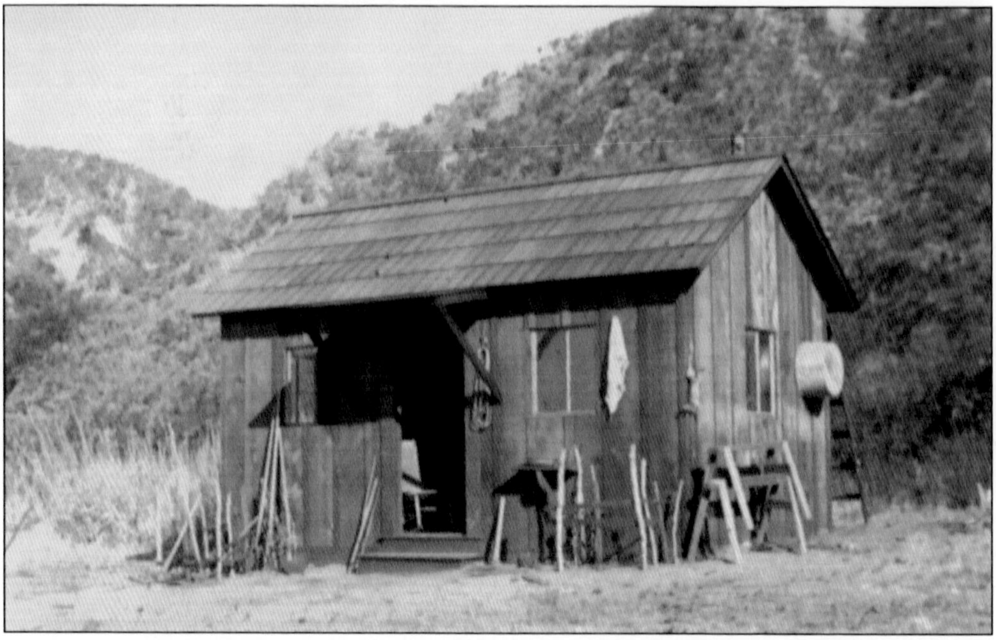

In February 1888, Stephen Janus, an early settler, came to Banning from Washington to officially represent the Indian Bureau. His special mission was to see that settlers and squatters vacated certain lands reserved for the Native Americans in the Water Canyon area above Banning. Janus left Banning for a while, but later returned and built the cabin pictured above to live in while recovering from a lung problem. He later married Betty Stewart and farmed a peach orchard on the bench—the flat mountainside area north of Banning. (Courtesy of Nara Haskell.)

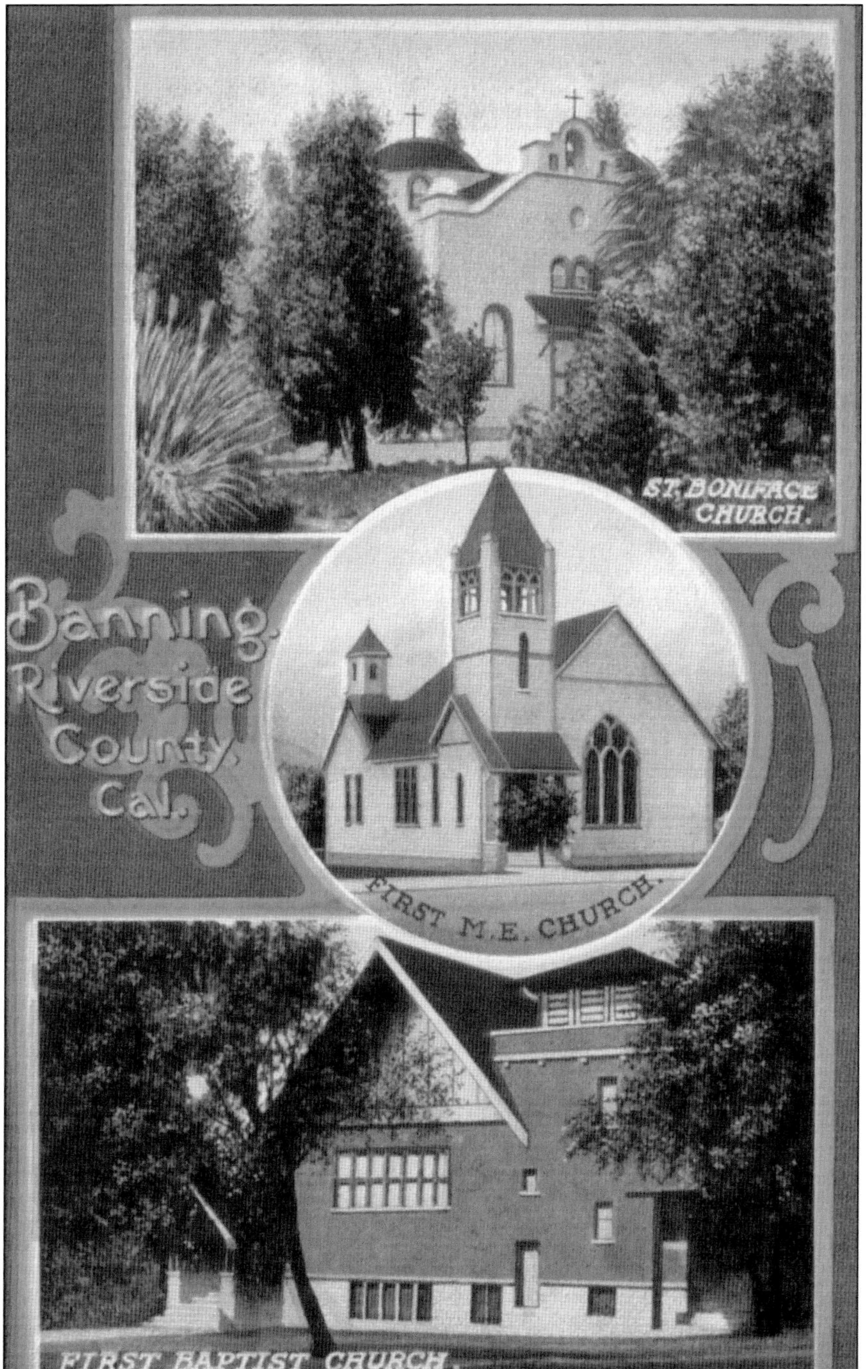

Only nostalgia for these three early churches remains because all have been razed. However, their legacy lingers on in the form of new churches that have been built to replace them, with the exception of St. Boniface Church, which once served the Native American school that no longer exists. The Baptist and Methodist churches remain active entities today and serve the community well. (Courtesy of Steve Lech.)

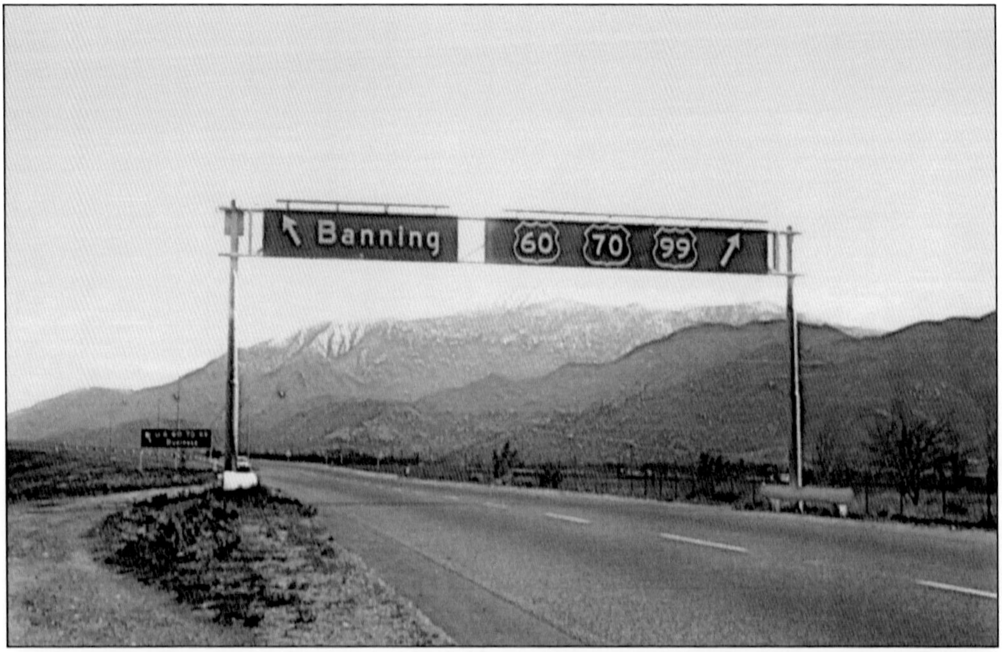

This rural highway once passed through the heart of Banning. It was later replaced by Interstate 10, which bypassed Banning to the south and drastically slowed the town's business activities. The picturesque landscape that it traversed is witnessed by beautiful Mount San Jacinto, framed by the highway sign. (Courtesy of Steve Lech.)

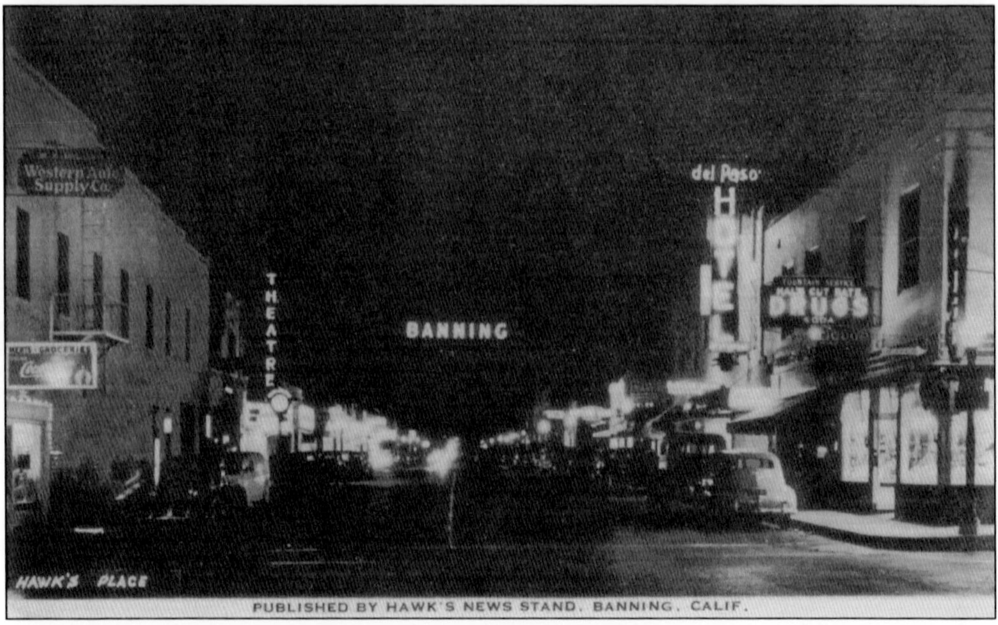

This picture was taken at night in the early 1940s, when precautionary blackouts were often enacted during World War II. Many cities on the West Coast became accustomed to not having lights at night during such times. Banning, however, was exempt because the demarcation line ran between Beaumont and Banning; Beaumont was forced to have blackouts but Banning was not. (Courtesy of Joan Coombs.)

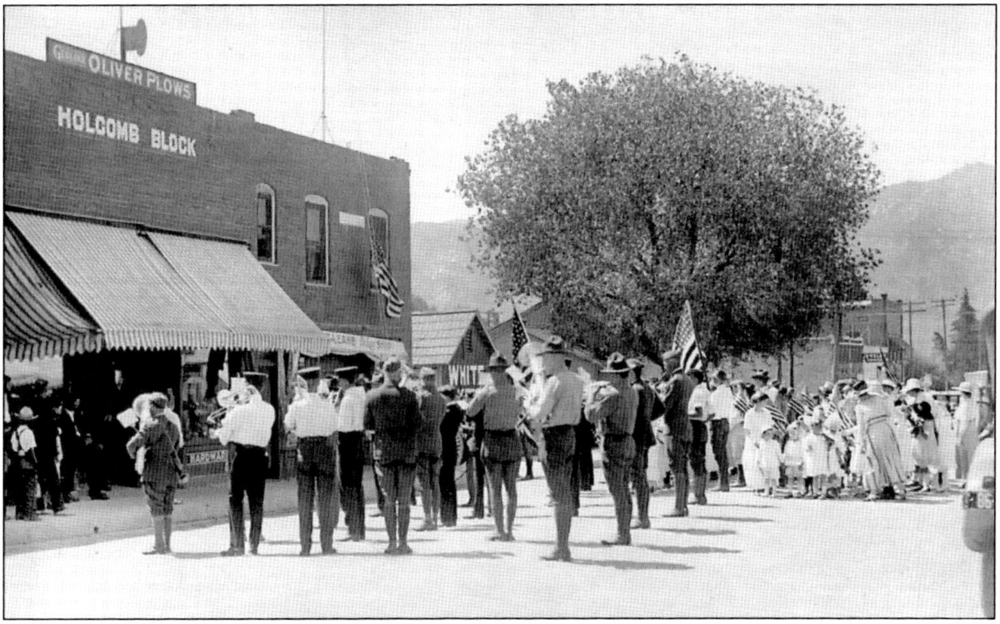

This celebratory scene, looking south on San Gorgonio Avenue around 1919 or 1920, shows a welcome home for veterans of World War I being conducted in Banning. The picture is filled with patriotism, as evidenced by the many flags and uniformed militia. The war had been a traumatic shock to those Banning residents who had sent their sons to fight in Europe. (Courtesy of Joan Coombs.)

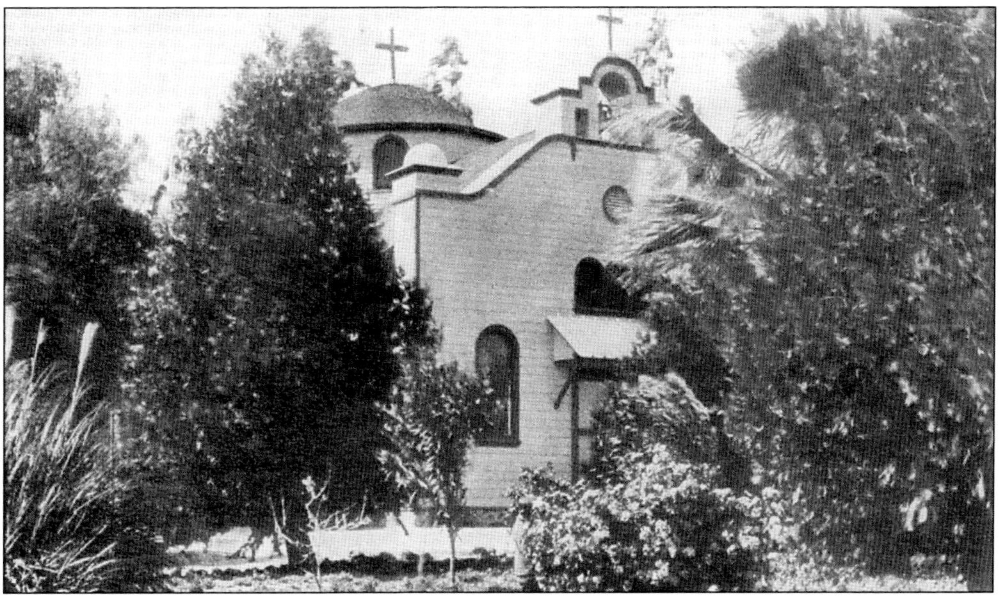

St. Boniface Church in Banning was located north of Gilman Street and west of Eighth Street. It was part of the St. Boniface Indian School complex, which was rebuilt after a 1900 earthquake almost totally destroyed it. The church served the community well for many years and was an integral part of the St. Boniface School. In later years, the school lost its standing and, along with other buildings, was razed.

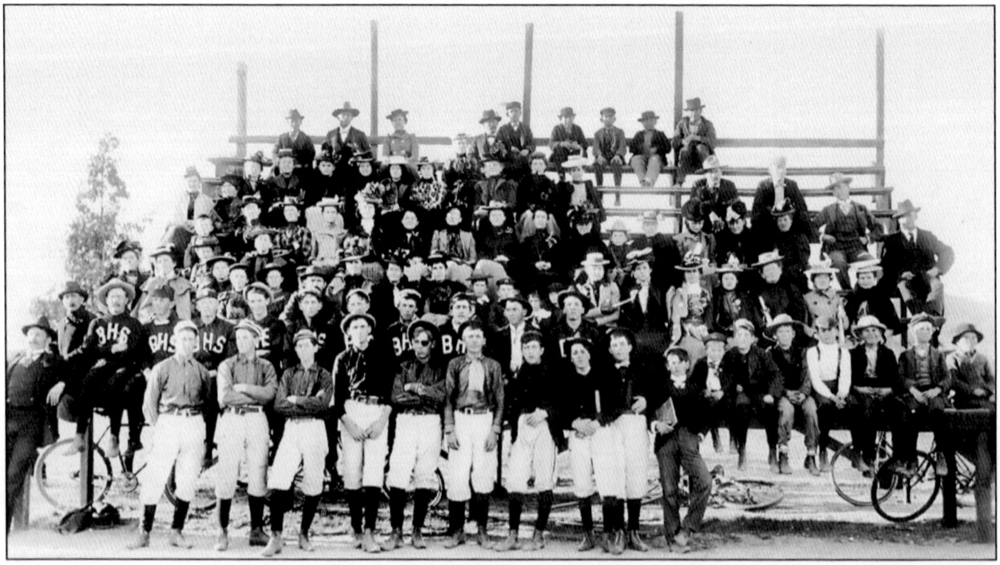

This 1896 photograph shows the Banning High School baseball team at a game outing. Banning has always been very competitive in sports against its nearby Beaumont rival to the west. This was an era when baseball was becoming quite popular and this popularity can be witnessed by the town's large turnout. (Courtesy of Joan Coombs.)

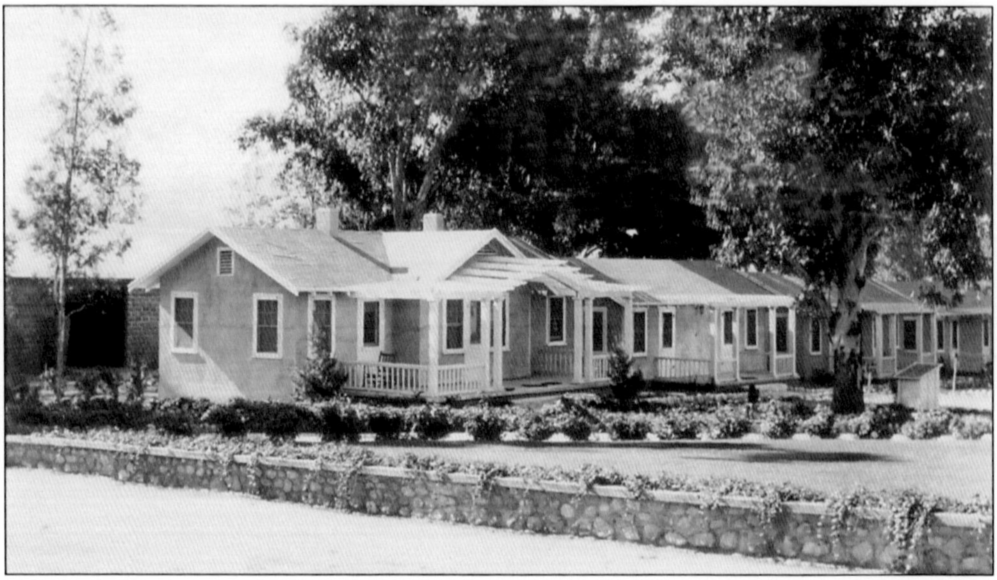

When The Banning Hotel and its entire block were purchased by two San Francisco developers, they added a number of bungalows to the property. Pictured here are several of the bungalows in their quaint setting surrounding both sides and the rear of The Banning. Fortunately, the 1930 fire that brought the hotel to shambles did not spread and destroy the bungalows. However, they were razed later. (Courtesy of Steve Lech.)

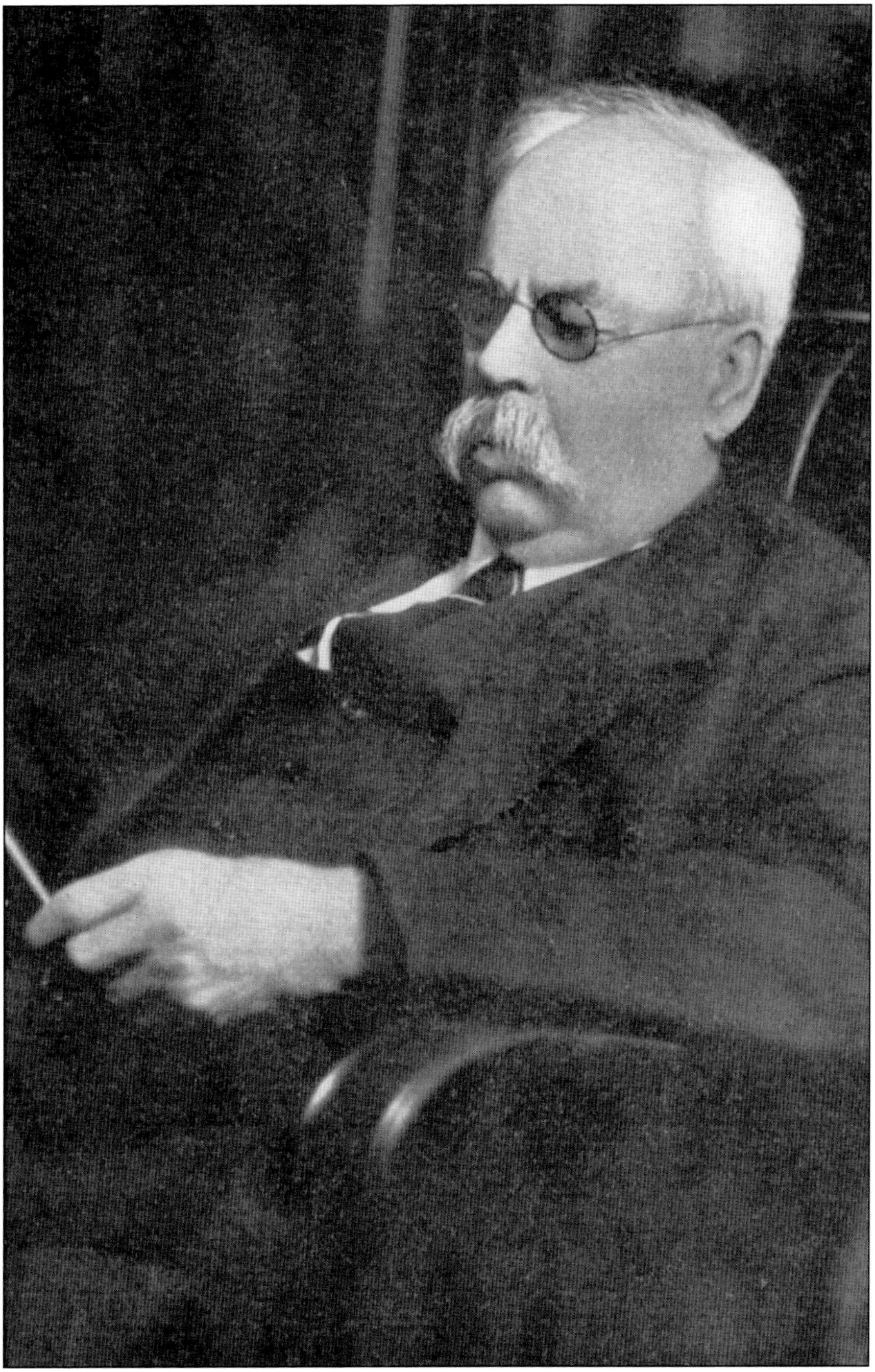

Charles Omar Barker, for many years Banning's most prominent citizen, was born July 4, 1858, near Yates City, Illinois. He arrived in Banning from Riverside on June 6, 1884, spending his first night on a cot in the Southern Pacific Railroad depot. In 1892, Barker was elected to the State Assembly from San Bernardino County. On January 9, 1893, he introduced Assembly Bill No. 130, thereby creating Riverside County. (Courtesy of Tom Hughes.)

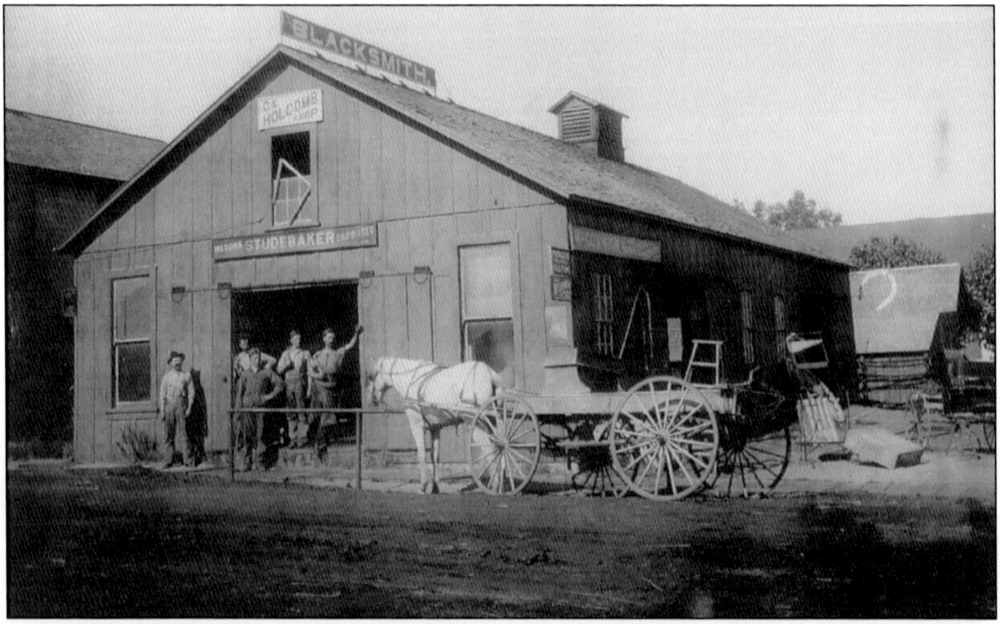

In the early days of Banning's history, before the advent of mechanized automobiles and trucks, the town relied totally upon horse-drawn buggies and wagons. Like the garages and body shops of today that care for fleets of cars and trucks, residents then relied upon blacksmith shops and livery stables to accommodate the buggies, wagons, and horses. Pictured here is one of the early blacksmith shops in Banning that provided such service. (Courtesy of the Banning Public Library.)

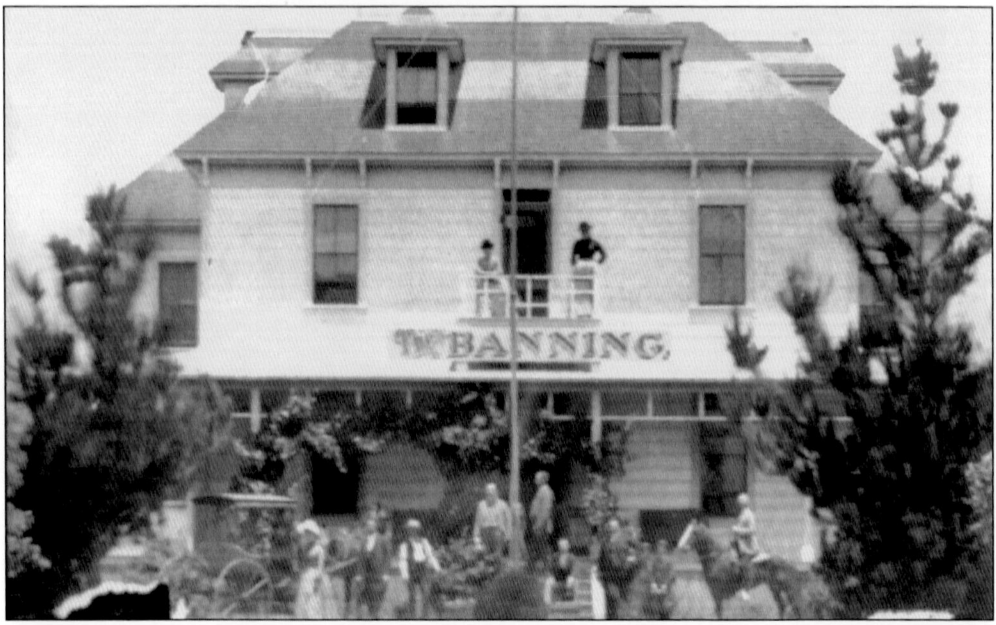

In 1888, Captain and Mrs. Fraser bought the Bryant House from Mr. and Mrs. Crosley, the developers of the hotel, and changed its name to The Banning. In 1920, John Livacich and J. Kurtal of San Francisco bought The Banning and its entire block from Mrs. Fraser. They renamed it the San Gorgonio Inn. On April 15, 1930, it was heavily damaged by fire and practically destroyed. However, it was soon rebuilt. (Courtesy of Joan Coombs.)

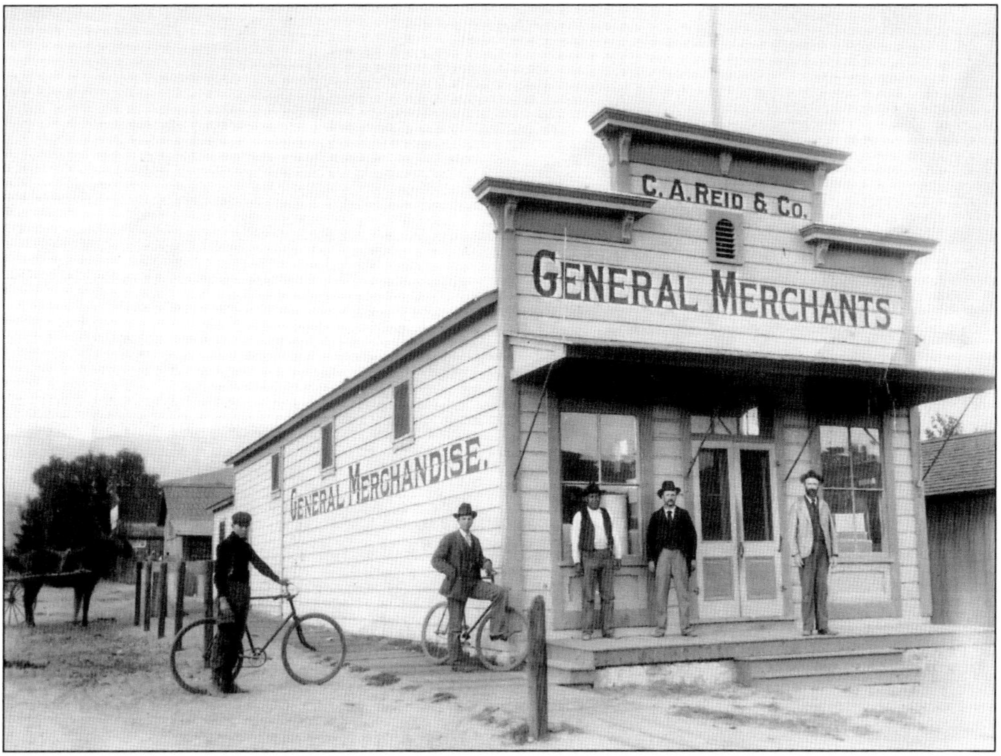

As Banning's population began to increase, businesses prospered. This 1898 photograph of the Reid Building seems to indicate that business activity has begun to pick up, as witnessed by the activity on the street. Also to be noted is that a number of structures have been built in the back of the C. A. Reid and Company General Merchants Store as well as on its east side. (Courtesy of Joan Coombs.)

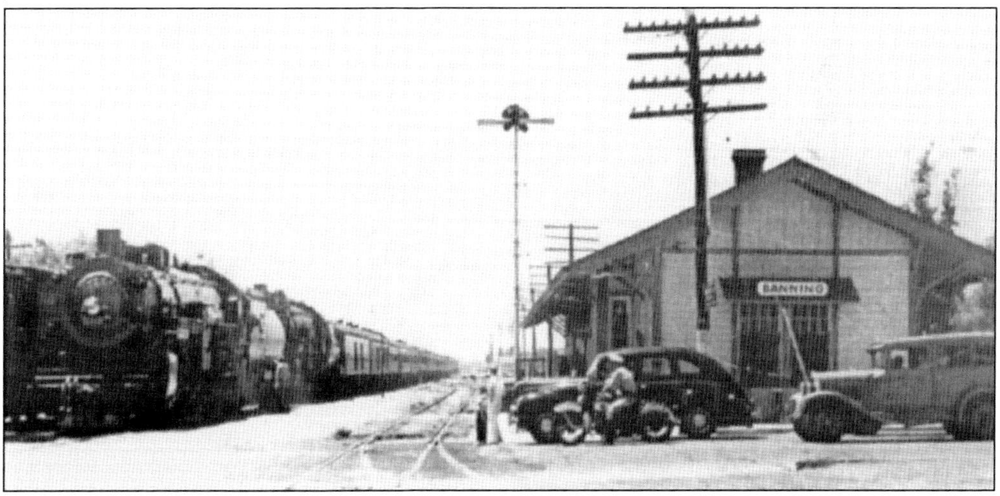

As the population of Banning grew and rail was laid through the San Gorgonio Pass, demand soon arose for a railroad station. The Southern Pacific station (pictured) was built in Banning to accommodate passenger and freight service. In later years, the station was partially destroyed by fire and the remnant of the remaining building razed. The train station was never rebuilt. (Courtesy of the Banning Public Library.)

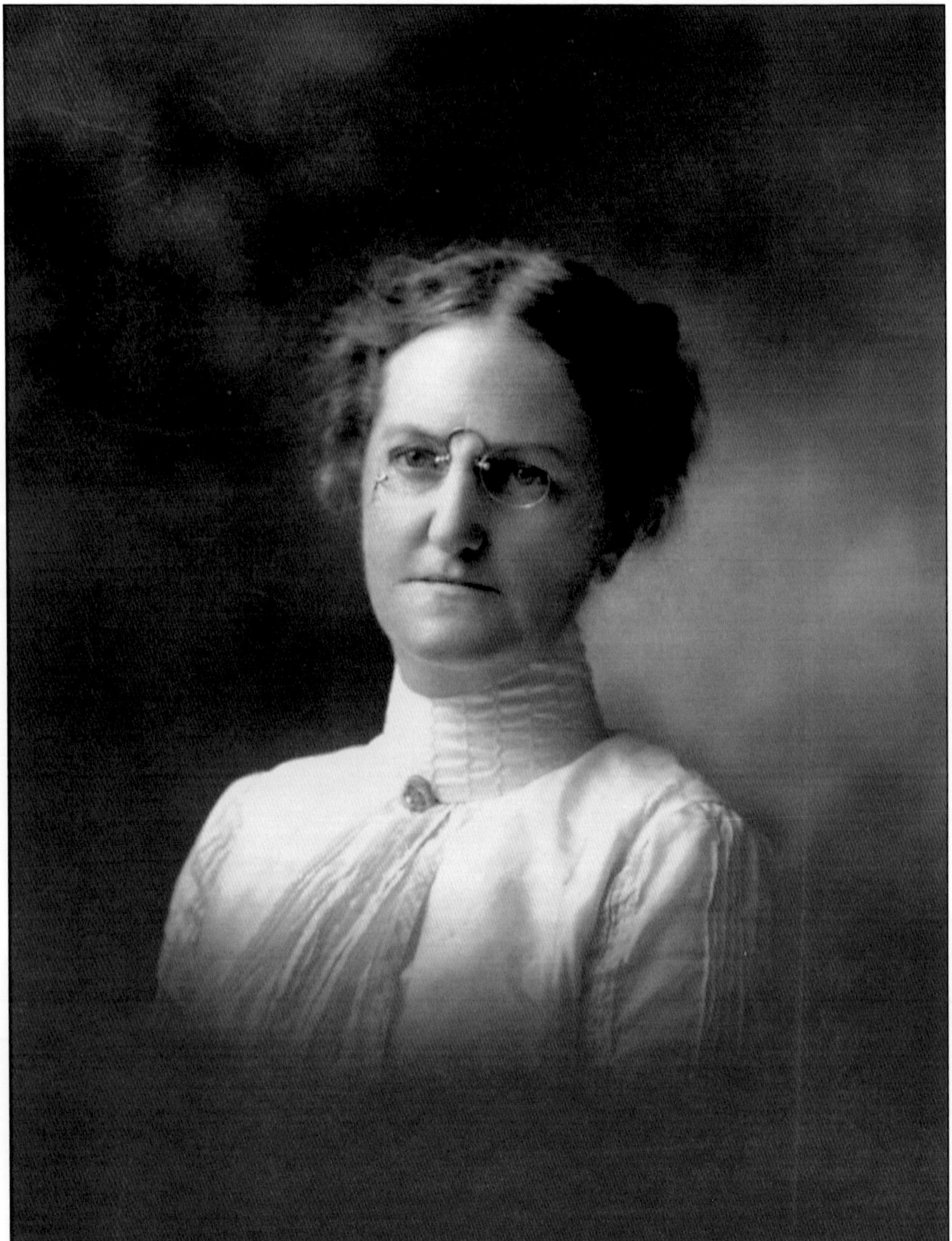

Ida Bird reached her future home at the edge of the desert in Banning around 1890. Although she found Banning quite remote from the culture and activity of Chicago, she nevertheless clung to what little civilization she found in Banning and labored hard to improve it. The church, the Saturday Afternoon Club, and all local social activities had her ardent support and her help in organizing. (Courtesy of Joan Coombs.)

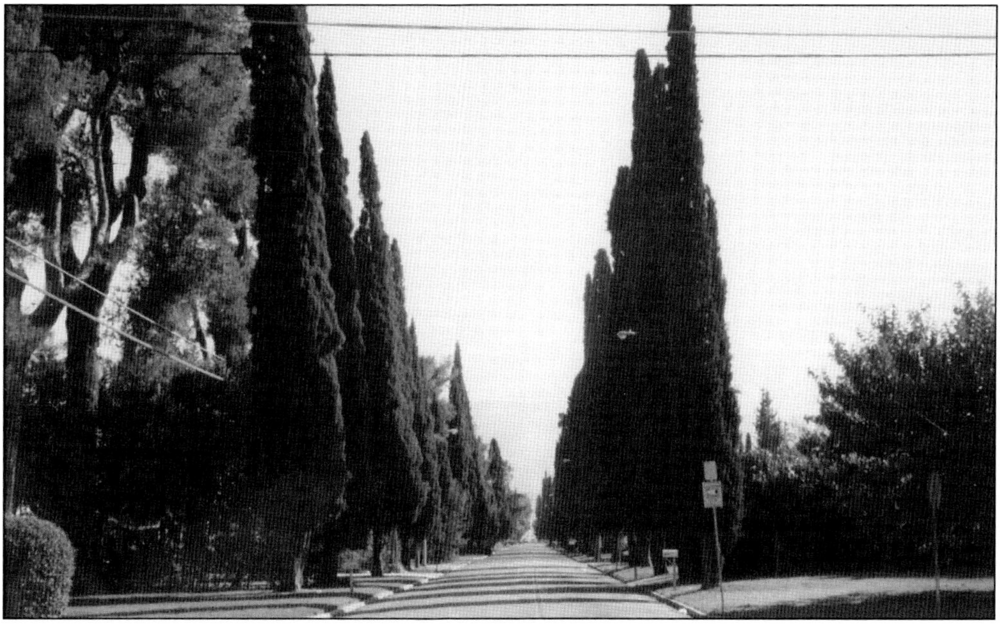

San Gorgonio Avenue is depicted here looking south from the intersection of Indian School Lane. The beautiful Italian cypress trees bordering both sides of San Gorgonio Avenue were planted by John G. Repplier. Two months after Banning was incorporated in 1913, Repplier became its first tree warden. Under his direction, seven miles of trees were planted, mostly with acacias and peppers. (Courtesy of the author.)

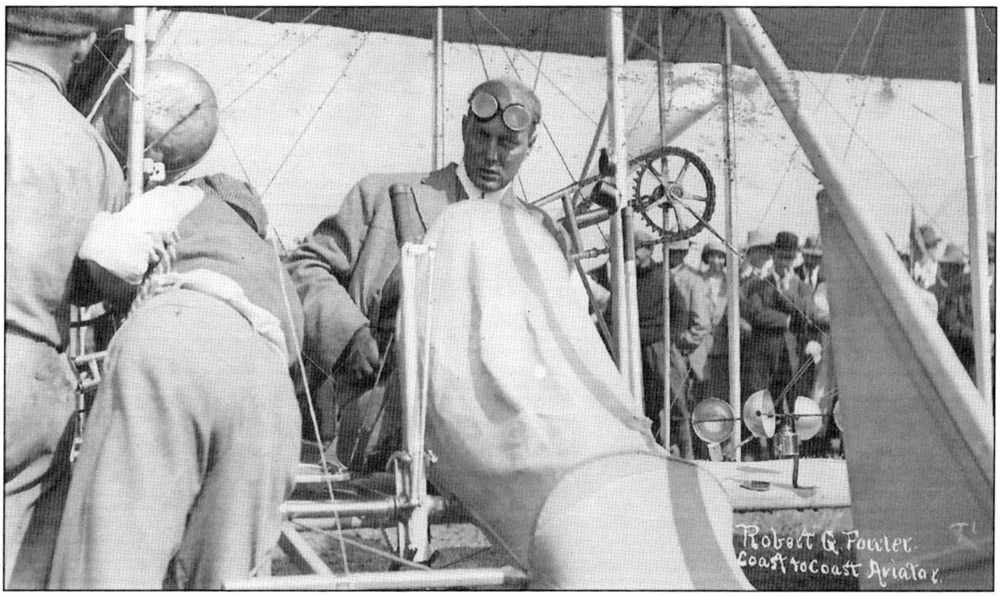

Orville Wright's historic flight in 1903 spurred aviation forward. An improved Wright Model B plane was later made available and in 1911, William Randolph Hearst offered $50,000 to the first person to fly coast to coast within 30 days. Robert Fowler (pictured) accepted the challenge and left Los Angeles in 1911. He was forced down in Banning by gale winds at Stewart's Ranch, and although he completed his flight, he failed to do so in 30 days. (Courtesy of the Historical Gilman Ranch and Wagon Museum.)

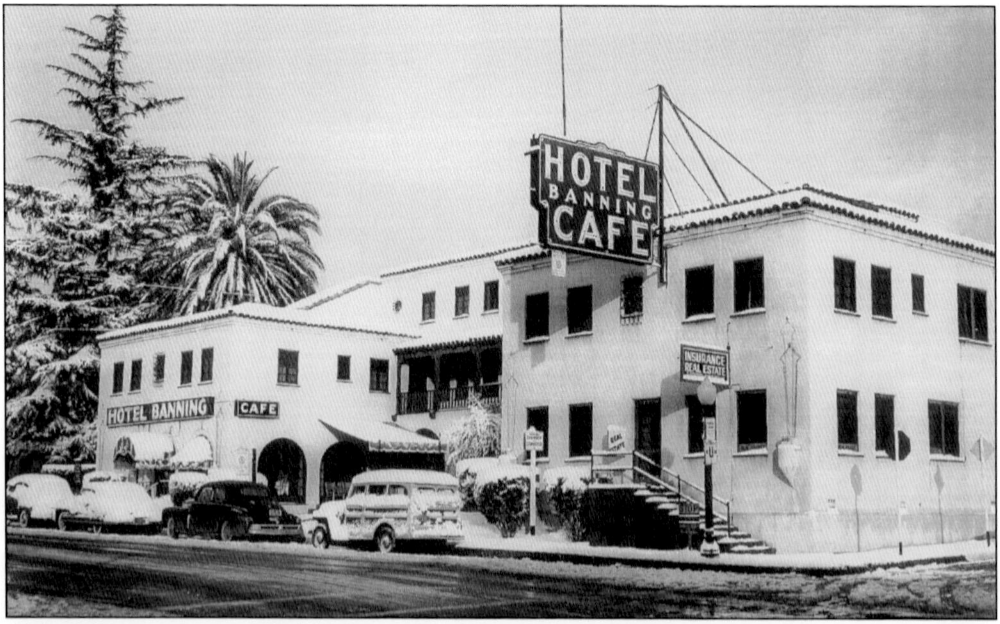

Although Banning is cradled between two mountains that are snow capped for several months of every year, it is seldom that significant amounts of snow fall upon the town and its surroundings. This picture, however, shows that it does sometimes snow in Banning and, that enough can fall to cover the large valley and make its green golf courses appear glistening white. (Courtesy of Bud Mathewson.)

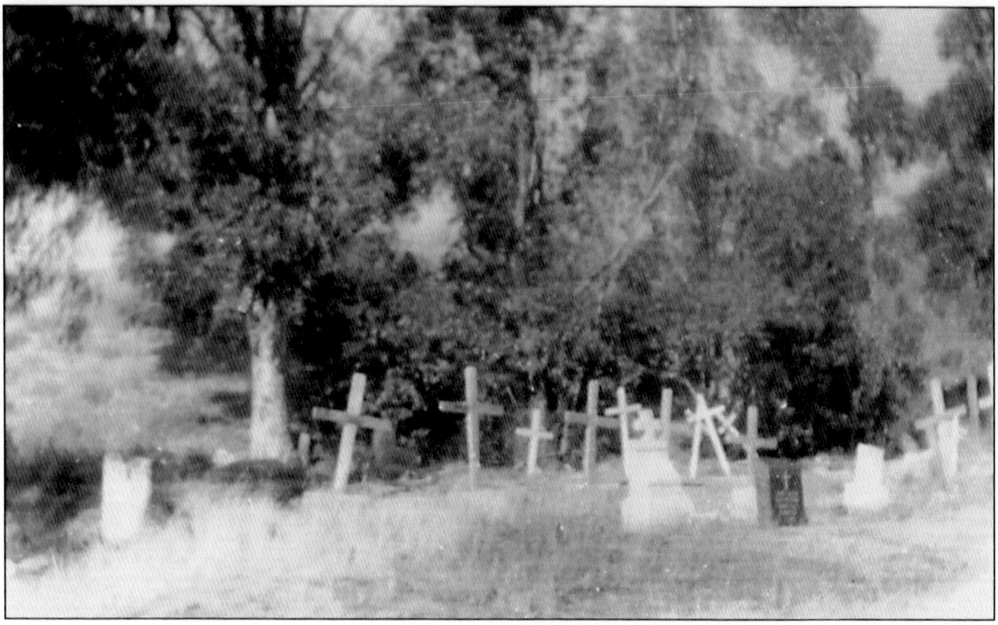

St. Boniface Indian School and Church were located north of Gilman Street and west of Eighth Street in the early years of Banning's history. Both are gone now, but the cemetery that was established still remains, although it has been vandalized and is in poor condition. This picture was probably taken when the school was still in operation, because the cemetery is in relatively good care. (Courtesy of Joan Coombs.)

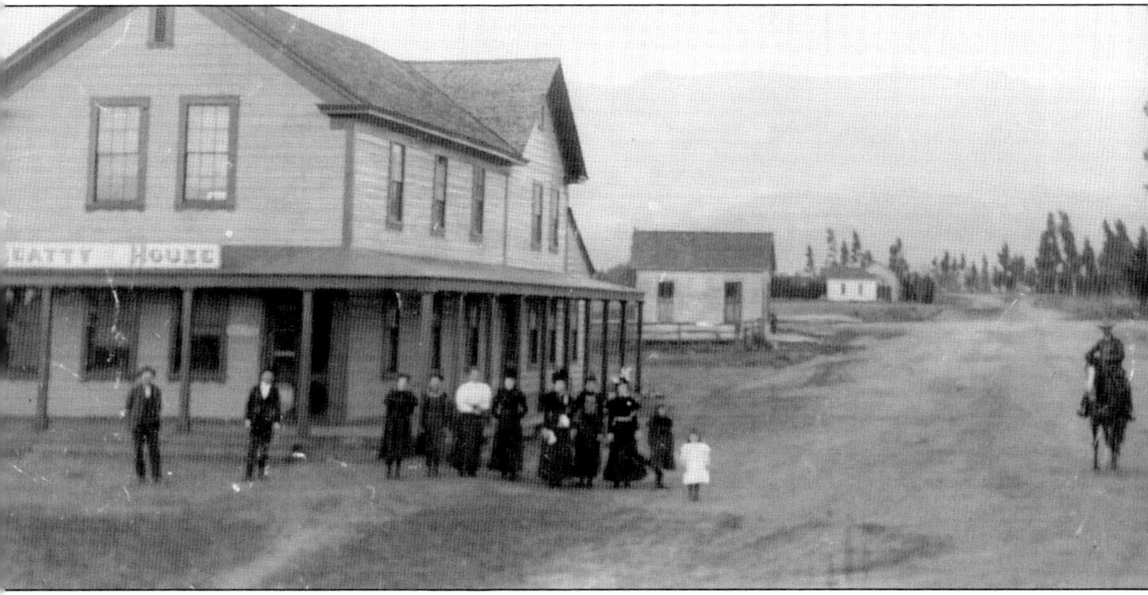

Beatty House was an early boardinghouse in Beaumont, Banning's adjoining western neighbor. The gathering outside probably consists of the boardinghouse's working crew. Note the wide rural street that today is filled with bustling auto traffic and at that time consisted of just one horse and rider. Boardinghouses during this era served to accommodate new arrivals. (Courtesy of Marilyn Vonderheide.)

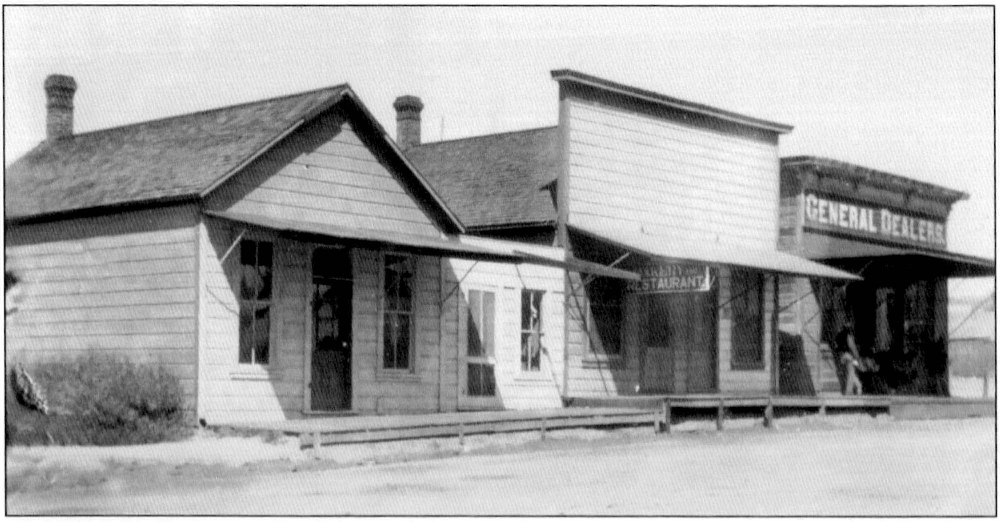

This photograph portrays how some of the early businesses in Banning appeared in the 1890s. The building housing the General Dealers store at the right was owned by Banning's first mayor, Walter Hathaway. The architecture of the bakery and restaurant next to the General Dealers store incorporates a high, false front that was commonly used on buildings in Banning. (Courtesy of Joan Coombs.)

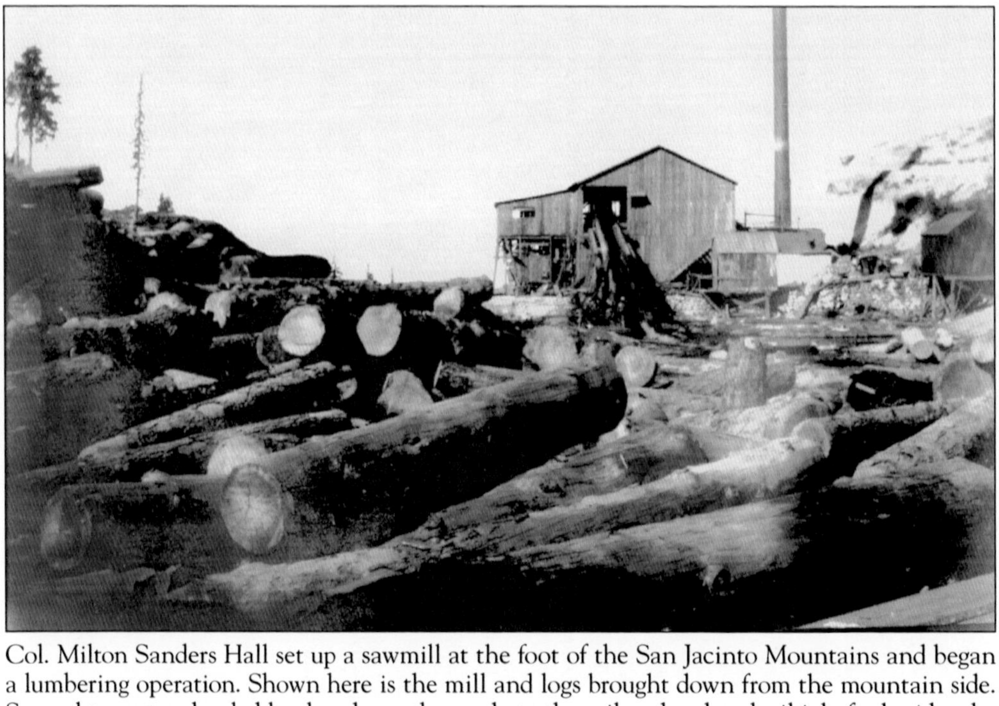

Col. Milton Sanders Hall set up a sawmill at the foot of the San Jacinto Mountains and began a lumbering operation. Shown here is the mill and logs brought down from the mountain side. Several teamsters hauled lumber down the grade to the railroad, a daredevil job, for besides the regular brakes they had to tie logs and trees behind loads to drag in the dirt and keep loads off the rumps of the horses. (Courtesy of Joan Coombs.)

Three

Banning Becomes a City

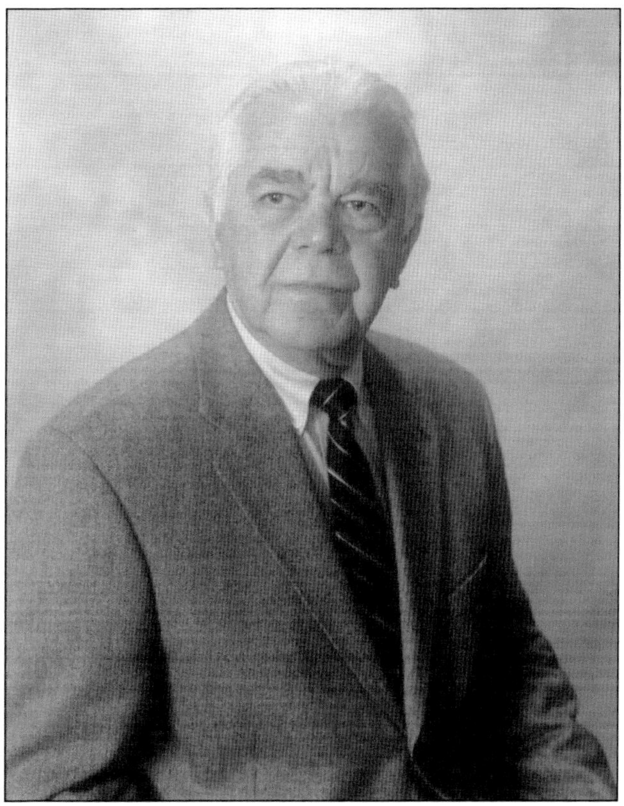

On December 10, 2004, John Machisic replaced Art Welsh as mayor of Banning. He was born in Turtle Creek, Pennsylvania, in July 1931, and came to California in 1956. After receiving his master and doctorate at the University of Southern California while living in Lakewood, California, he worked in the educational field before moving to Banning in 1994. Since then he has served on the school board, the board of directors of the Sun Lakes Country Club, and Banning City Council. Mayor Machisic has been married 52 years, and he and his wife, Peggy, have three children and nine grandchildren. (Courtesy of John Machisic.)

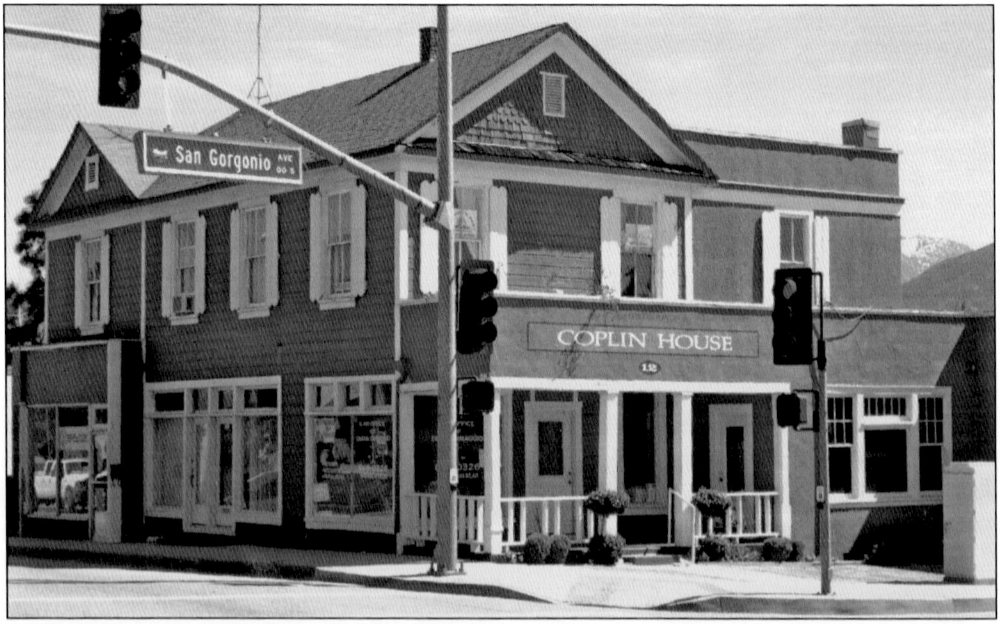

The Coplin House still stands in the heart of Banning on the southeast corner of Ramsey Street and San Gorgonio Avenue. William Salisbury, who once ran Banning's opera house in the Holcomb block to the south, built it in 1900 and named it the Coplin House after his mother, who purchased the property in 1887. Due to changes of ownership, it has also been called the Spokane Hotel and El Camino Real Hotel. (Courtesy of the author.)

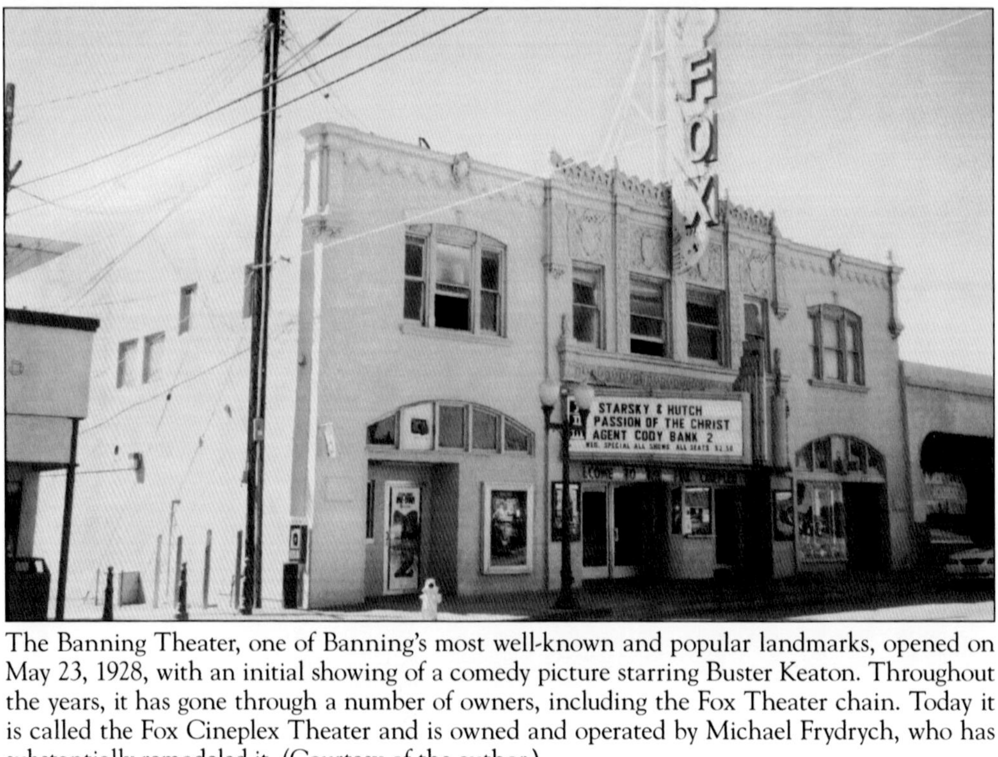

The Banning Theater, one of Banning's most well-known and popular landmarks, opened on May 23, 1928, with an initial showing of a comedy picture starring Buster Keaton. Throughout the years, it has gone through a number of owners, including the Fox Theater chain. Today it is called the Fox Cineplex Theater and is owned and operated by Michael Frydrych, who has substantially remodeled it. (Courtesy of the author.)

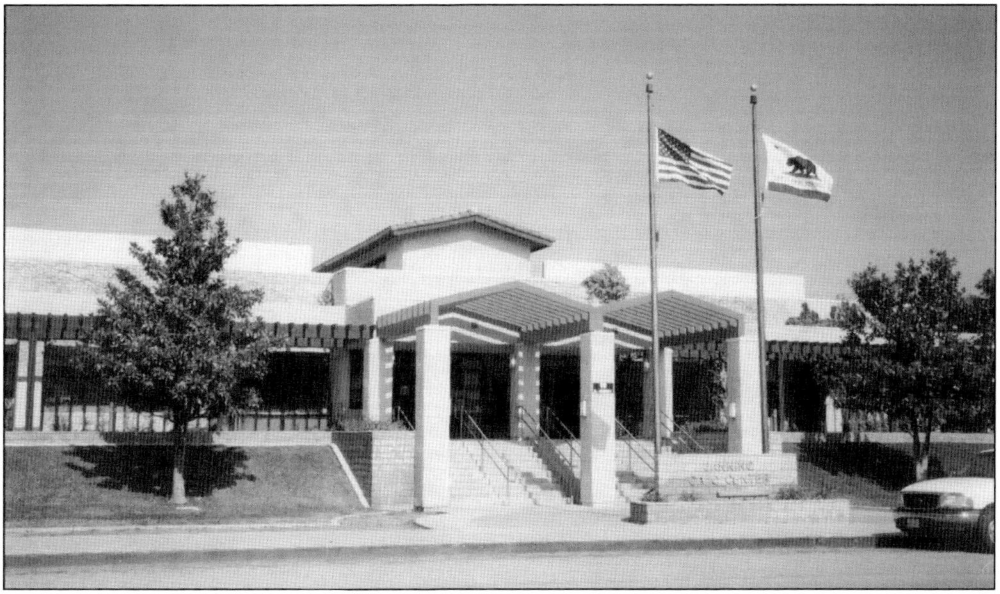

The Banning Civic Center is located on the north side of Ramsey between San Gorgonio Avenue and Alessandro Street. The complex of buildings houses all the city's major facilities. The city council chamber is located in the building with reserved parking on the side for city officials. The chamber of commerce office is toward the right facing Ramsey Street. The police facility is housed next to the main building. (Courtesy of the author.)

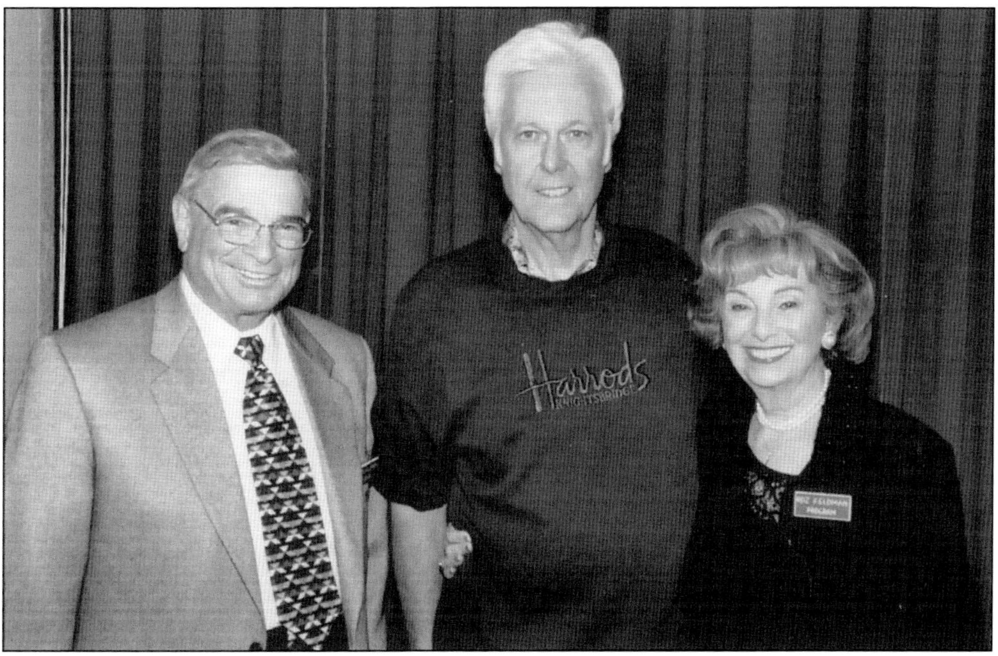

Pictured here are Bert and Roz Feldman, with entertainer Jack Jones in the center. Bert is president of the Sun Lakes Country Club's Friendship Club and his wife, Roz, is the club's program chairperson. The Friendship Club began about 1996 with only 12 couples, but today has blossomed into 931 members, due to the enduring efforts of Roz Feldman to bring in exceptional entertainment, such as Jack Jones, who was featured here November 14, 2004. (Courtesy of Bernice Schoen.)

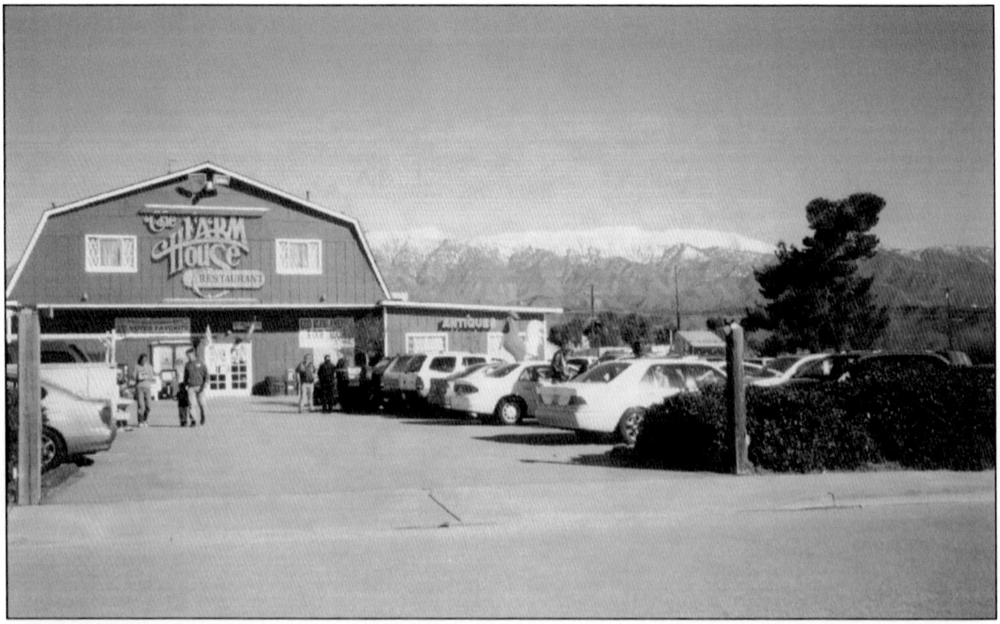

The Farmhouse Restaurant, one of Banning's best known, long-established restaurants, is a popular stop for many travelers and vacationers along Interstate 10 through Banning, as well as a favorite gathering and eatery for locals. Adjoining the restaurant is an antiques shop, which attracts many of those who stop by to dine. It is owned and operated by Jackie Palmer Kennedy. (Courtesy of the author.)

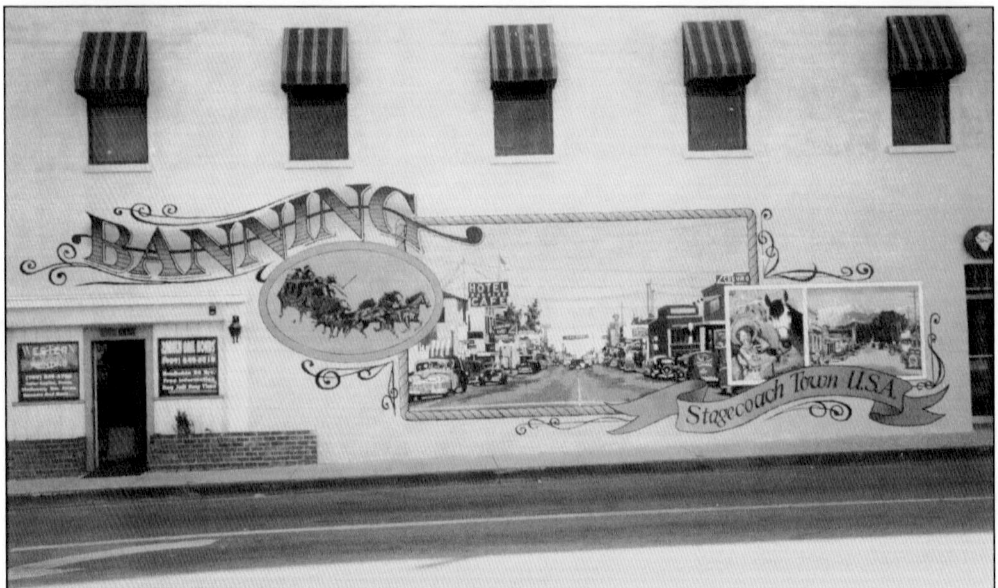

This mural-in-a-day project was completed by artist Art Mortimer and helpers during the 47th-annual Stagecoach Days celebration. The 52-foot-long, 12-foot-high mural is on a building at 42 West Ramsey Street. Completed in a day, the mural pays tribute to first lieutenant Joshua Palmer, a Banning native who died in Iraq while leading his troops into an enemy occupied building in Fallujah. (Courtesy of the author.)

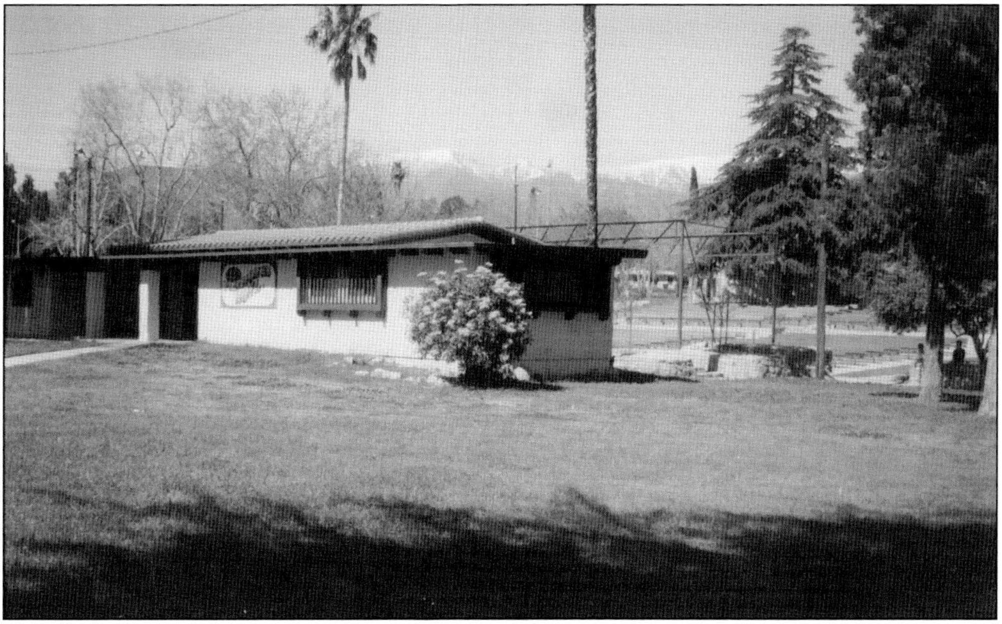

Seen here is the main building and ticket booth of the Playhouse Bowl, which stands in front of an amphitheater in Repplier Park in Banning. Numerous cultural events have taken place at this open-air site over the many years since it was instituted in the park, and its events are highly anticipated and enjoyed by not only Banning residents, but also by people from outlying areas. (Courtesy of the author.)

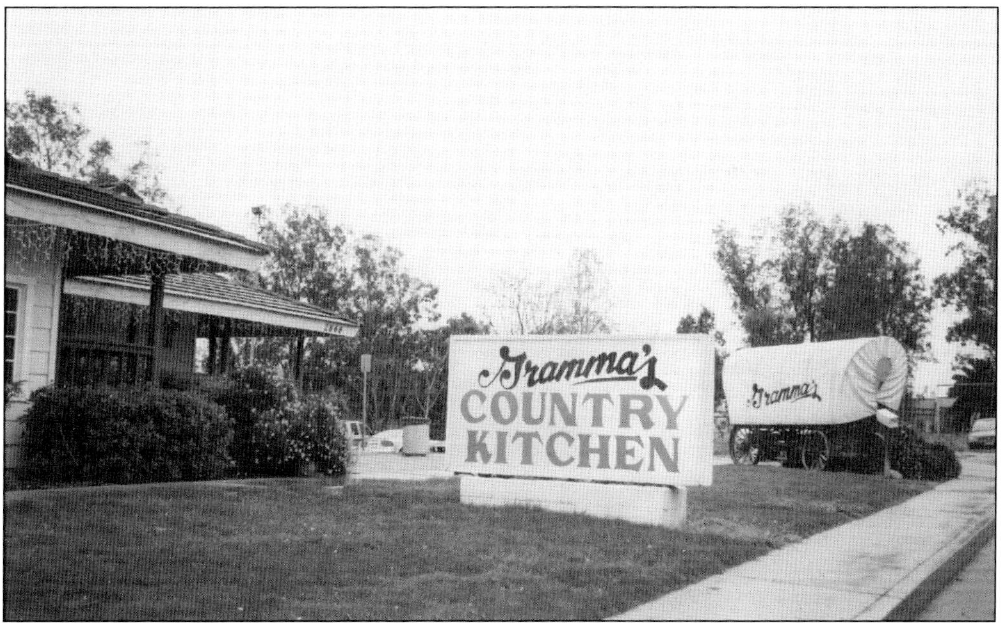

Shown here is another popular eatery in Banning now located on the south side of Ramsey Street south of Sunset Avenue. Co-owned and operated by Kathy Kennedy and Frank Ramirez, it was originally established on the northeast corner of Woodland Street and Ramsey Avenue before being relocated to its present site. The old covered wagon pictured here has become a landmark. (Courtesy of the author.)

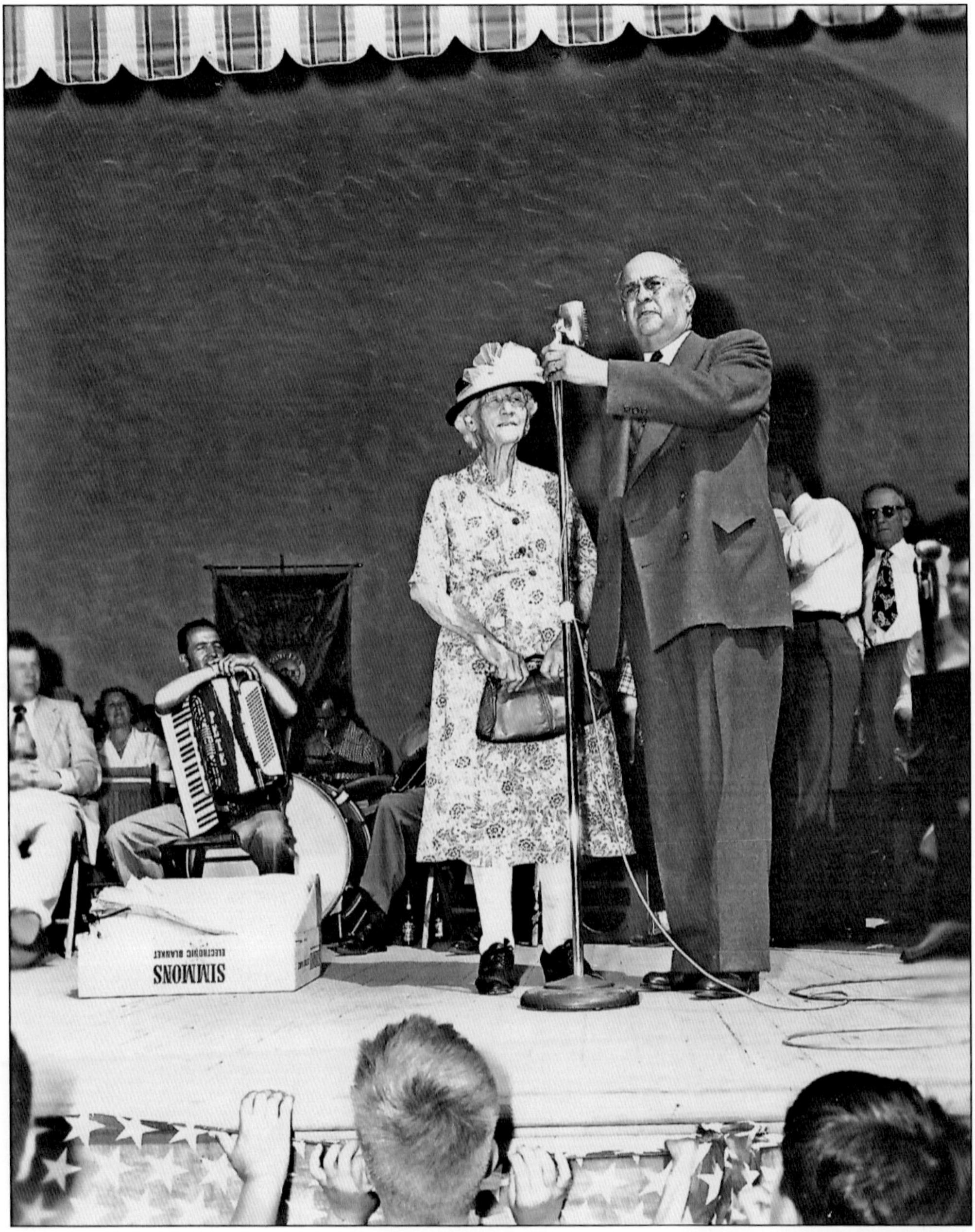

Pioneer Nellie Bailiff made quite an impression with the Southern Pacific Railroad echelon. She was not only a telegrapher who helped the railroad run smoothly, but often held out the message hoop that was then grabbed by someone reaching out to get it while hanging from the train car. Here she is being honored by Southern Pacific president A. T. Mercier on a visit to Los Angeles. (Courtesy of Marianne Bailiff.)

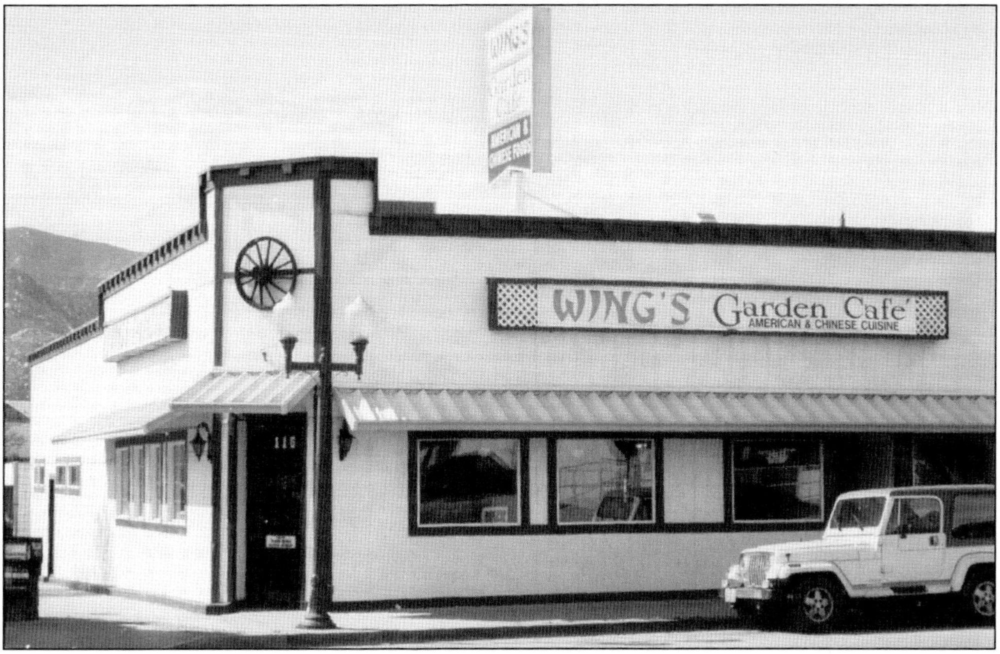

The Wings Garden Restaurant on the southwest corner of Ramsey and First Streets in Banning occupies space that was built in 1942 and once included four businesses: a soda fountain, shoe store, garage, and doctor's office. In the 1950s, the soda fountain became Gray's ice cream store. In 1973, Mr. Roberts bought the property and converted all businesses under one roof as Roberts' Restaurant. In 1986, Mr. Wing Wong purchased the building and in 1992 changed its name to Wings Garden Restaurant. (Courtesy of the author.)

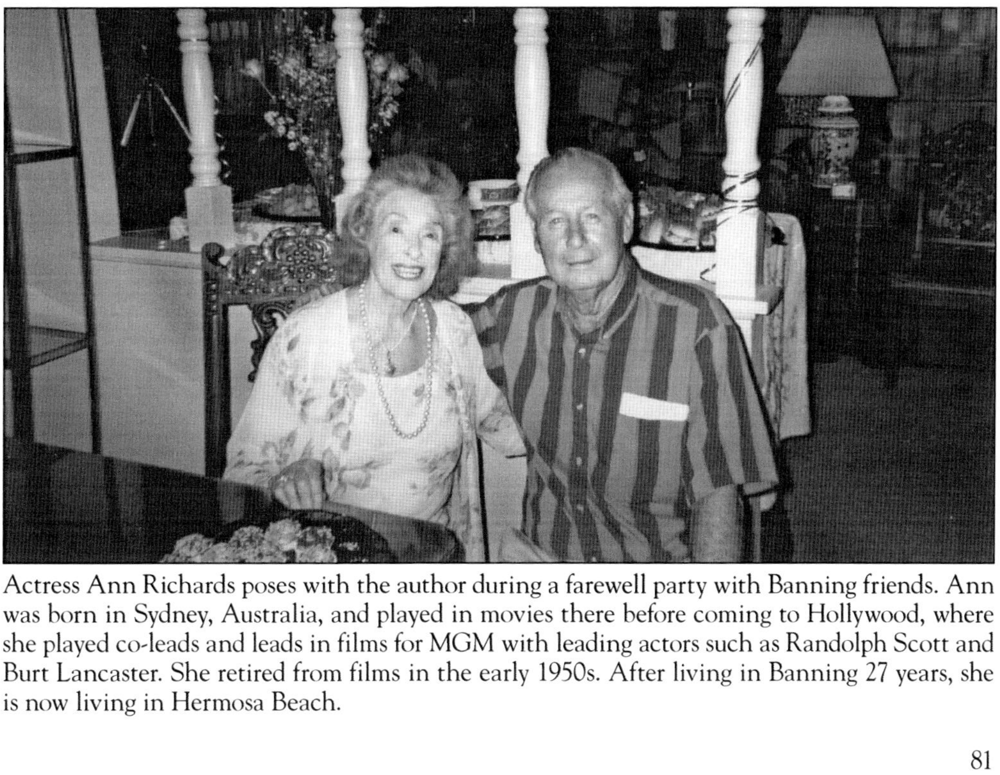

Actress Ann Richards poses with the author during a farewell party with Banning friends. Ann was born in Sydney, Australia, and played in movies there before coming to Hollywood, where she played co-leads and leads in films for MGM with leading actors such as Randolph Scott and Burt Lancaster. She retired from films in the early 1950s. After living in Banning 27 years, she is now living in Hermosa Beach.

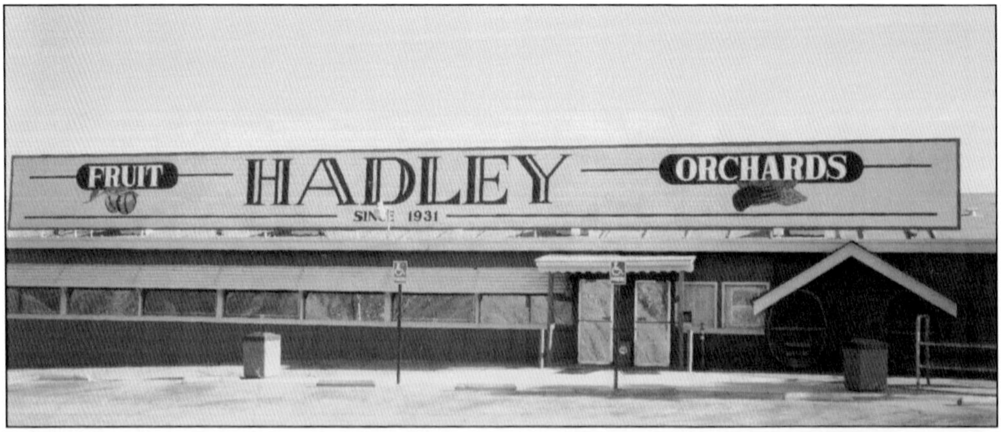

Hadley Fruit Company was founded by Paul and Peggy Hadley in 1931 in Banning, but eventually the fruit stand was moved north of old Highway 99 in Cabazon, east of Banning. Thanks to the high quality of their merchandise and a tremendous amount of hard work, the single road stand prospered, eventually selling more dates, nuts, and fruits than most wholesalers. Today Hadleys is owned and operated by the nearby Morongo Indian Reservation. (Courtesy of the author.)

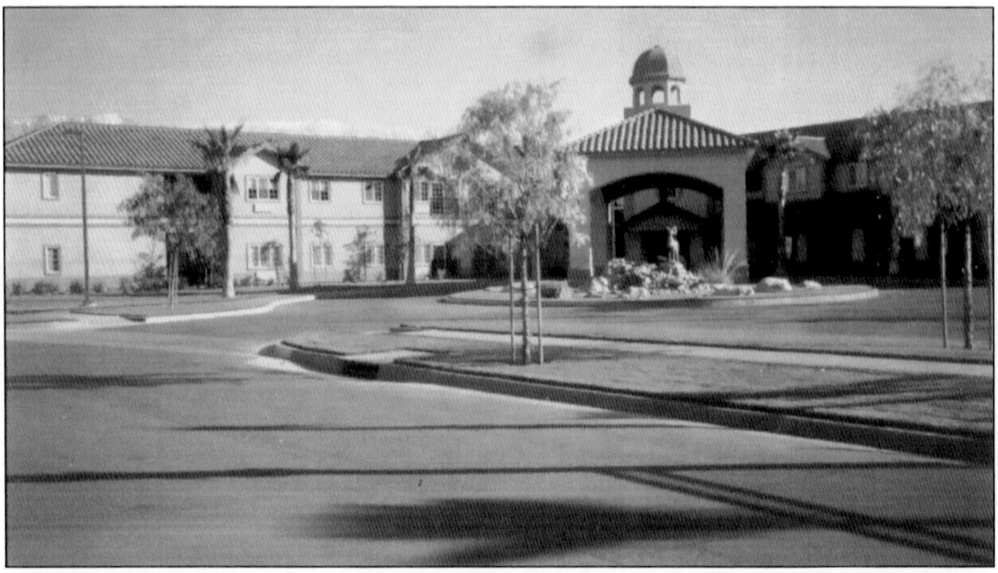

A modern, community assistance living facility, The Lakes was recently built in Banning at 5801 Sun Lakes Boulevard. It contains 70 individual living quarters and 50 assistance quarters. People have come here from around the world to enjoy the good weather and healthful living. The facility opened April 2004 and has become quite popular. The many amenities include a large swimming pool, a game room, and a gym. (Courtesy of the author.)

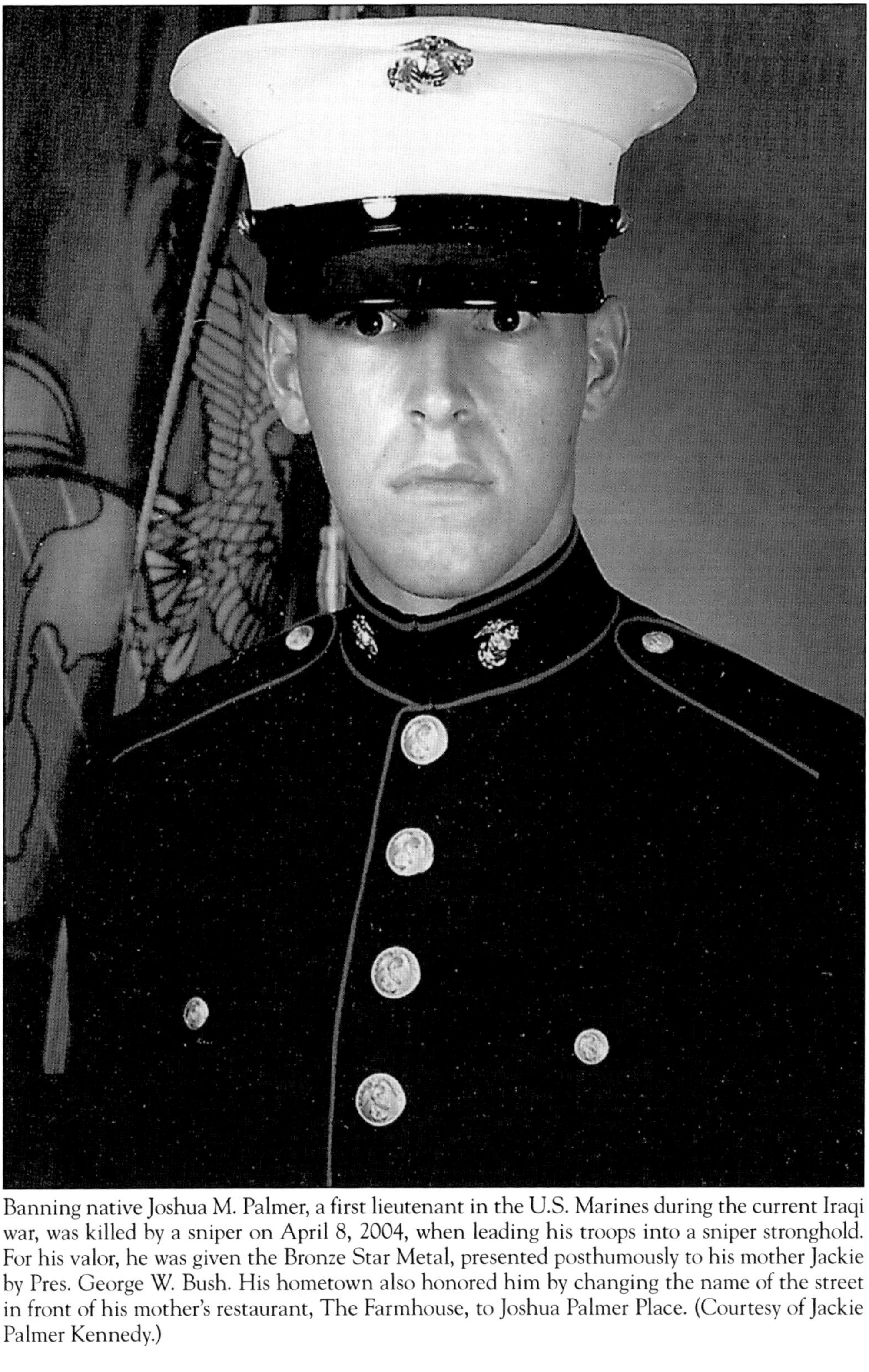

Banning native Joshua M. Palmer, a first lieutenant in the U.S. Marines during the current Iraqi war, was killed by a sniper on April 8, 2004, when leading his troops into a sniper stronghold. For his valor, he was given the Bronze Star Metal, presented posthumously to his mother Jackie by Pres. George W. Bush. His hometown also honored him by changing the name of the street in front of his mother's restaurant, The Farmhouse, to Joshua Palmer Place. (Courtesy of Jackie Palmer Kennedy.)

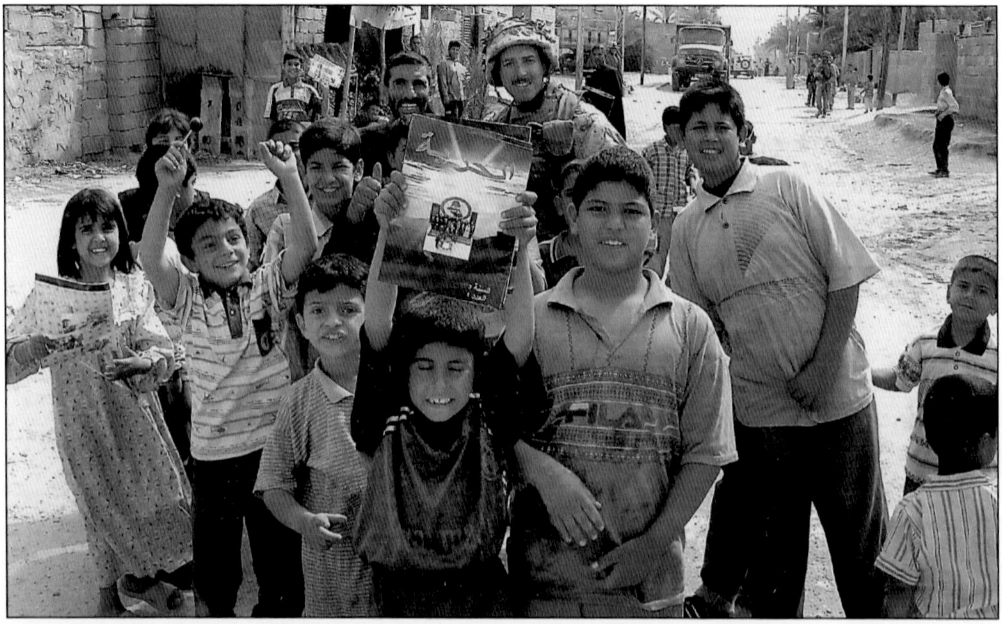

Lieutenant Palmer is pictured here in a camouflaged hat standing next to a friend and behind a group of Iraqi children. A graduate from San Diego Sate University with a degree in International Relations, his love for children made him determined to fight for the future of all the world's children. Previously, he had worked with children in Mexico on a drug program. (Courtesy of Jackie Palmer Kennedy.)

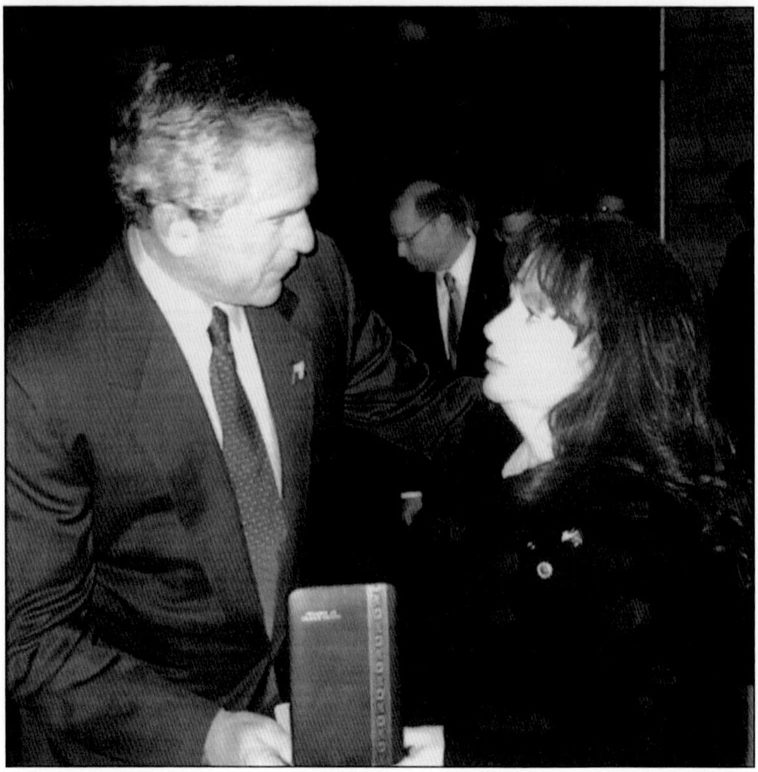

President Bush presents the Bronze Star Medal to Jackie Palmer Kennedy at Camp Pendleton. The award was made posthumously to her son Joshua Palmer, who was killed while serving in Iraq. Members of her family were also present to view the ceremony, which was gratifying to everyone and heightened the pride they all held for Joshua Palmer. (Courtesy of Jackie Palmer Kennedy.)

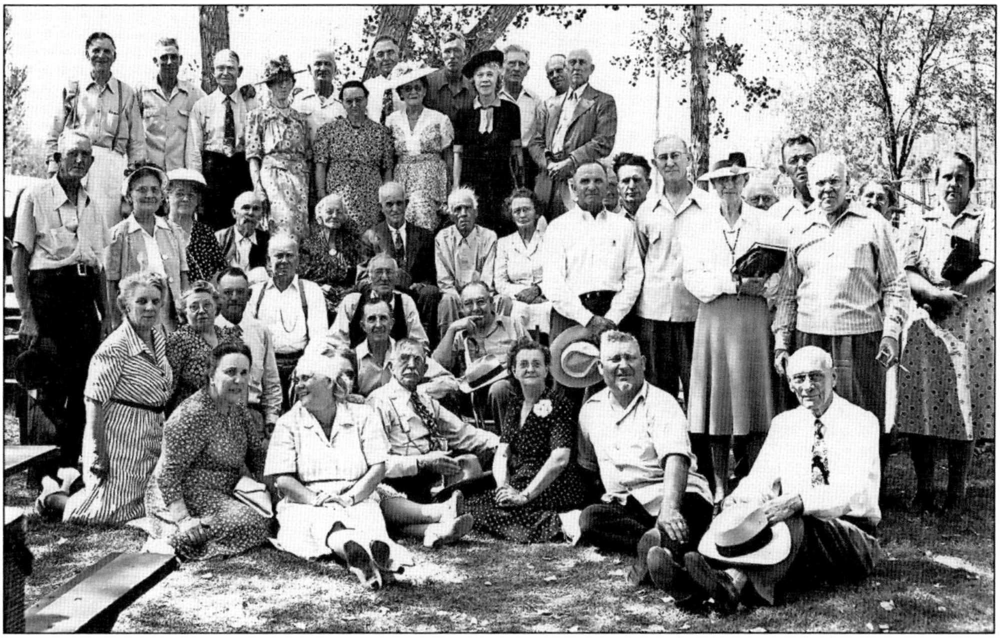

This is an undated photograph of an old-timer's picnic in Banning. Picnics like this were held year after year to honor Banning pioneers of 30 years or more and, later, for pioneers of up to 50 years. The faces seen here represent many of the men and women who formed the nucleus of Banning's business community. (Courtesy of Marianne Bailiff.)

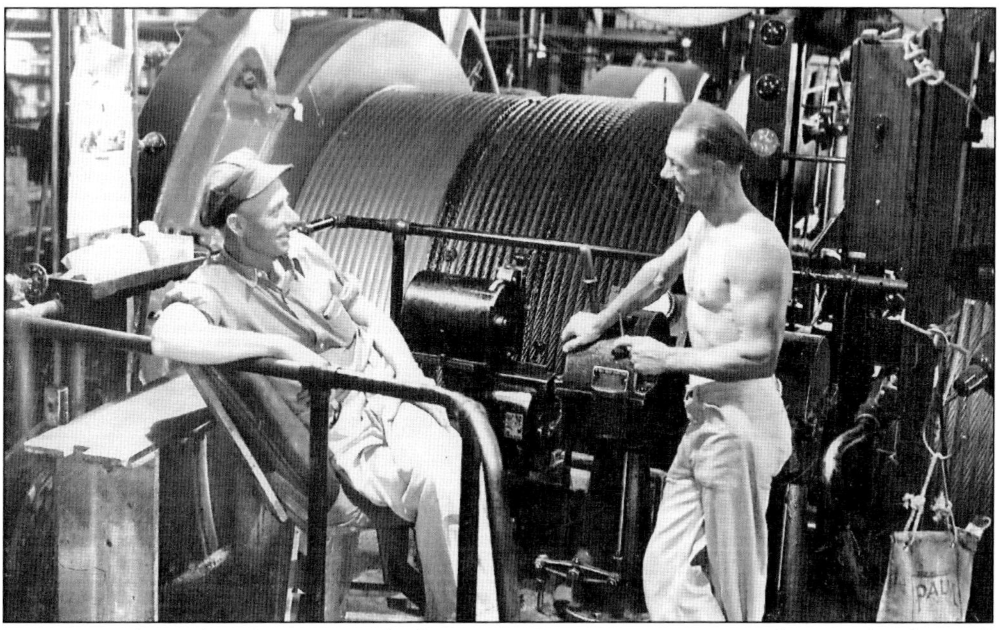

In 1931, in the midst of a nationwide depression, Banning was sustained on a tide of payroll prosperity initiated by the Metropolitan Water District's construction of the Colorado Aqueduct, of which Banning was made its headquarters. This scene depicts the complexity and magnitude of the drilling operation through the 17-foot-diameter, mile-plus tunnel through the base of Mount San Jacinto southeast of Banning. (Courtesy of Marianne Bailiff.)

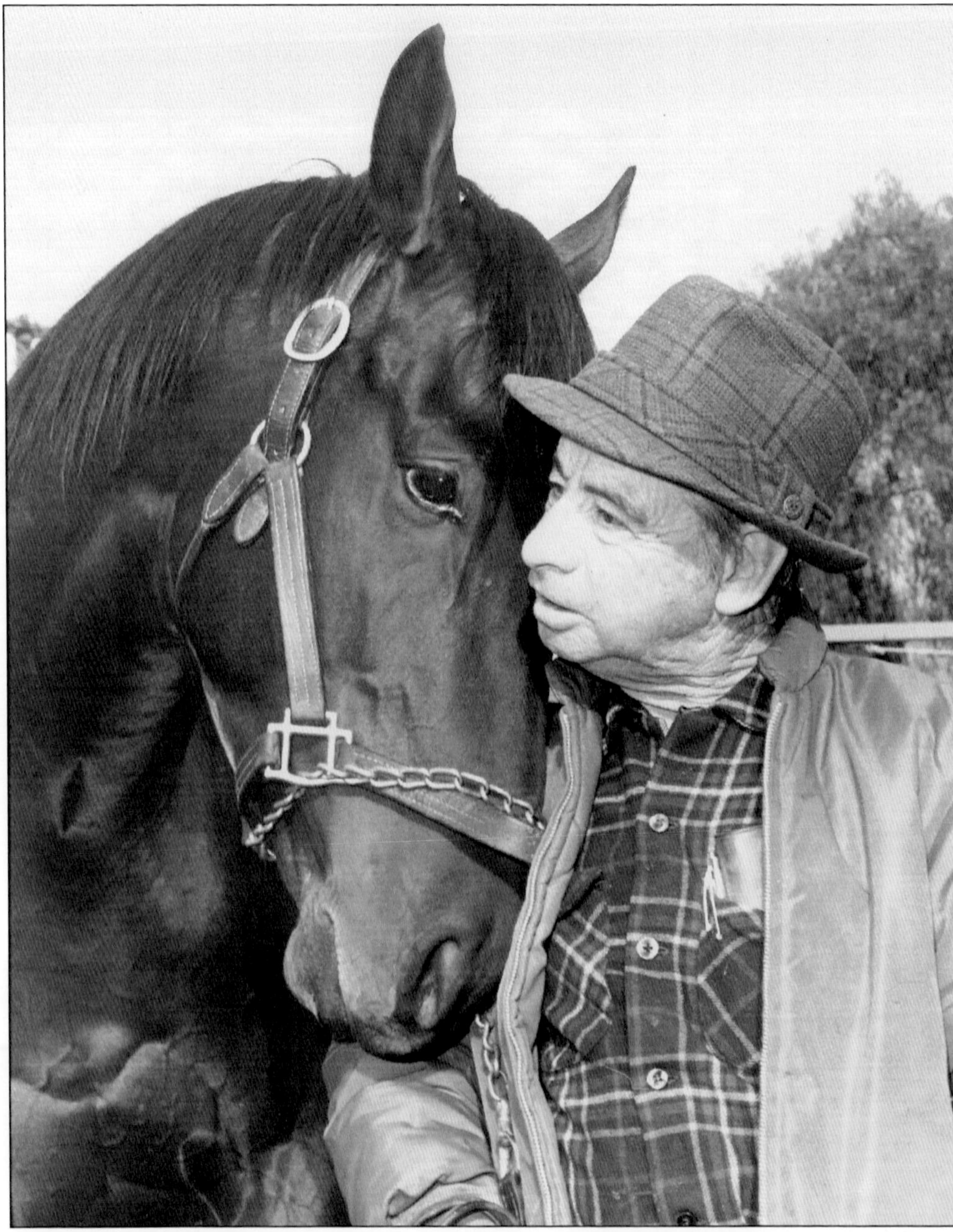

Former Banning resident and racehorse jockey Johnny Longden poses with one of his beloved horses, Money Lender. Longden's admiration of Money Lender is apparent and seems to be reciprocated by the horse, which is perhaps not surprising considering the many relationships that have existed between Longden and the horses he has associated with during his 40-year career as a jockey and racehorse trainer. (Courtesy of Doris McCoy.)

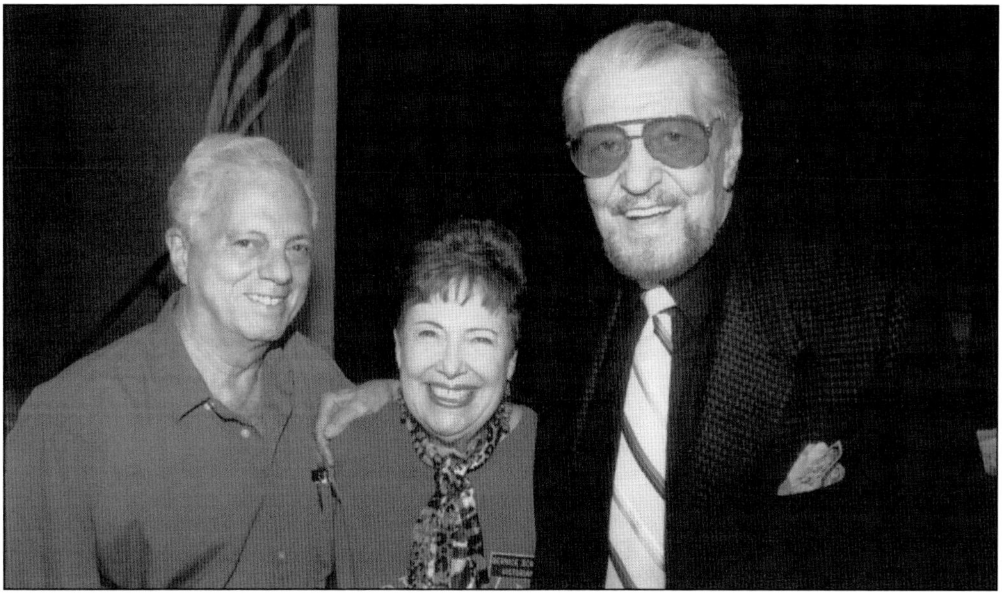

Joe and Bernice Schoen pose for a picture with Herb Jeffries on his 90th birthday. Jeffries was invited to perform for the Friendship Club in Sun Lakes Country Club's theater in Banning in 2001, presenting a superb performance with singer Helen Gee. He became famous during the early years of movies for his cowboy roles. Bernice Schoen is the Friendship Club's historian and her husband, Joe, is an organizer of the memorial committee that helps deceased members' families. (Courtesy of Bernice Schoen.)

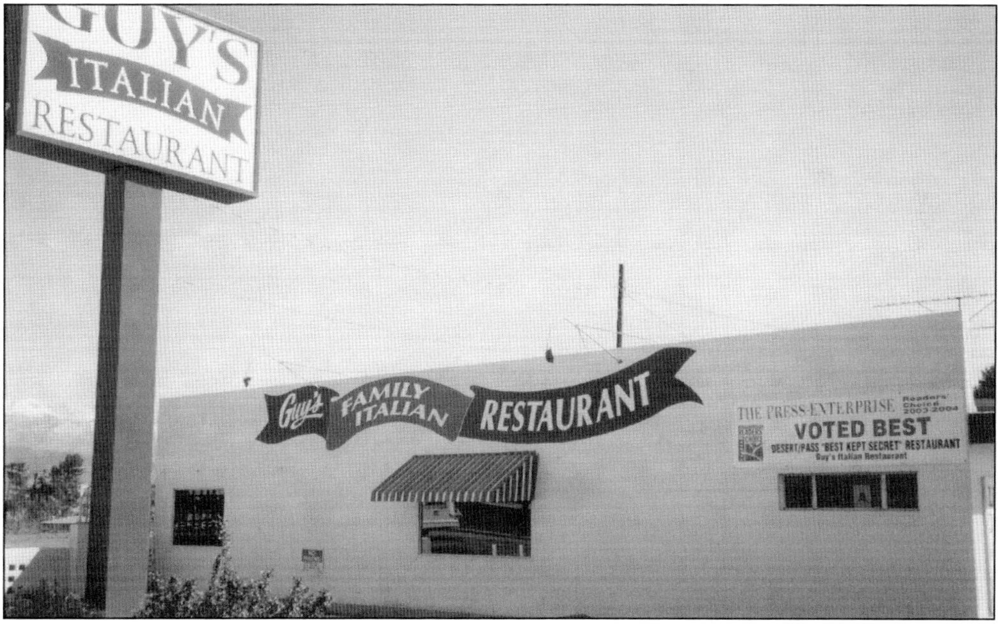

Guy's Family Italian Restaurant is located on West Ramsey Street in Banning. Owner Teresa Bagnar is from Italy where she married her late husband, Giosue Bagnar, who operated restaurants at Pacific Ocean Park Pier in Santa Monica and San Pedro's Ports of Call. Teresa's domestic career ended in 1977 when her husband died. To support her family, she opened Guy's with her sister Nina Mazzella, who remains her partner. (Courtesy of the author.)

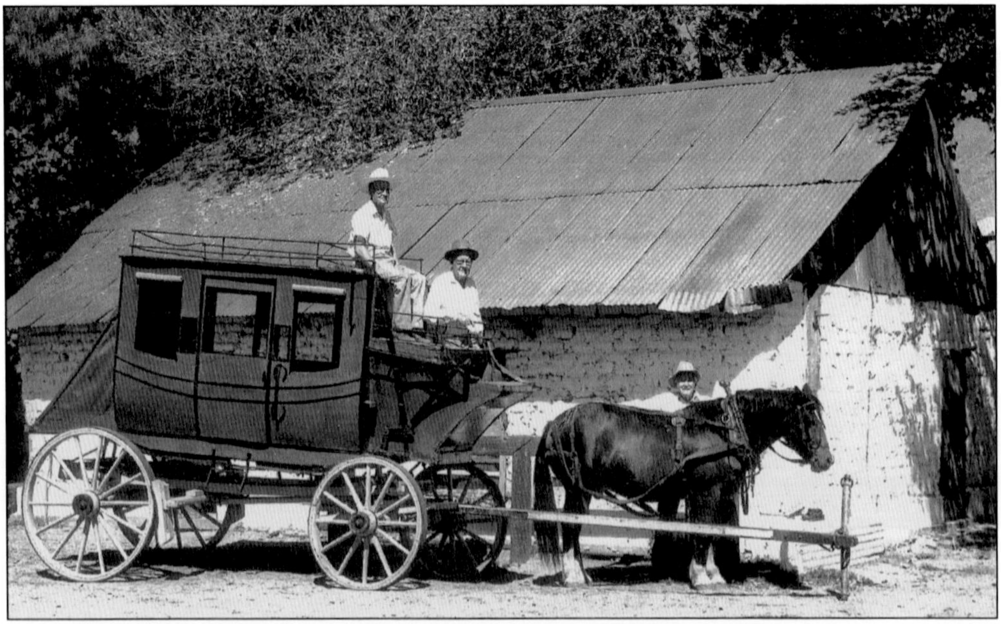

This photograph was taken during an early Stagecoach Days celebration in front of the old Gilman adobe before its demise. Only the foundation of the adobe remains after it was damaged by an earthquake. Banning conducts a yearly Stagecoach Days celebration, which always includes a parade that Banningites and others eagerly look forward to. (Courtesy of the Banning Public Library.)

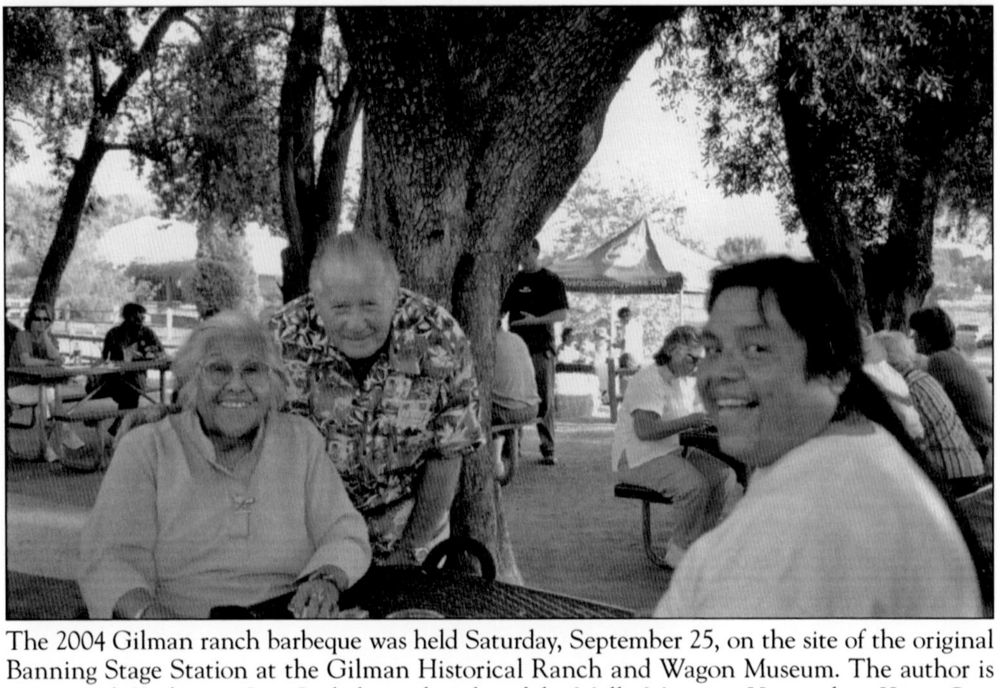

The 2004 Gilman ranch barbeque was held Saturday, September 25, on the site of the original Banning Stage Station at the Gilman Historical Ranch and Wagon Museum. The author is posing with Katherine Siva Saubel, a cofounder of the Malki Museum. Her nephew Kevin Siva is to the right. The barbecue is one of the Stagecoach Days' regularly scheduled events and is highly anticipated each year. (Courtesy of the author.)

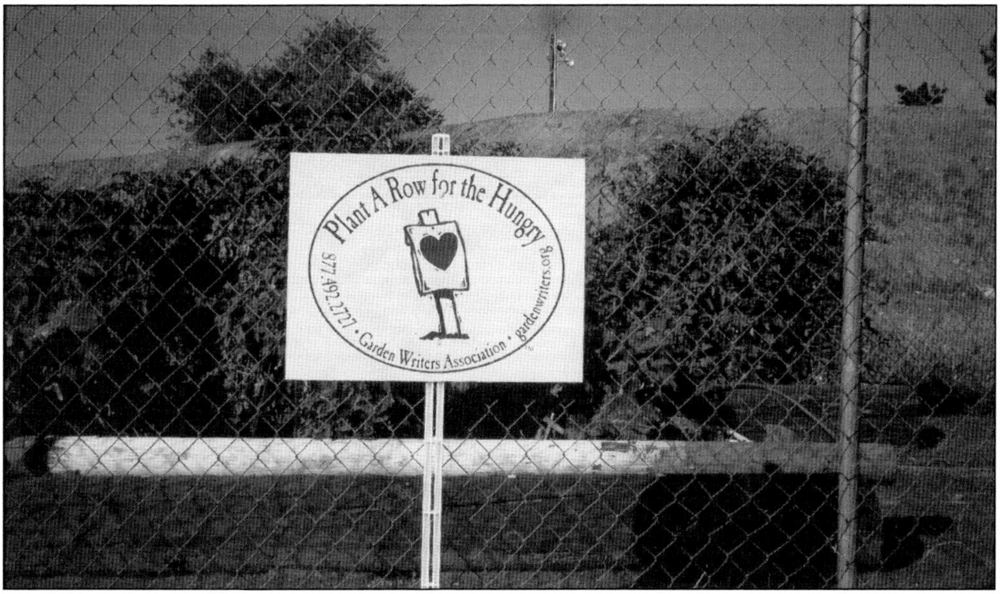

This sign with the logo "Plant a Row for the Hungry" is sponsored by the Garden Writer's Association. The garden plot is located in Dysart Park in Banning and is maintained by 16 volunteers of the garden club at Sun Lakes Country Club. The garden prospers under the management of coordinator Doris Harrison and advice of retired farm advisor Hunter Johnson. The many vegetable types grown are donated to the charitable organizations Carol's Kitchen and Help Center. (Courtesy of the author.)

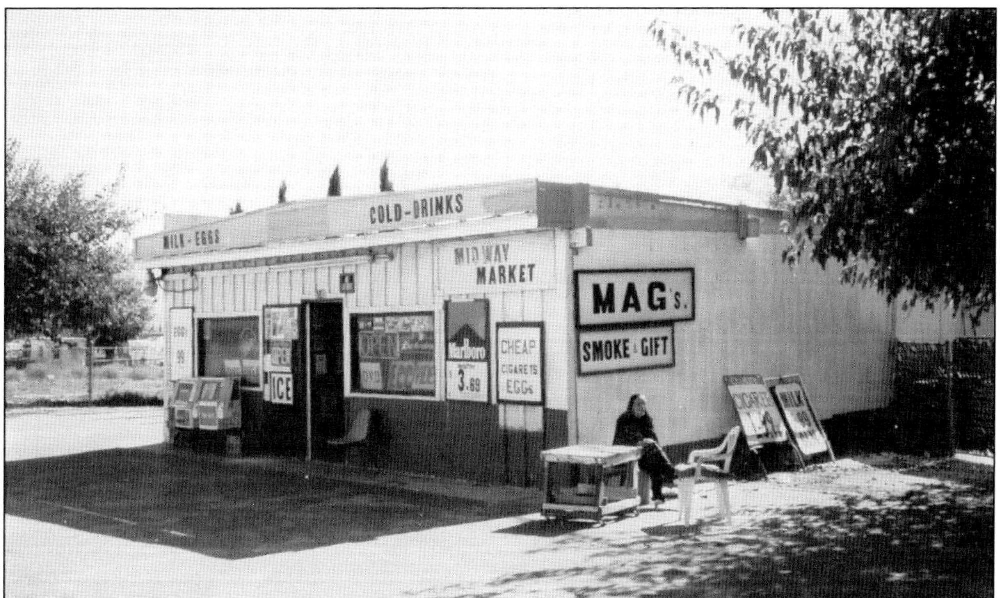

Banning's growth slowed after Interstate 10 bypassed it; however, it has grown some since then. Although new housing development has encompassed some of the farm land, this latest growth has not taken a large toll on most little mom and pop stores like the one shown here, thereby maintaining the serenity that has made the community such an alluring place to be. (Courtesy of the author.)

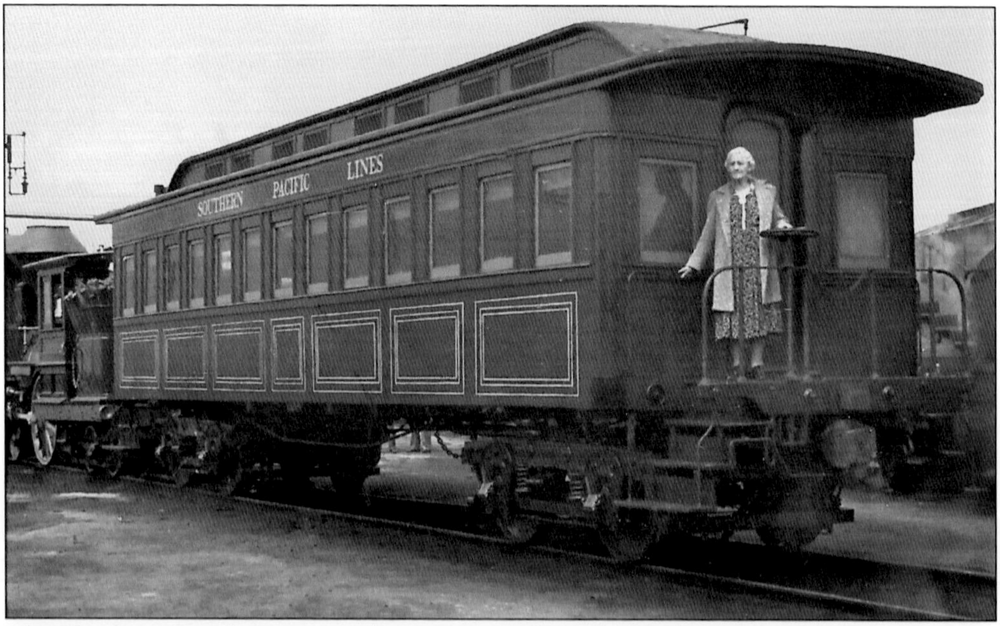

This Southern Pacific Lines coach once stopped at Banning's train station as well as the Cabazon and Beaumont stations to its east and west. Telegraphy Nellie Bailiff often commuted these short distances and is seen here just after boarding the back of a coach. Sometimes she would take her grandchildren along just to give them the thrill of riding a train. (Courtesy of Marianne Bailiff.)

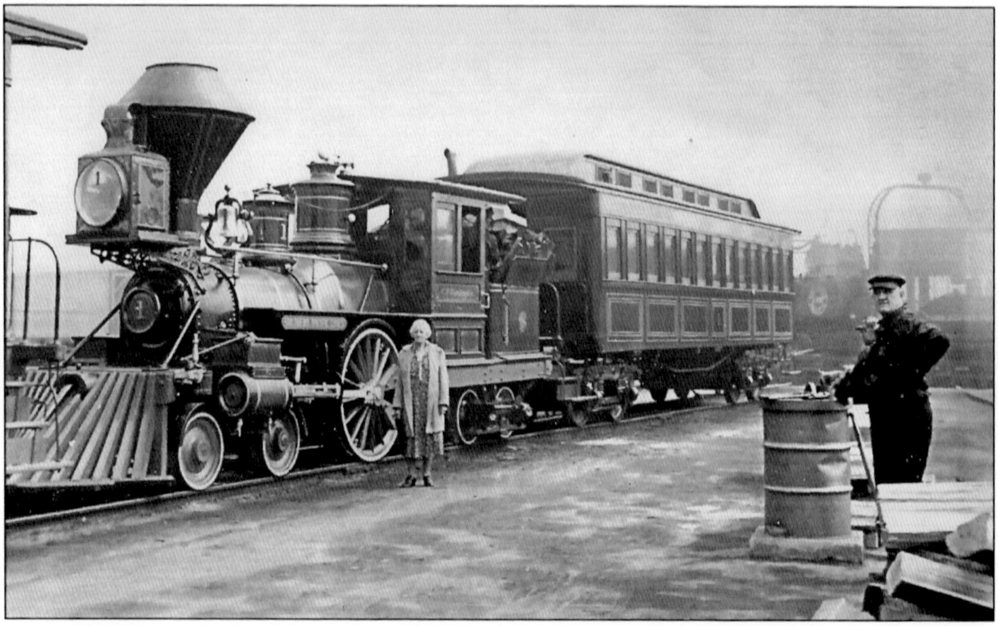

Nellie Bailiff, a pioneer to the area, poses in front of a large wood-burning locomotive that routinely traveled through Banning. Note the wood in the bin at the rear of the engine. Nellie worked for the Southern Pacific Railroad for many years as a telegrapher at the nearby Cabazon railroad station. She was a valued employee of Southern Pacific and was held in high esteem by everyone. (Courtesy of Marianne Bailiff.)

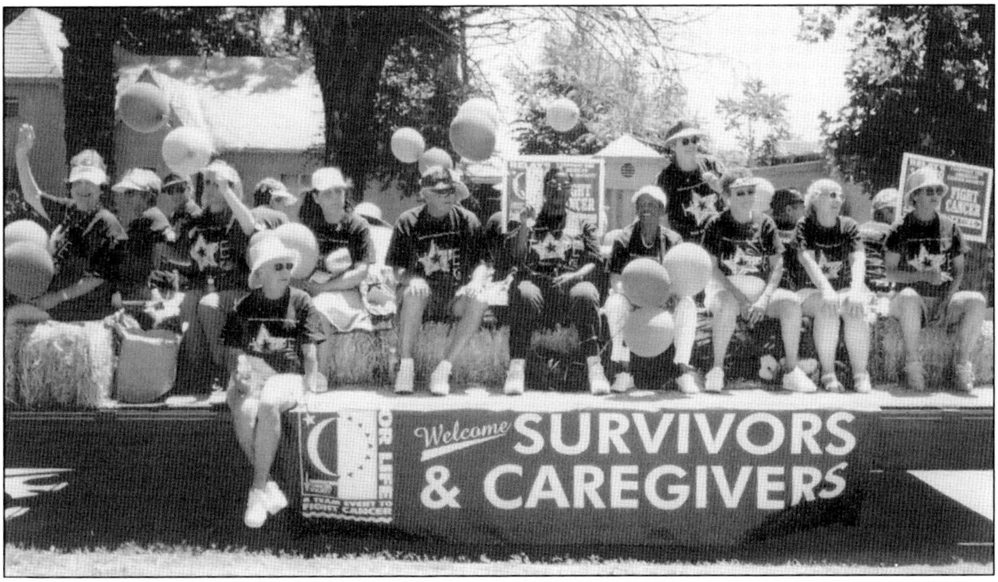

This group of San Gorgonio Pass area residents participated in the 2004 American Cancer Society's Relay for Life. Cancer survivors and caregivers circled the track rimmed with glowing luminaries purchased for $5 each at Beaumont Sports Park. The names of survivors and those lost to the disease were then read aloud. Plans are for continued relays in the future. (Courtesy of Sahara Quinn.)

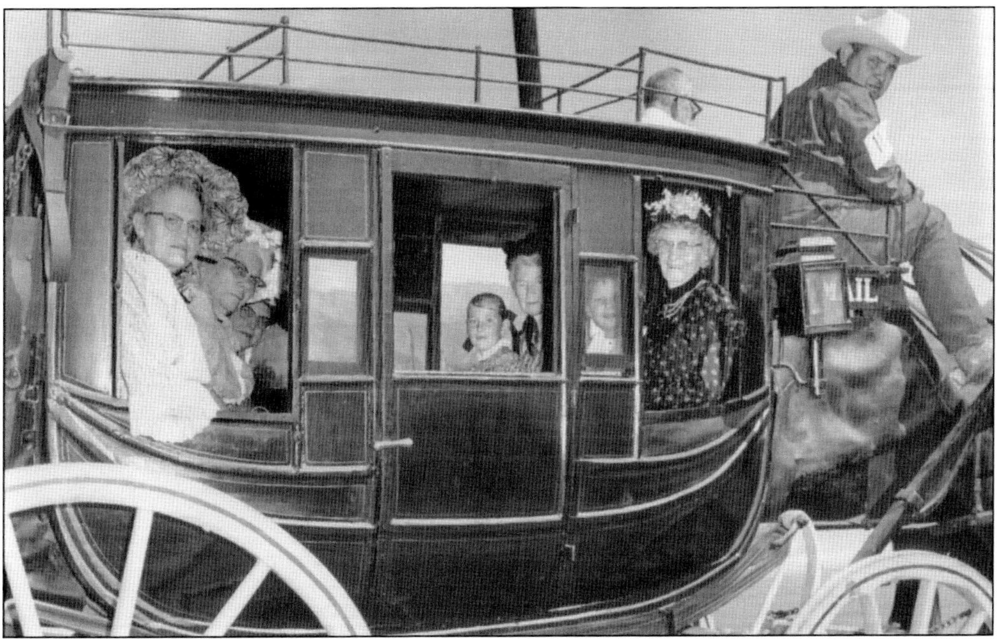

Banning is famous for its Stagecoach Days celebration, which includes a parade centered along Ramsey Street in Banning. The parade depicted here took place on October 10, 1964. Seated in the stagecoach, from left to right, are Ruth Mack (Gandy), Rohena Hemmerling (Innes), Francis Mitchell (Pierce), Ruth Little (Forintain) and her granddaughter Laura, and Susan Coombs (Bird) and granddaughter Beth. All women were daughters of pioneers arriving in the pass between 1880 and 1890. (Photo by Bob Purcell; courtesy of Joan Coombs.)

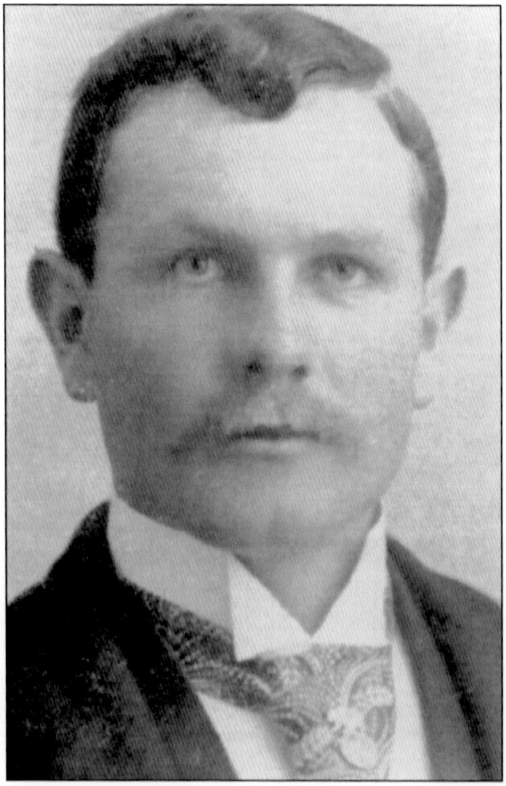

James M. Gilman was one of Banning's most prominent pioneers. Born June 9, 1842, at Meredith Village, New Hampshire, he was well known for having bought the old Chapin sheep ranch from Newton Noble and establishing a store and stage stop at the old adobe on his ranch. He married Martha Smith, and they raised six children. He was always active in civic and political affairs. (Courtesy of Tom Hughes.)

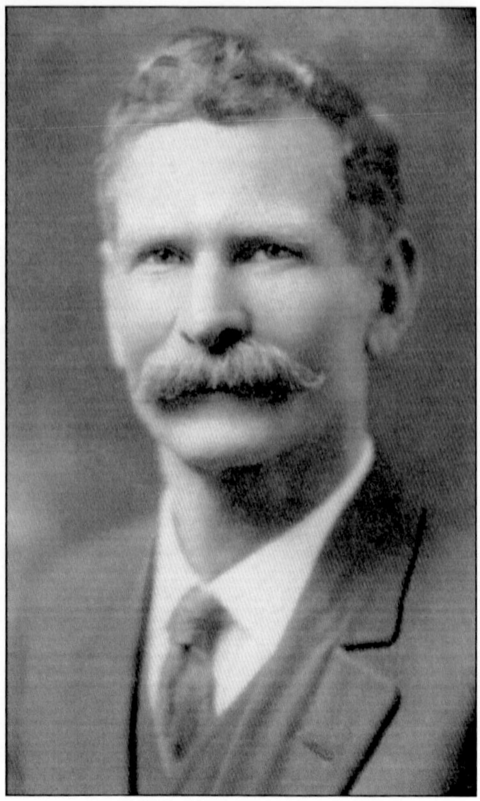

Marshall French Gilman has long been prominent in the history of botanical and ornithological research in America. He made extensive botanical studies and collections of desert plants in Southern California. He was the eldest son of James and Martha Gilman and was born on the Gilman ranch in Banning on November 12, 1871. He was Banning's mayor from July 18 to October 23, 1933. (Courtesy of Tom Hughes.)

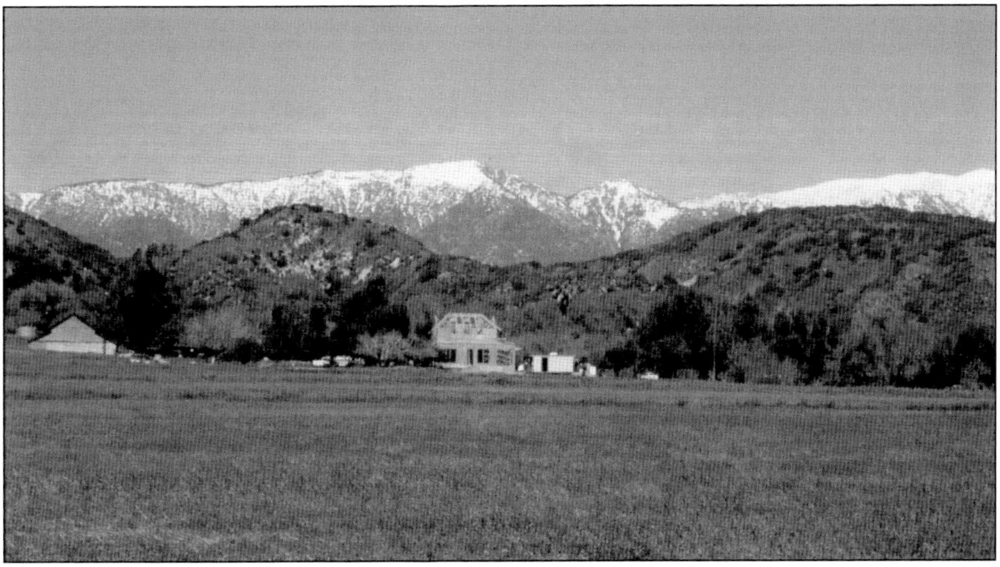

This panoramic view shows the Gilman Historical Ranch and Wagon Museum, nestled on a plain below Mount San Gorgonio, just north of Wilson Street in Banning. The current reconstruction of the original Gilman ranch house is pictured center, in progress. The remains of an adobe that was once the Gilman Stagecoach Station can be seen between the ranch house and the Gilman barn at the extreme left. (Courtesy of the author.)

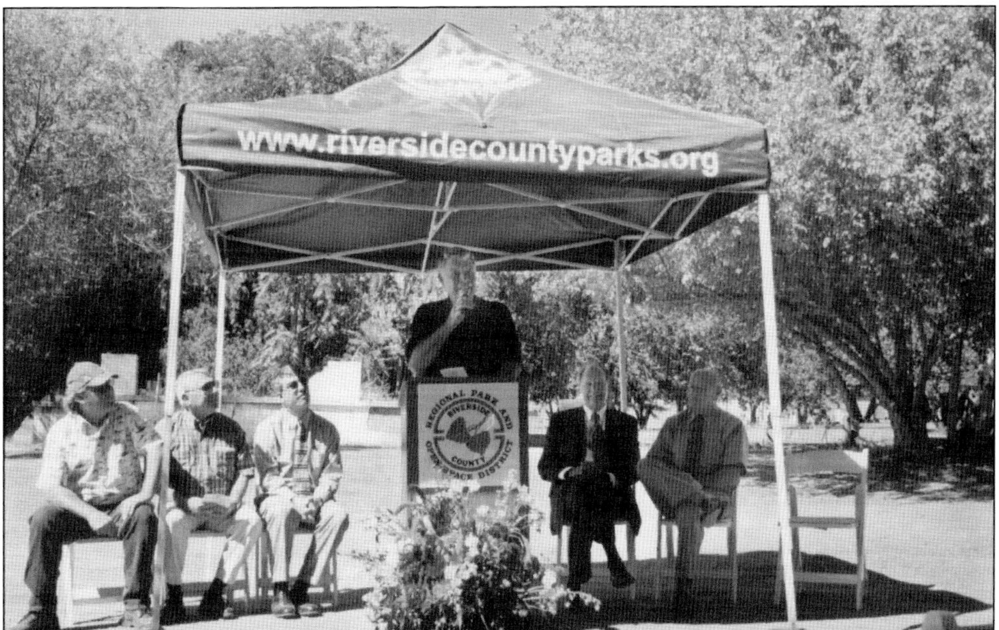

Mayor Art Walsh stands at the podium under the canopy where he, county officials, and Ranch Hands president Herb Spencer (center left) are officially dedicating the rebuilding of the Gilman ranch house at the Gilman Historic Ranch and Wagon Museum. Note the old foundation of the Gilman ranch house in the background. The dedication was held on October 4, 2004. (Courtesy of the author.)

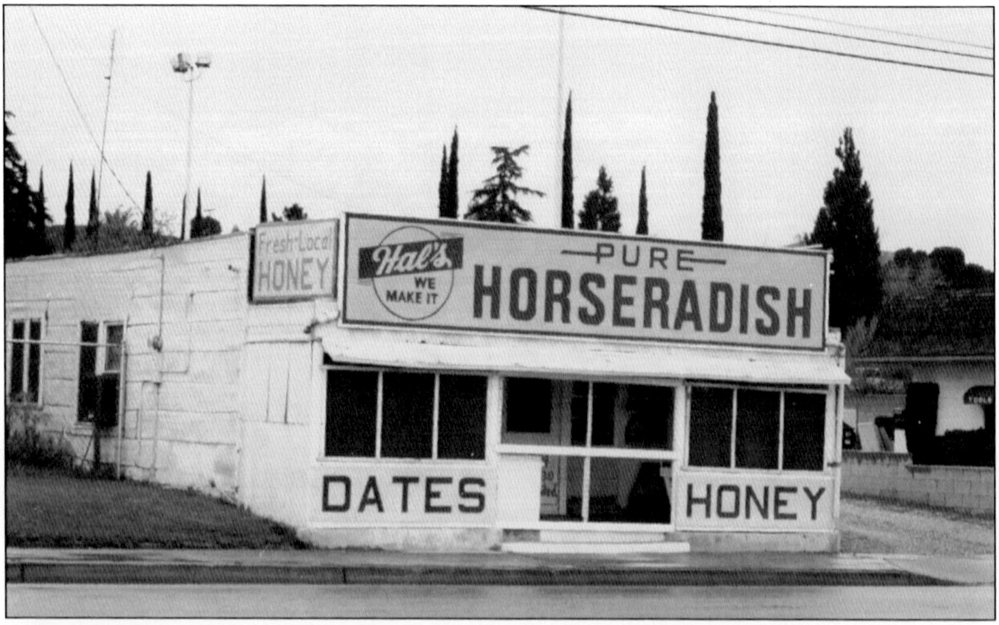

A few buildings in Banning along Ramsey Street date back to before Interstate 10 bypassed the town. At that time, motorists could pull to the curb while passing through town to buy such sought after items as seen advertised on the face of this little building. Honey was heavily produced in Banning at one time, especially during the era of abundant fruit production. (Courtesy of Margaret Holtzclaw.)

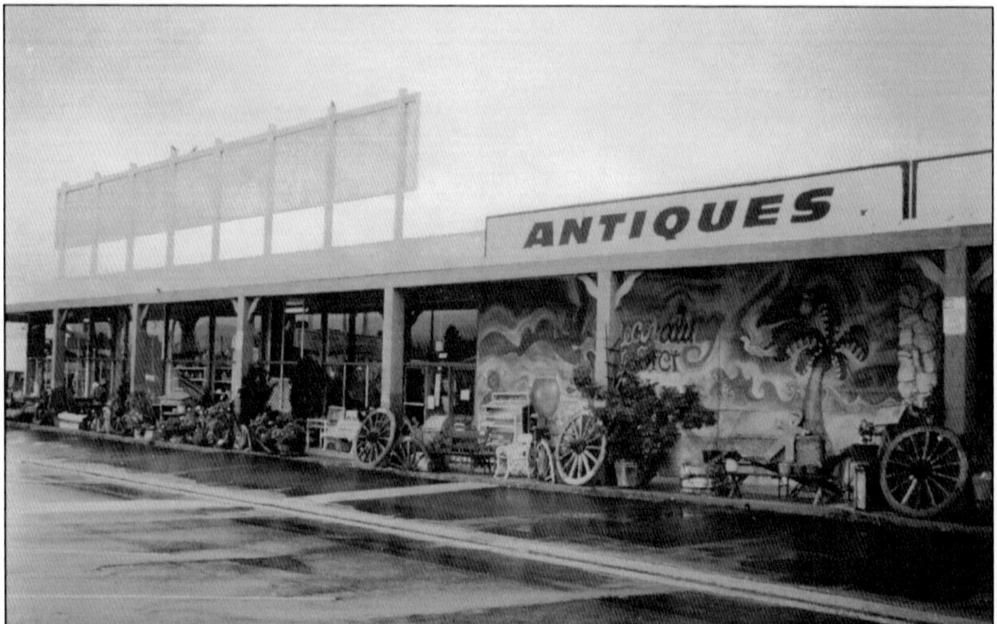

There are many antiques stores throughout the San Gorgonio Pass, and Banning is no exception. Pictured here is an antiques store on Ramsey Street in a strip mall that contains a number of them. Shoppers from both Banning and nearby Beaumont frequent these stores, while others come from long distances to buy. (Courtesy of Margaret Holtzclaw.)

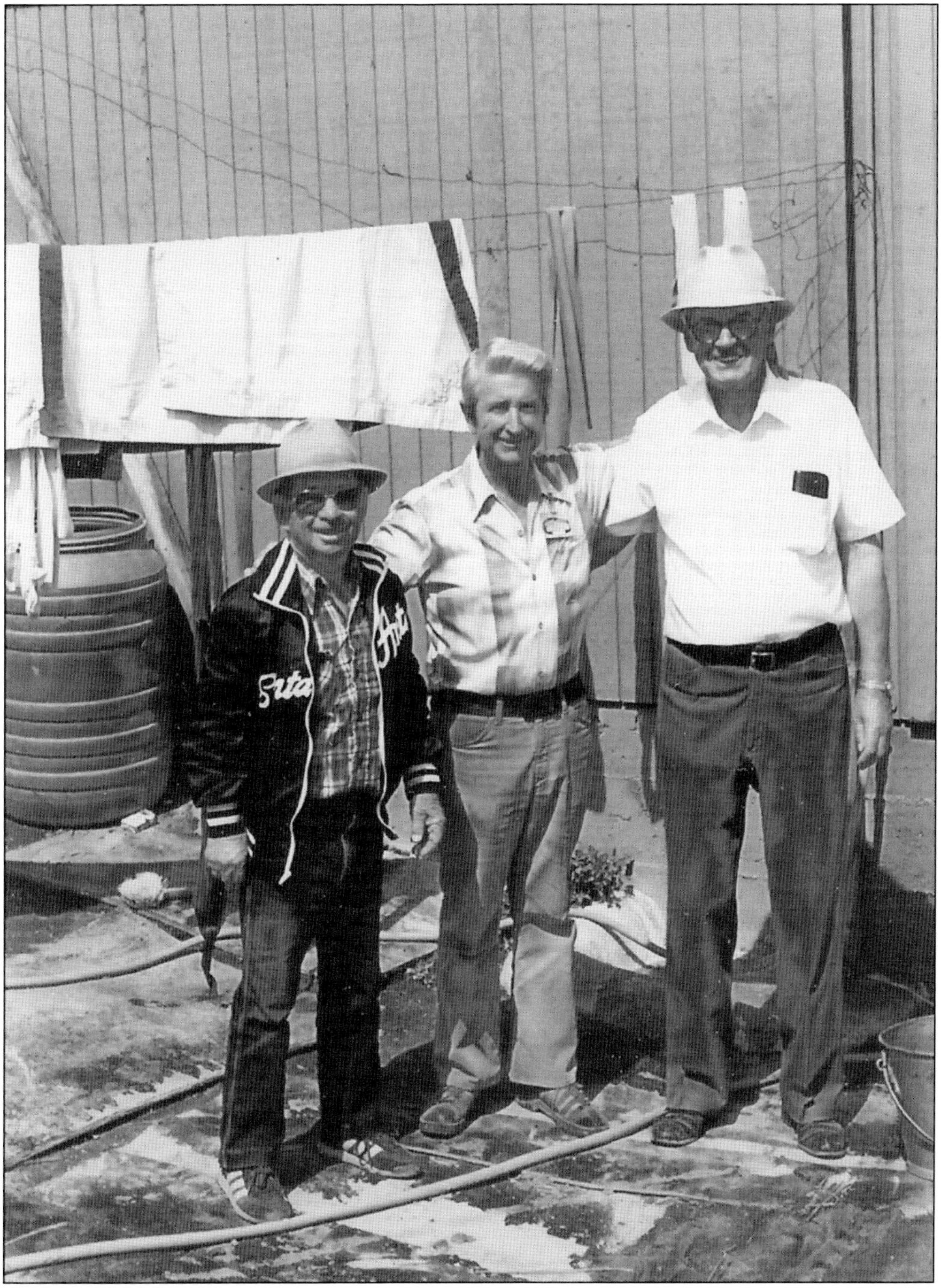

These well-known horseracing men, from left to right, are Johnny Longden, Chase McCoy, and Wally Dunne, the only non-Banning resident. McCoy was a horse owner who had many stake winners. His T. V. Lark won at the Los Angeles Handicap Race at Hollywood Park in 1961 ridden by jockey Johnny Longden, and was voted turf horse of the year in 1962. Dunne was a racehorse trainer. Longden and his wife, Kathy, were former Banning residents while Chase and wife, Doris, remain residents today. (Courtesy of Chase McCoy.)

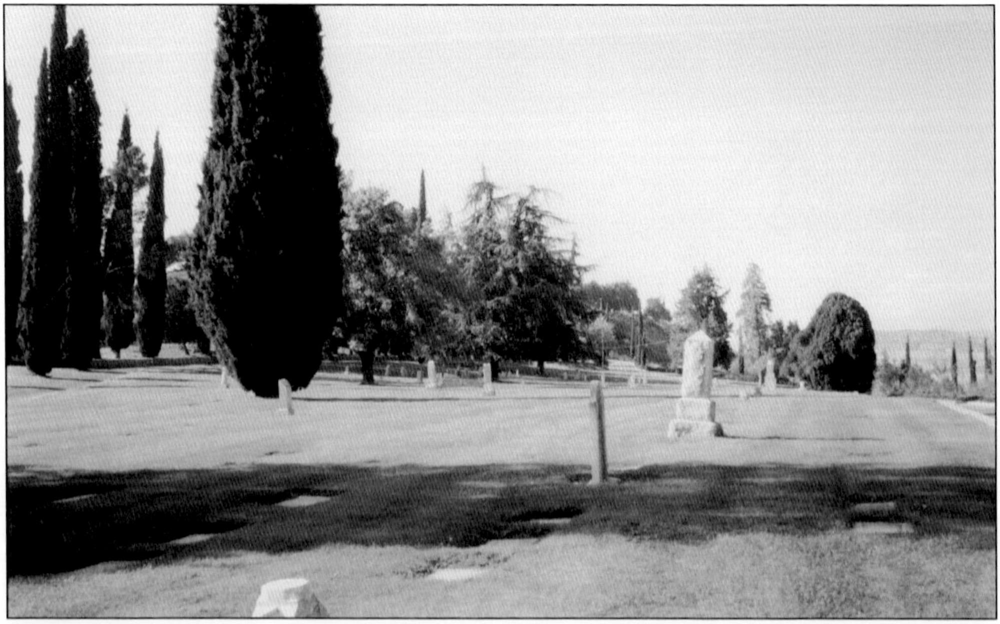

The Banning cemetery was once part of the Morongo Indian reservation, but through an exchange made by an act of Congress in 1905, this portion passed into the hands of the Southern Pacific Railroad, which sold it to F. E. Dudley. He, in return, sold the 3.74 acres to five citizens of Banning, incorporated under the name of the Banning Cemetery Association. Since then, it has been enlarged and is now known as San Gorgonio Memorial Park. (Courtesy of the author.)

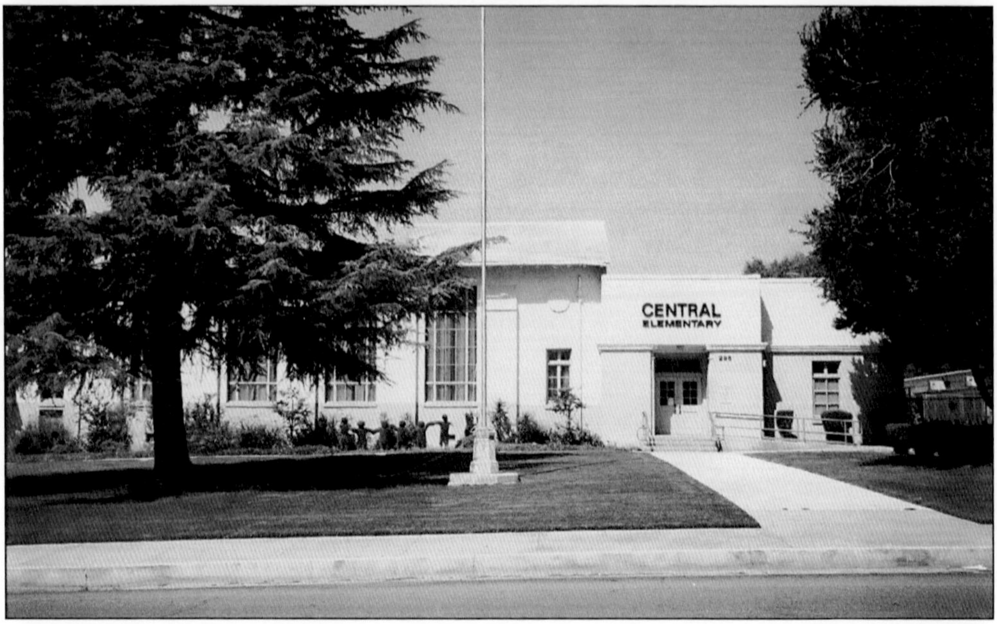

Banning's first one-room grammar school opened June 3, 1877, and had no blackboard. A larger two-room school was built in 1885 on Murray Street and a room for a kindergarten was added later. It served Banning for 18 years until it burned down. In 1903, a five-room school was built at First and Williams Streets. It burned down in 1907. Pictured is the present school on San Gorgonio Avenue, built in 1928. (Courtesy of the author.)

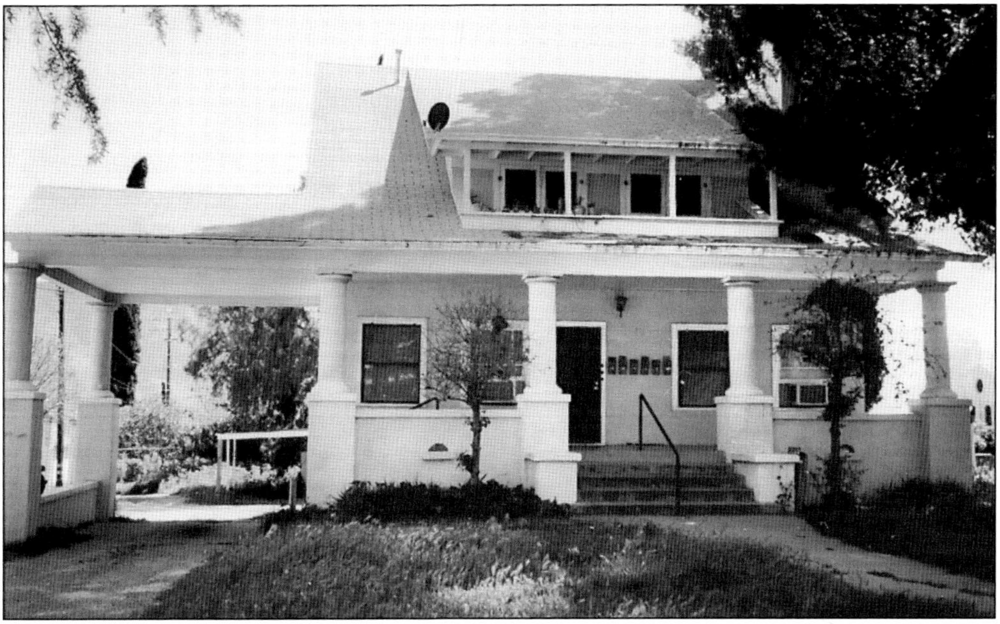

This esteemed Banning landmark is one of the few extant old residences still remaining today. The former residence of pioneer C. D. Hamilton and his wife, Pearl Theodora Noble, a native of Riverside, it is located on the southeast corner of Second and Williams Streets. Hamilton was born in Elwin, Illinois, July 15, 1885, and educated in a one-room, one-teacher school as far as the eighth grade. (Courtesy of the author.)

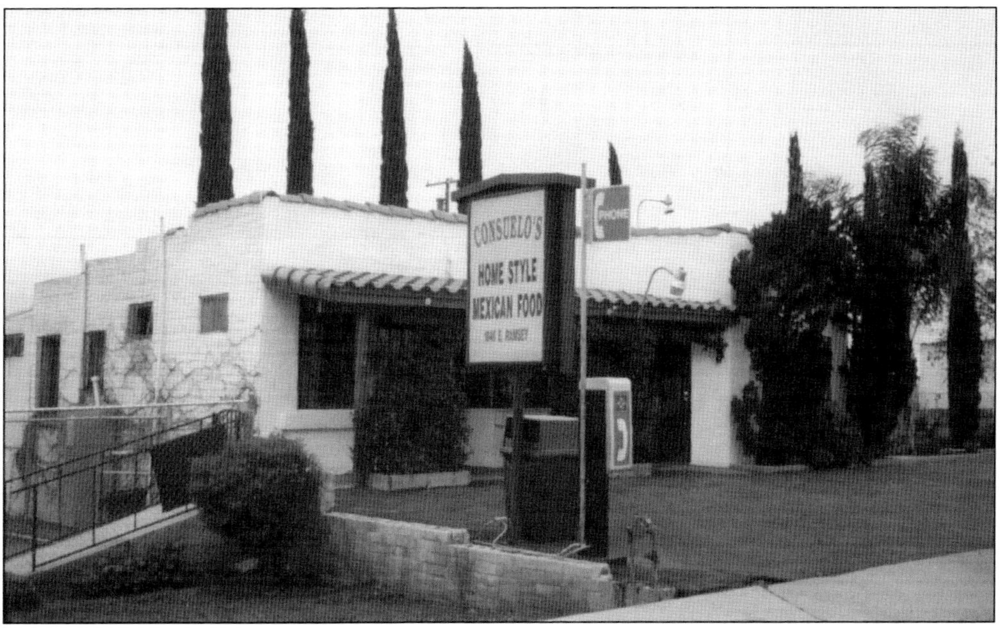

Consuelo's Restaurant on East Ramsey Street features home-style Mexican food and has operated in the same location for over 33 years. It began as a small market in 1960 and changed to a restaurant in the 1970s. Run by Connie and Greg Hernandez until 1995, it was then handed down to their daughter Yvonne Aguilera and son-in-law Frank Aguilera. The couple has built it into a thriving business. (Courtesy of the author.)

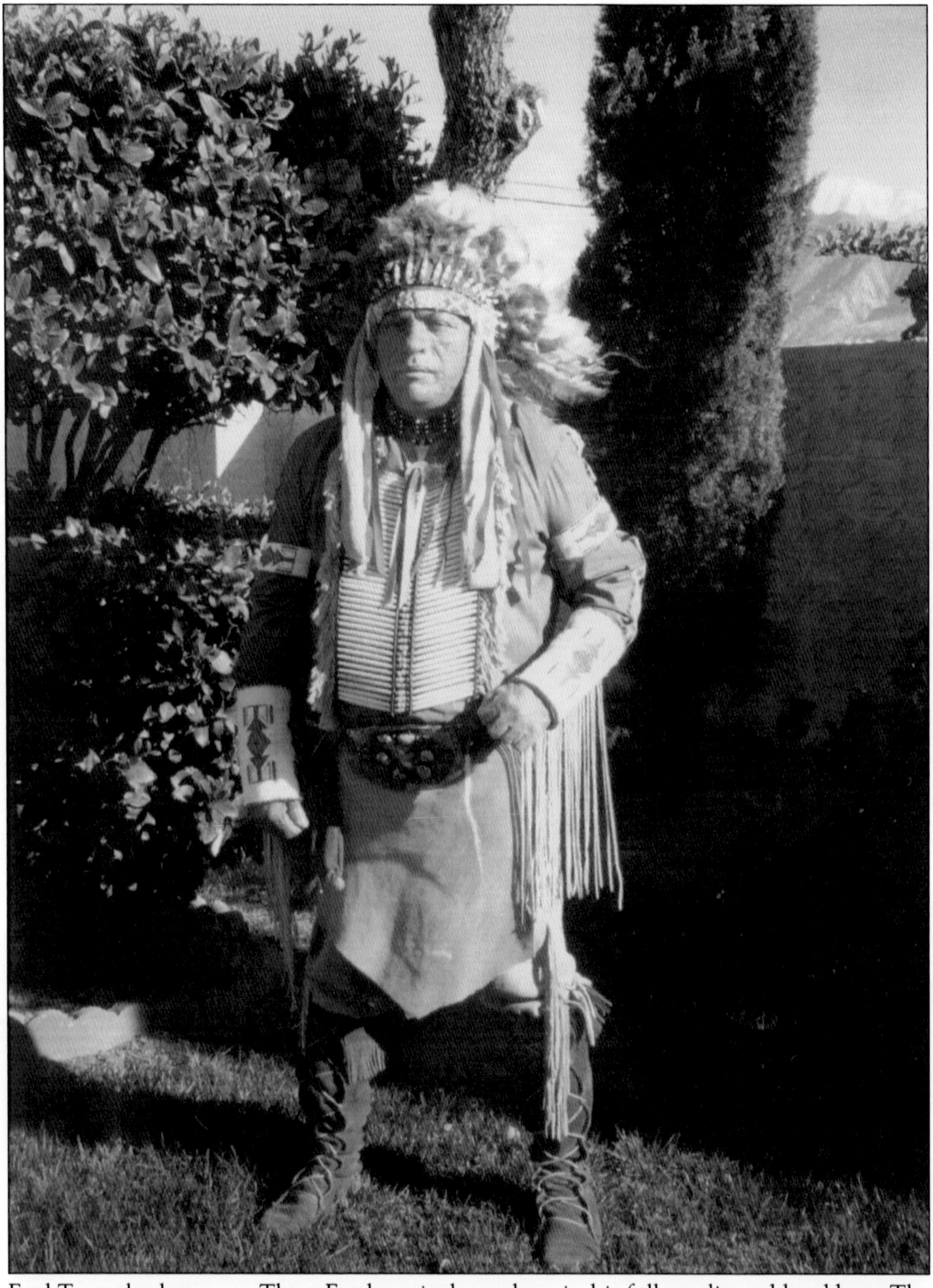

Fred Toro, also known as Three Feathers, is shown here in his full regalia and headdress. The headdress was given to him by Black Buffalo in nearby Hemet, the regalia by Grandpa White Cloud in Apple Valley, and the brown leather medicine bag on his side by an Apache friend. Fred has worked with Stephen Seagal in movies, and also uses this attire for school performances and other activities. He lives with his two daughters at his home on the Morongo Indian Reservation. (Courtesy of the author.)

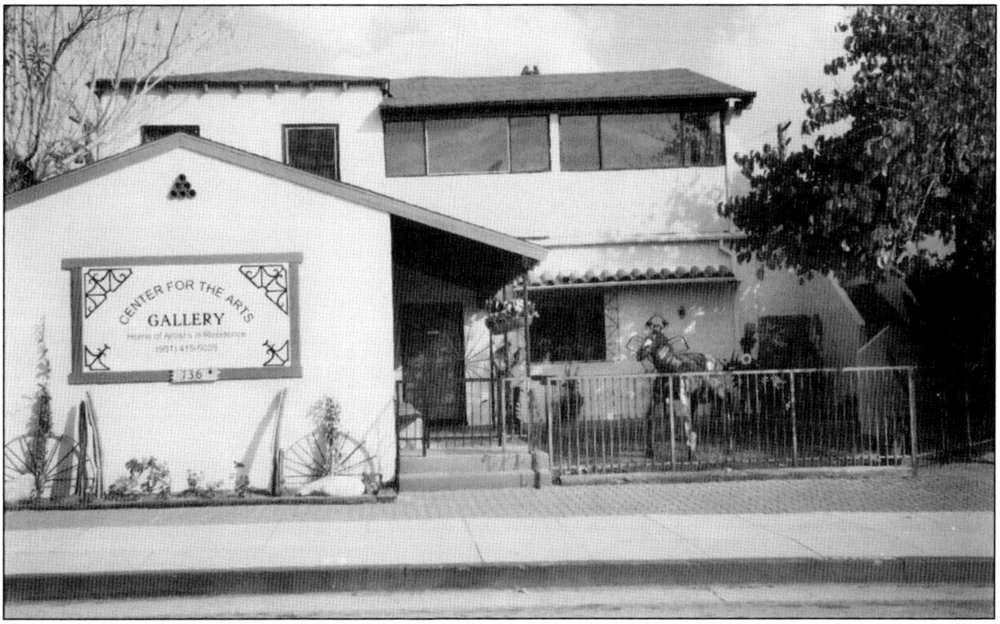

Downtown Banning recently got this Center for the Arts Gallery. Its logo, the letters AIR, represents Artists in Residence, a group of Banning artists that previously had to meet in a local restaurant. Art Cocarro from Long Island, New York, spearheaded the purchase and rehabilitation of the AIR space. Member Ron Corda, a painter and sculptor, runs his own gallery across the street. (Courtesy of the author.)

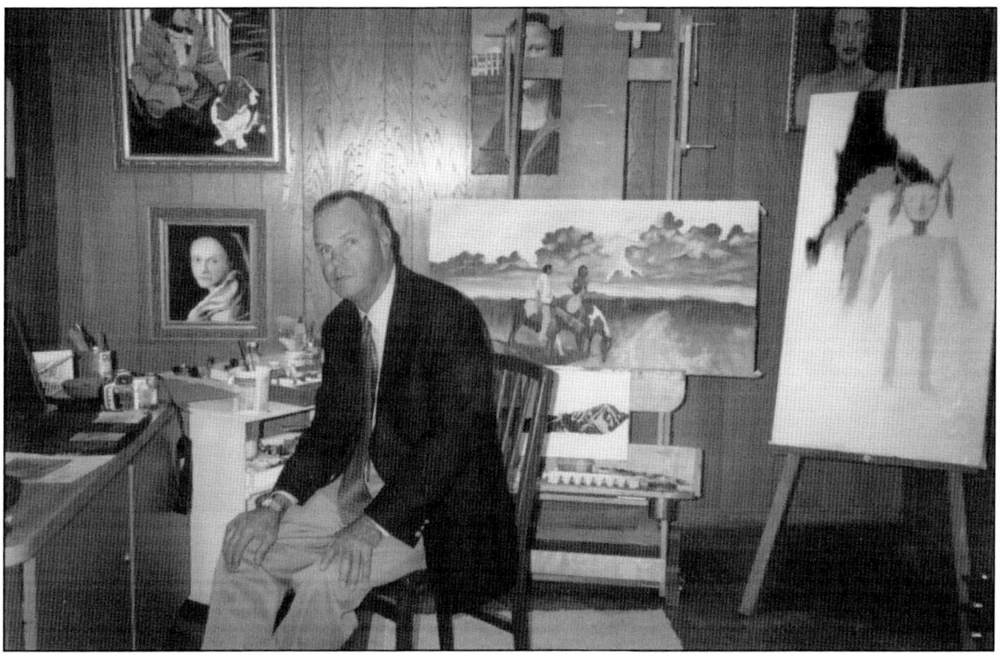

Art Cocarro poses in his studio at the new Center for the Arts Gallery. In this building he has brought together numerous artists such as Jolene Biss, who works in oils, Paul "Bear" Bradford, sculptor Ron Singerton, and Joe Corda, a painter and sculptor. Art Cocarro himself is an artist who paints realistic street scenes. (Courtesy of the author.)

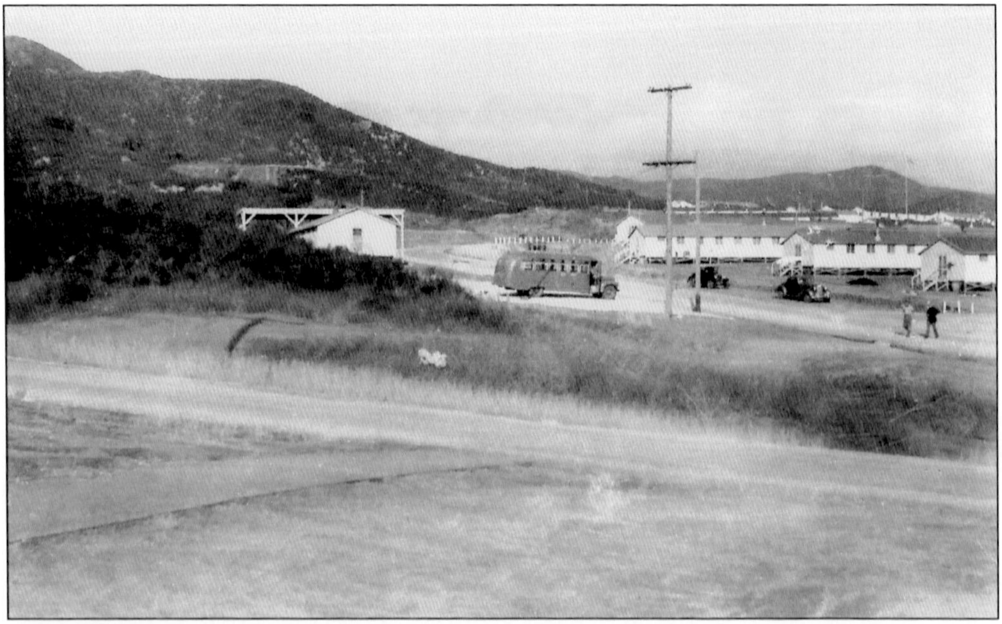

This 1944 photograph shows two hospitals that were renovated by U.S. Navy corpsmen after General Patton abandoned the army hospitals to begin his North African campaign. One facility was located near the heart of Banning and the other in the rolling hills northwest of the town. Each covered around 100 acres and had 30 or so barrack-like structures. The small building in the left of the photograph is a fire station. (Courtesy of Homer Shockey.)

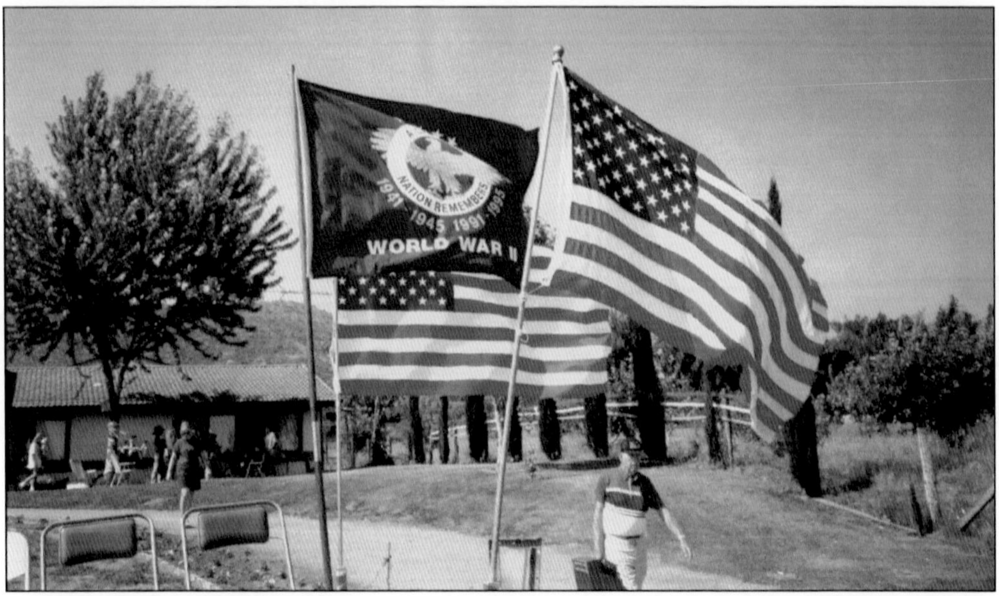

A 50th reunion was held in 1994 for the "Dirty Thirty," as they were known for their cleanup activities and rehabilitation of General Patton's two army hospitals in Banning and Beaumont after he abandoned them. The grounds had been inhabited by cows and overgrown with weeds. Note the memorial World War II flag that was donated by March Air Force Field for the occasion. Pictured walking beneath the flags is Homer Shockey, who arranged the reunion. (Courtesy of Homer Shockey.)

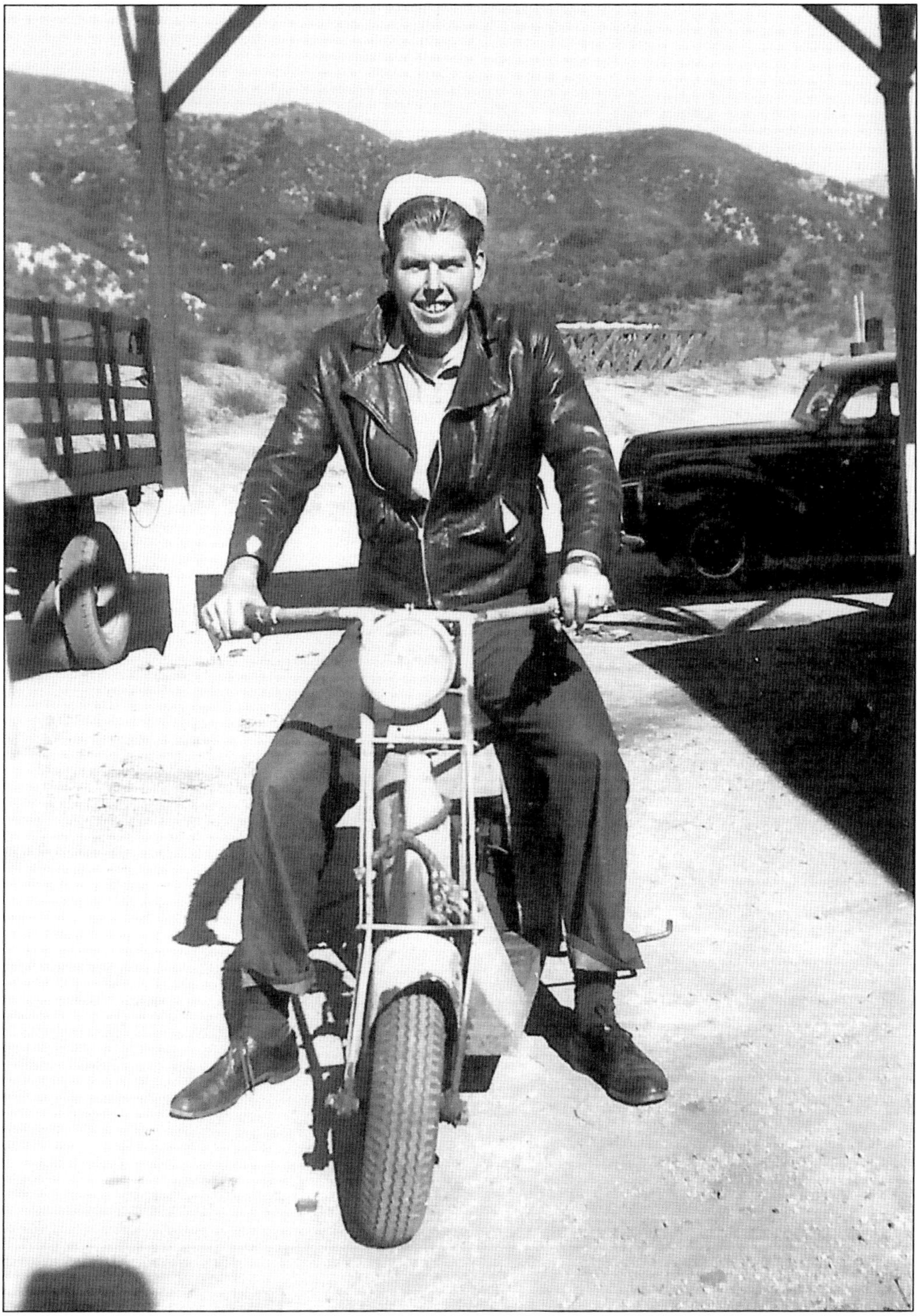

Homer Shockey was one of 30 navy corpsmen who came to Banning to renovate and convert General Patton's deserted army hospitals into navy hospitals. Today he lives in Banning with his wife, Margaret, and is nearly 80 years old. He was also a past president of the San Gorgonio Pass Historical Society. (Courtesy of Homer Shockey.)

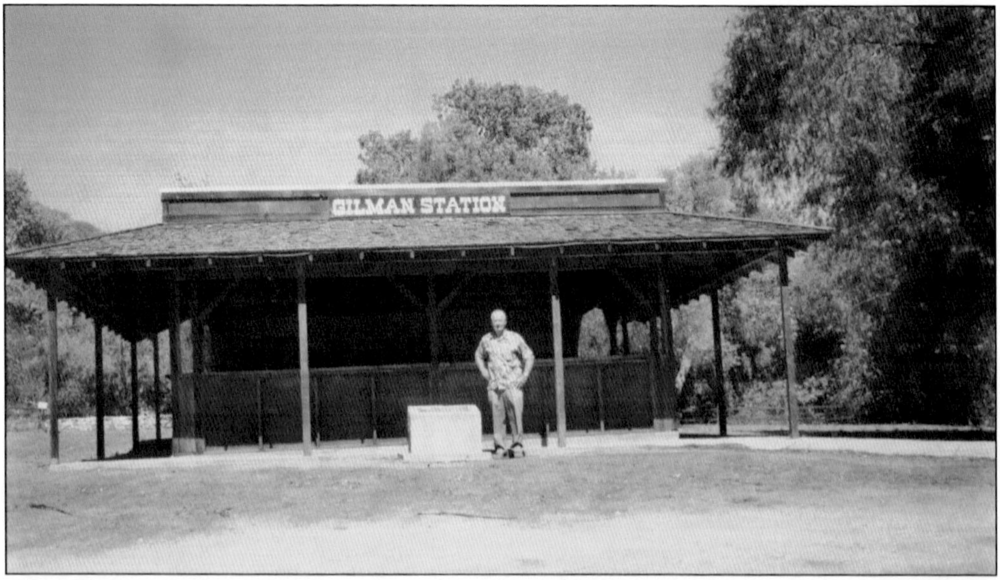

The author is standing by what was once a beautiful adobe building on the Gilman Ranch site. It was quite active as a station during the stagecoach era. No longer used as a stage stop, it fell into disrepair and was later damaged by an earthquake. Only the foundation remains today. (Courtesy of the author.)

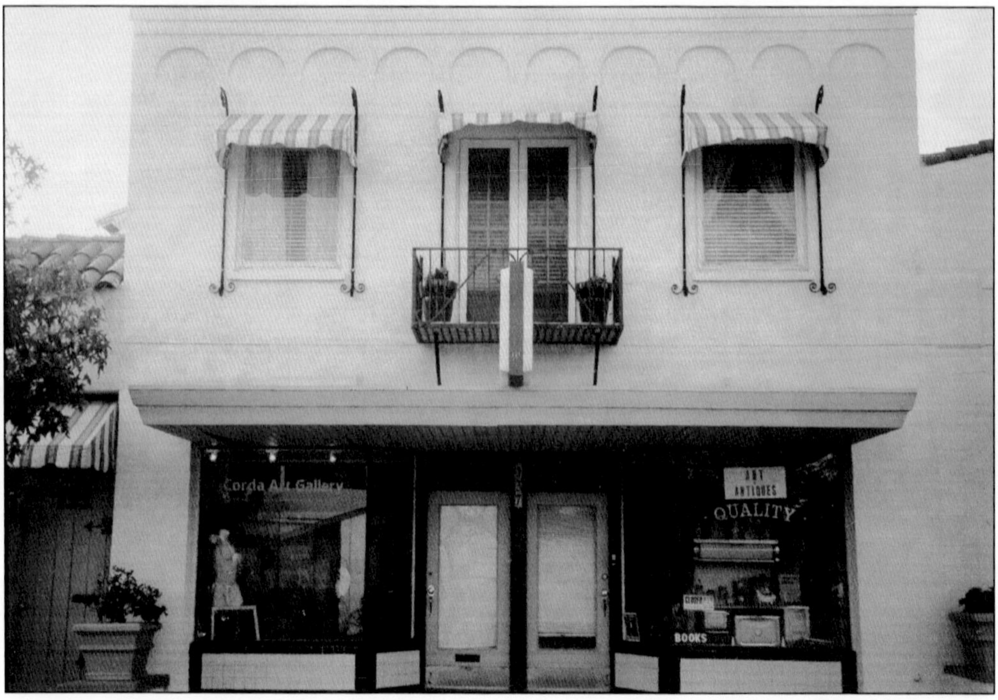

This art gallery on San Gorgonio Avenue is run by Joe Corda, a painter and sculptor, and is located directly across the street from Banning's new downtown art gallery with a front courtyard adorned with metal sculptures. Artists like to work and live in Banning because of its inspirational atmosphere under the snow-capped San Gorgonio and San Jacinto mountains. (Courtesy of the author.)

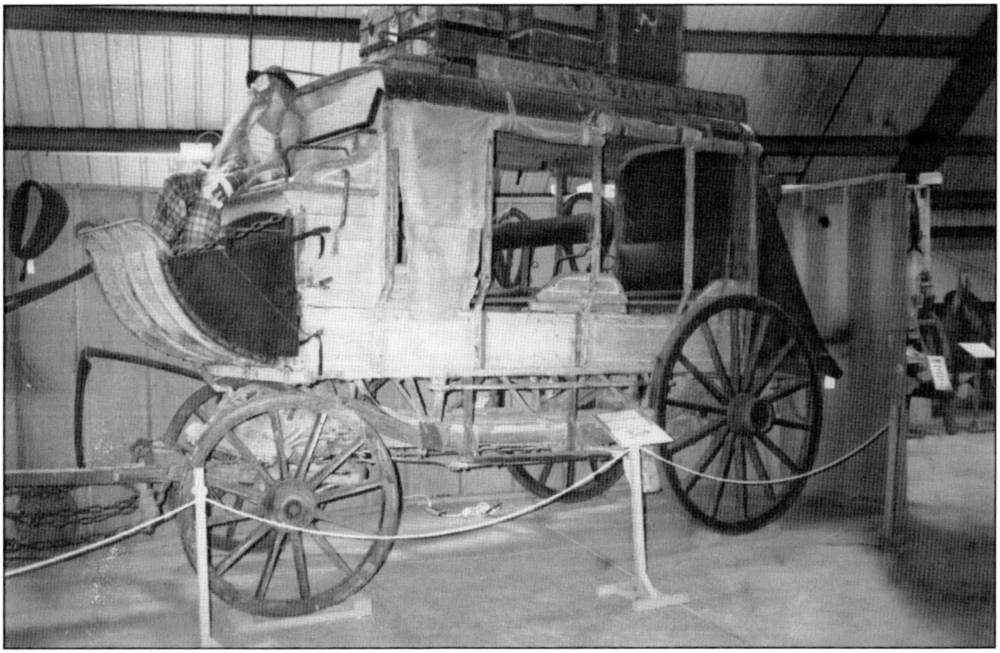

This Overland Stage Line stagecoach can today be seen in the Gilman Historic Ranch and Wagon Museum. It normally seated 12 people, but it has been reported that it once carried numerous others by putting some on the top of the coach where the luggage was carried. It was an active line during the era of the stagecoach but, like others after the emergence of the railroad, soon died away. (Courtesy of the author.)

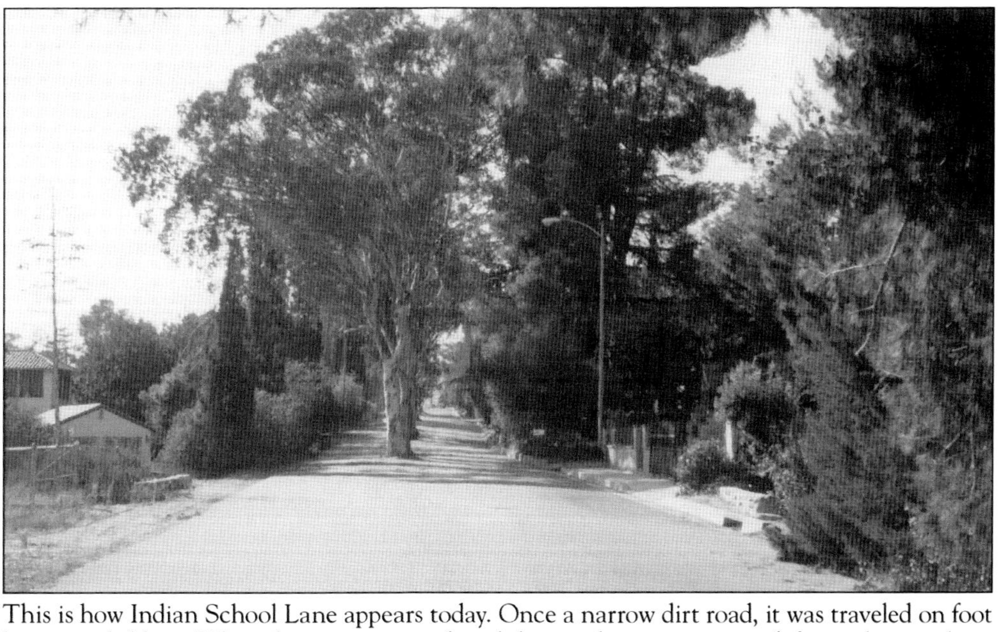

This is how Indian School Lane appears today. Once a narrow dirt road, it was traveled on foot by many children. When the street was widened the eucalyptus trees were left standing, making a divider in the road. It is of interest to note the bungalow on the grounds of Briargate Manor at the left, where Irving Berlin wrote the popular song "I'm Dreaming of a White Christmas." (Courtesy of the author.)

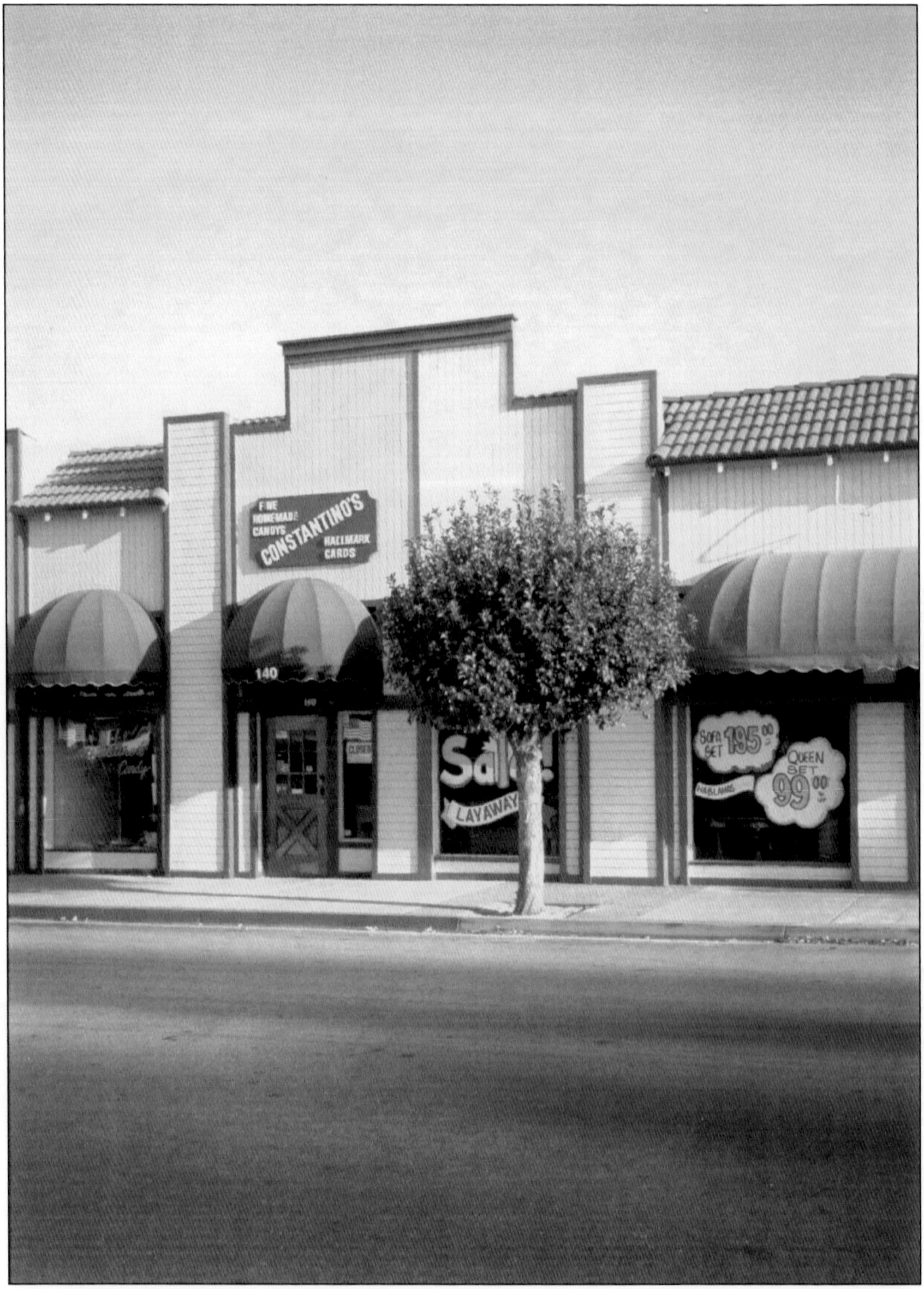

Since 1932, Constantino's candy store has been making and selling candies in Banning. Housed in a small building on Ramsey Street near the town's center, it warrants attention because it is the oldest, continuously owned business in Banning. It is currently owned and operated by Rachael and George Constantino, whose father came to Chicago from Italy in 1921, moved to Banning in 1932, and operated the candy store until 1945. (Courtesy of the author.)

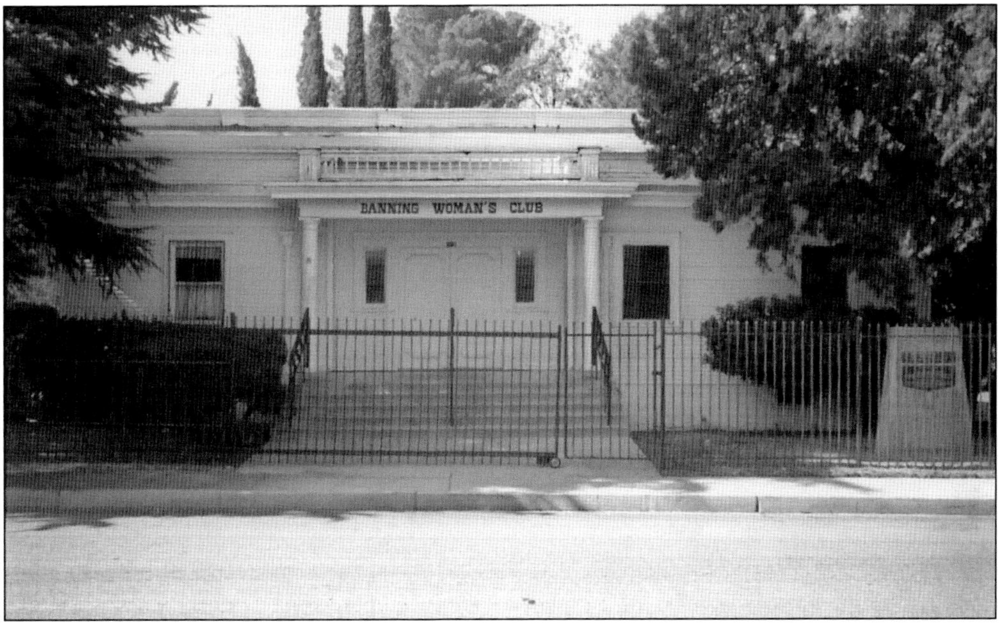

The Saturday Afternoon Club was the first service club in Banning and later changed its name to the Banning Women's Club. It began when a group of women met at the home of Mrs. Hamilton to organize it. In 1915, a formal club was built on the northeast corner of Hays and Williams. In the words of a past president, "The club was chamber of commerce, welfare association, and service club rolled into one."

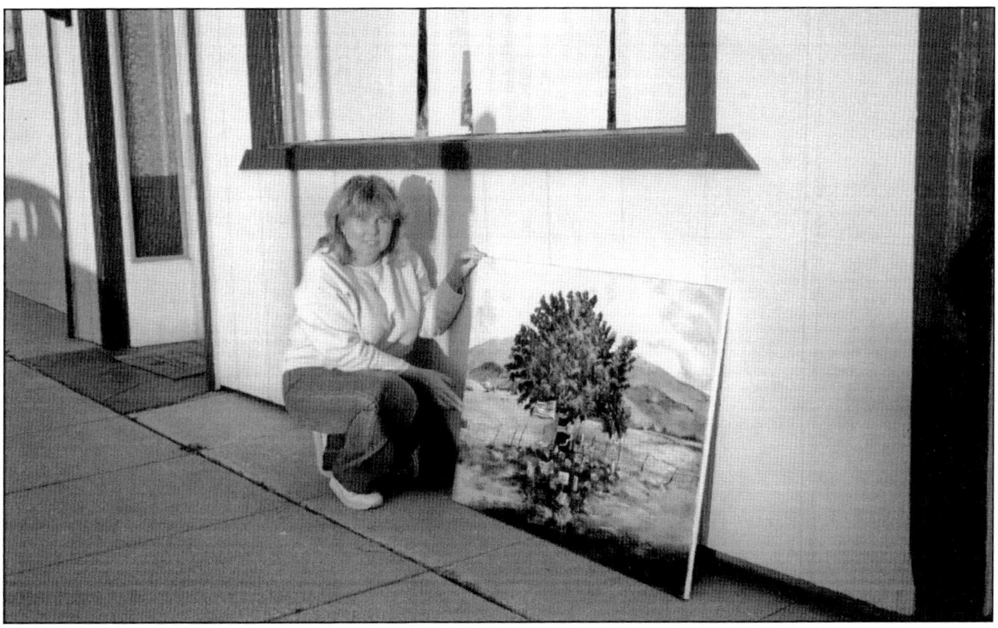

Artist Debi Elliott shows a picture that she painted for a charity raffle. The painting is entitled "Lone Tree Standing." It shows the large tree that stands alone along the side of the road on north Highland Avenue a mile or so in the country. The tree is unique because it has been adopted and decorated by citizens of Banning as a memorial to those serving in Iraq. (Courtesy of Debi Elliott.)

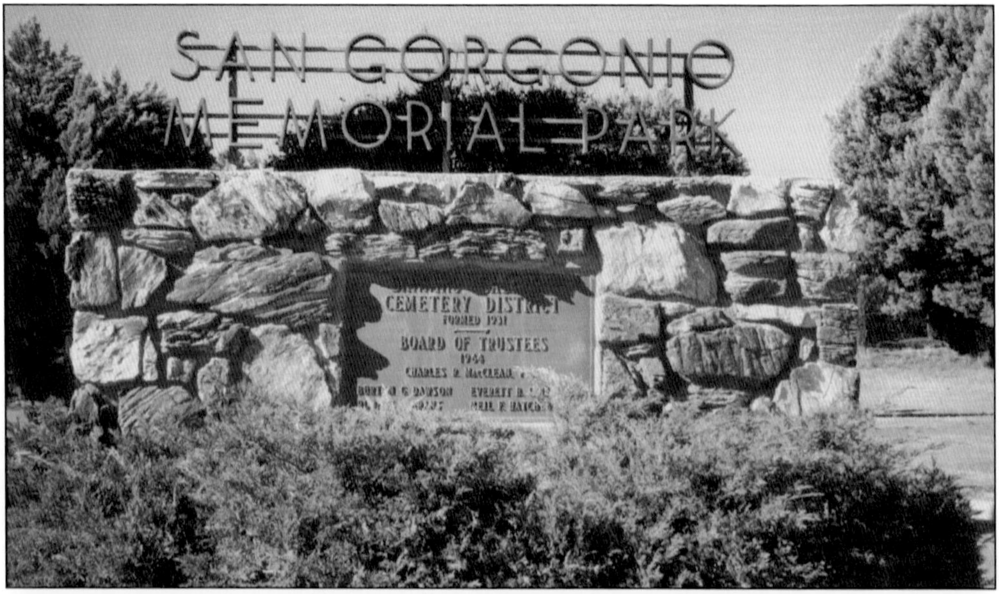

In 1905, the San Gorgonio Memorial Park cemetery, whose entrance is shown here, was operated under the Banning Cemetery Association with an elected board of directors all serving without pay. Sale of any lot had to be authorized, with lot owners acting as voting stockholders. On April 30, 1931, the association voted to deed all rights and title to the newly formed Banning-Cabazon Cemetery District, and the cemetery continues to operate under its jurisdiction. (Courtesy of the author.)

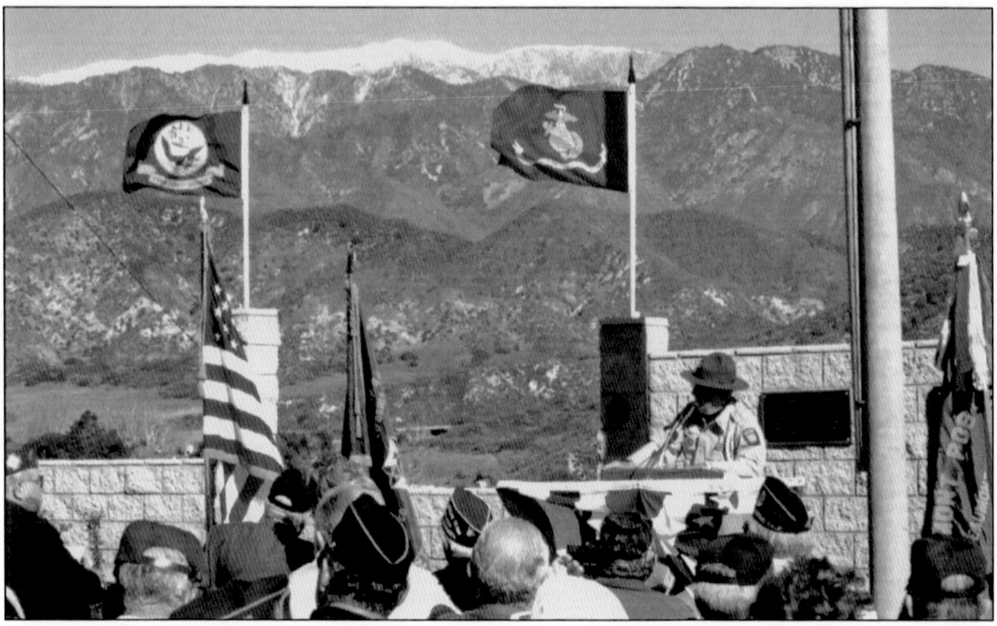

The dedication of the new Veterans Memorial Monument at San Gorgonio Memorial Cemetery in Banning was attended by some 200 veterans, community members, and public officials on Dec. 11, 2004. Tom Johnson, commander of VFW Post 4417, was master of ceremonies. Johnson, who initiate the project and brought it to fruition, received an official commendation from the California Legislature. Flags now fly over two memorials in Banning. (Courtesy of the author.)

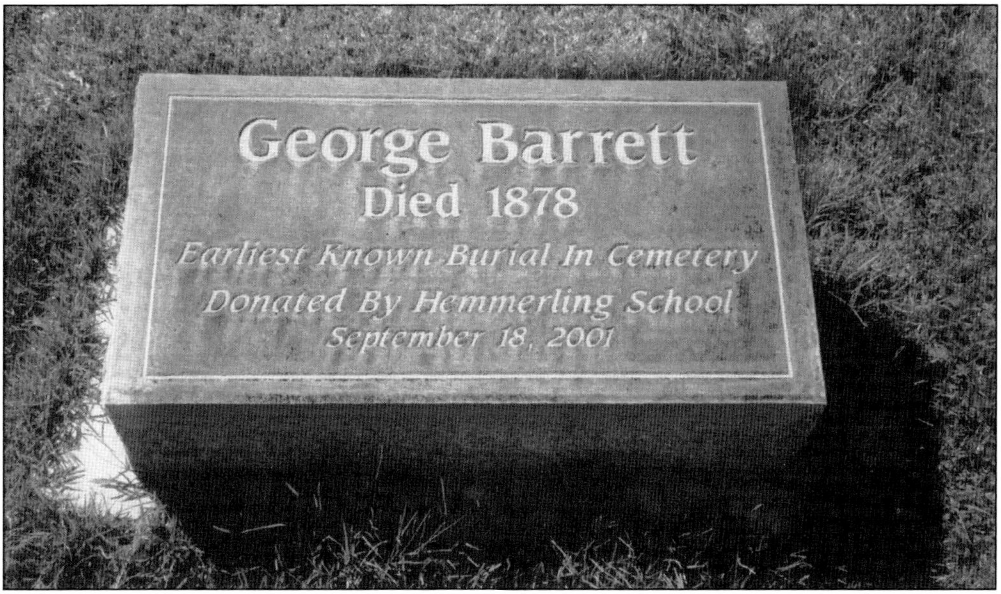

This marker is distinctive because it identifies the first man ever buried in the cemetery that later became San Gorgonio Memorial Park. In the spring of 1878, George Barrett, residing in a canyon above Banning, was murdered. His body was discarded on the hill where the current cemetery is located. When Barrett's body was discovered, several residents of Banning decided to bury him there. As years passed, other bodies were buried here, forming a cemetery. (Courtesy of the author.)

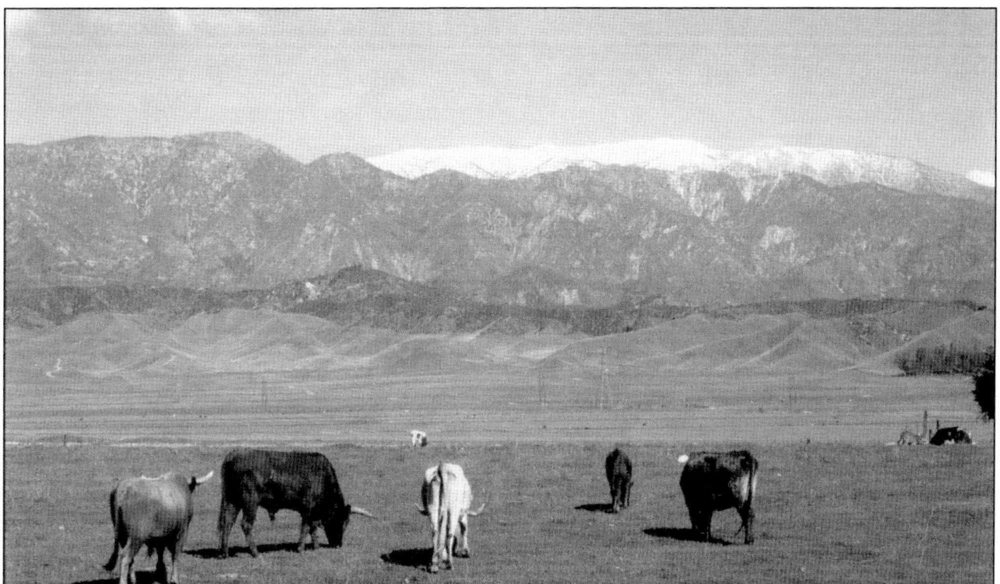

Cattle ranching ventures have been popular throughout the years in the Banning area. In this image, cattle graze on the range near the corner of Highland Springs Avenue and Wilson Street. In earlier years, sheep farming was extensively performed in the San Gorgonio Pass area. Today some sheep grazing continues, but the sheep are chiefly brought in from other areas. (Courtesy of the author.)

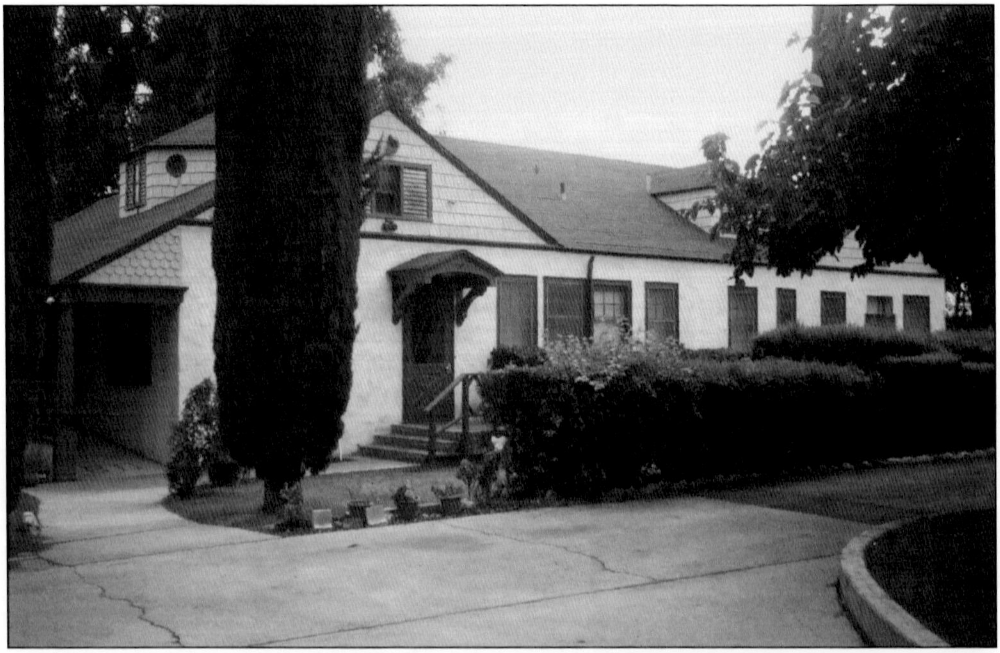

Pictured here is the main building of Briargate Manor. The sprawling 50-acre grounds of the original resort have been subdivided. Only one of 13 cottages remains, the others having burned to the ground in a fire. Briargate Manor once welcomed Hollywood personalities like John Wayne and Elizabeth Taylor. Briargate Manor was a popular vacation retreat but today is a home for the elderly. (Courtesy of the author.)

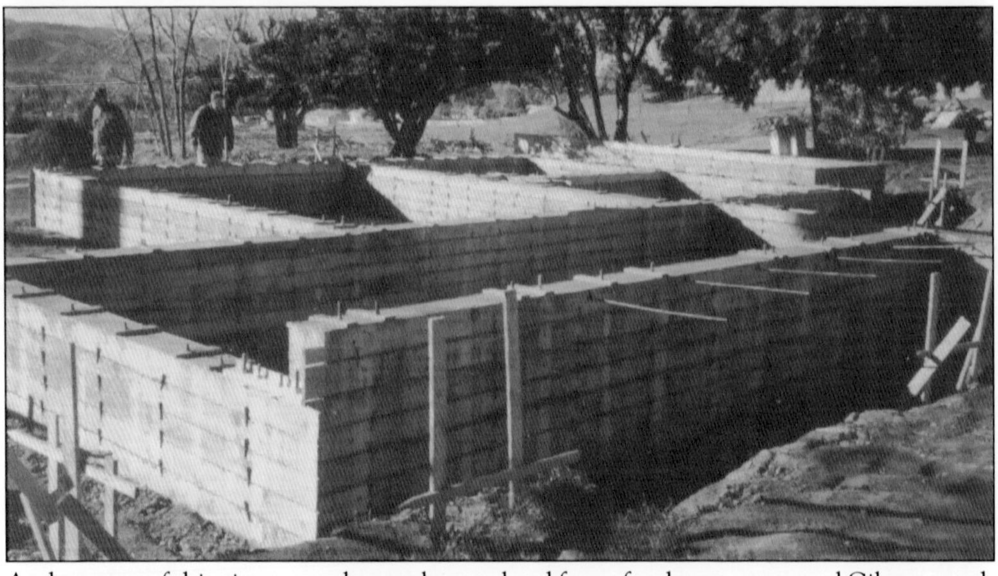

At the center of this picture are the nearly completed forms for the reconstructed Gilman ranch house. It has been the dream of the Gilman Ranch Hands, a group of volunteers dedicated to the preservation of the Gilman Historical Ranch and Wagon Museum, to bring this event to reality. The Riverside County Regional Parks and Open Space District is overseeing this county park project from start to finish under the supervision of its employee, Steve Lech. (Courtesy of the author.)

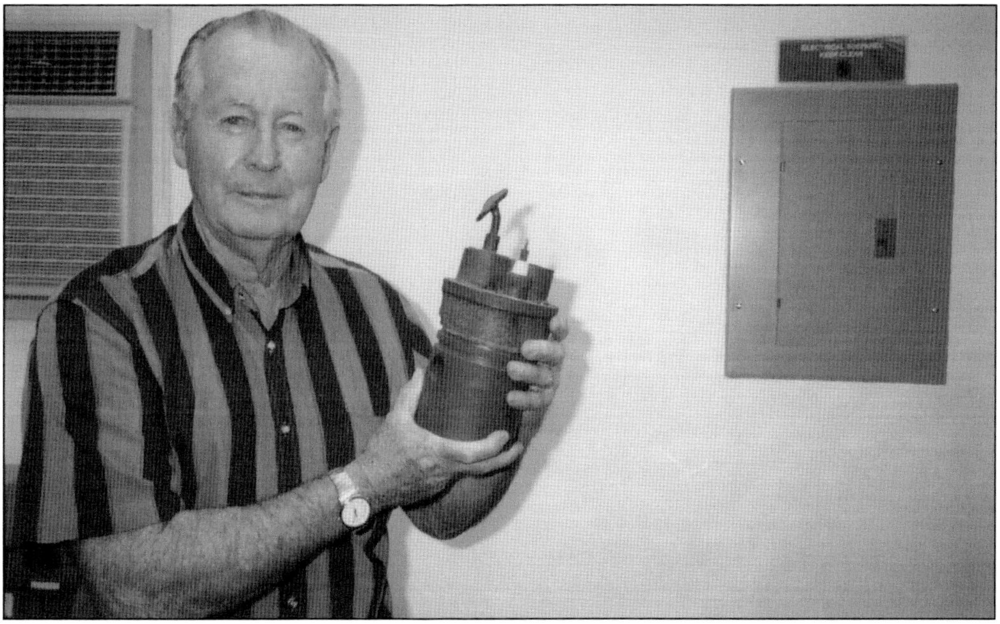

Here the author displays the component that failed and brought down aviator Calbraith Rogers's Wright Brothers Model B plane at Banning in 1911. It was donated to the Gilman Historic Ranch and Wagon Museum some years ago by C. O. Barker, one of Banning's early pioneers. The museum considers this to be a valued specimen, among the numerous others that can be seen at the facility. (Courtesy of Christie Mitchell.)

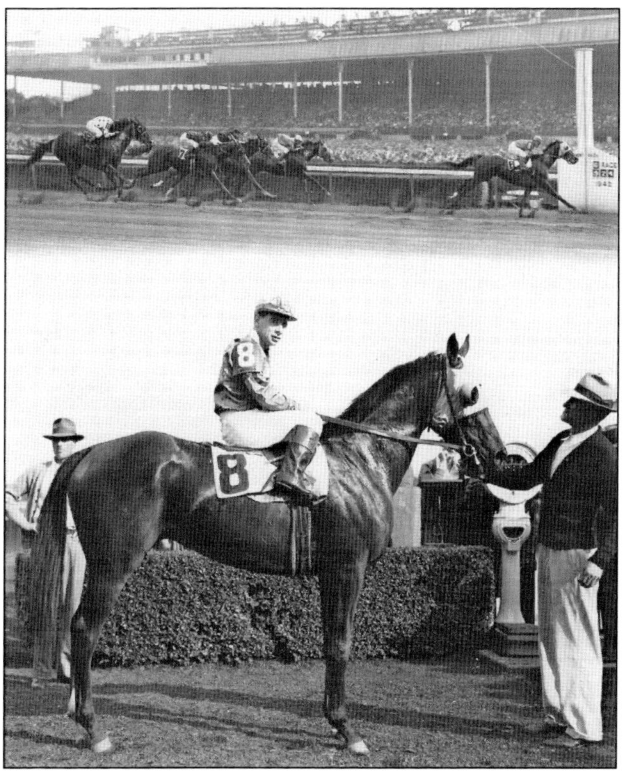

Legendary jockey Johnny Longden sits astride Count Fleet after winning the Morello Race at Belmont Park, September 14, 1942. He won the Kentucky Derby on Count Fleet in 1943 and retired from racing in 1966 at age 59. His 40-year career totaled 34,413 mounts and 6,032 winners. He had continued success as a racehorse trainer until he retired and moved to Banning's Sun Lake Country Club in 1990 with his wife, Kathy. He died at age 96 on February 14, 2003. (Courtesy of Chase McCoy.)

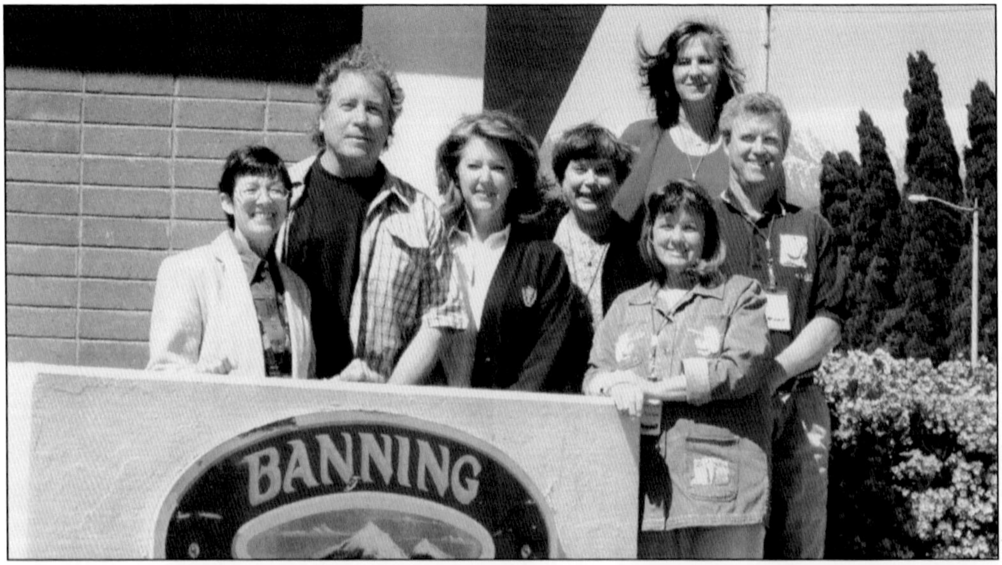

Pictured here is only a partial representation of the Banning Public Library staff, as several members are not present. Pictured, from left to right, are (first row) Ginger Hoiland, Bill Bell (head of interlibrary loan and reference), Delene Gonzalez (financial records), and Gloria Westerman; (second row) Janet Means and Lance Alloway (head of technical services); (third row) Lisa Rutherford (library director). By an election held August 21, 1916, citizens of Banning and Cabazon voted for a public library. Operations started in the Banning Union High School building with books loaned from the Riverside library. In 1954–1955, a library was built on the corner of Nicolet and San Gorgonio Avenues by renowned architect Albert Frey. The library's first books were donated by the Women's Club. Today the library has over 60,000 books. (Courtesy of Lisa Rutherford and Bill Bell.)

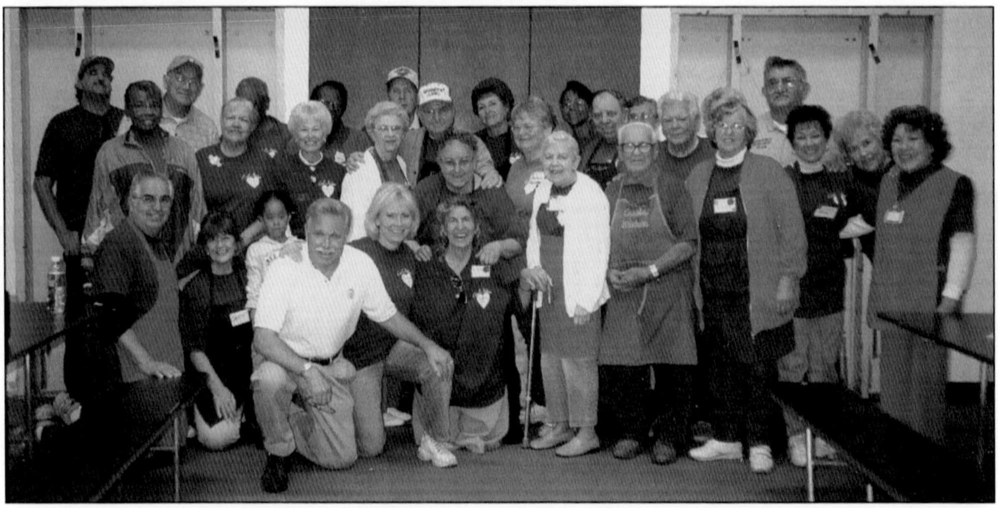

Pictured here are volunteers of Carol's Kitchen, an interdenominational, nonprofit, charitable corporation founded in 1998 by James and Arlene Ragan and James McConnell. Carol's Kitchen is a memorial to the Ragans' daughter, Carol, who was killed by a drunk driver in 1996. It first opened April 21, 1998, and fed 34 hungry people. Today it serves 1,000 meals a week at various locations in the San Gorgonio Pass area on different days of the week, operating solely on donations. (Courtesy of James McConnell.)

Four

BANNING'S NEIGHBORS, EAST AND WEST

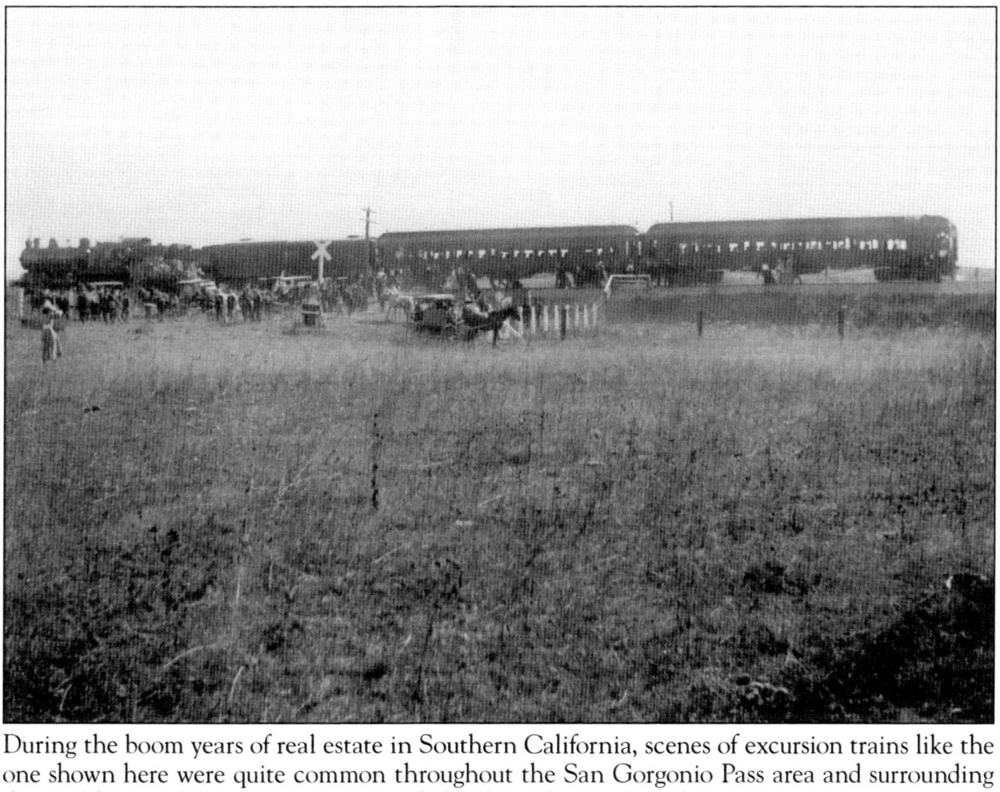

During the boom years of real estate in Southern California, scenes of excursion trains like the one shown here were quite common throughout the San Gorgonio Pass area and surrounding desert. This special excursion train, probably from the Los Angeles area, incorporated to bring prospective land buyers to the countryside. Many came to take advantage of the outing, others to buy. (Courtesy of Nara Haskell.)

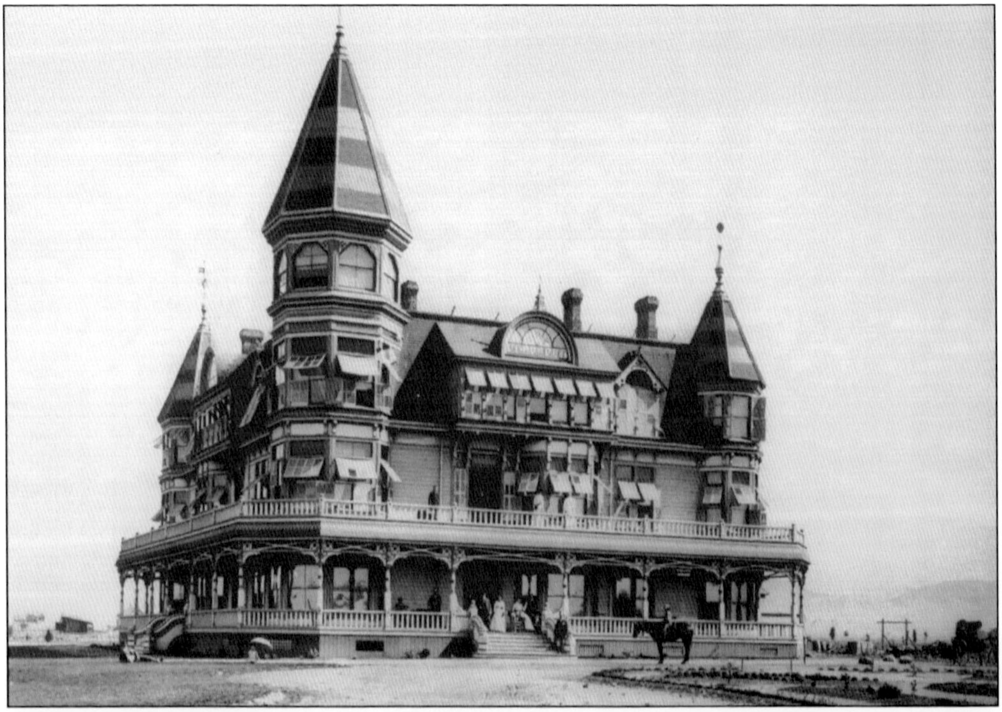

The Beaumont Hotel at Beaumont was built in the boom days by one Dr. Sigler. Three premium items for fostering real estate booms included impressive hotels, ample water, and land. Hotels and land and water companies were prevalent wherever land sales were to be promoted and Beaumont was no exception. The Beaumont Hotel, later named the Edenburgh Hotel, burned to the ground in August 1935. (Courtesy of San Gorgonio Pass Historical Society.)

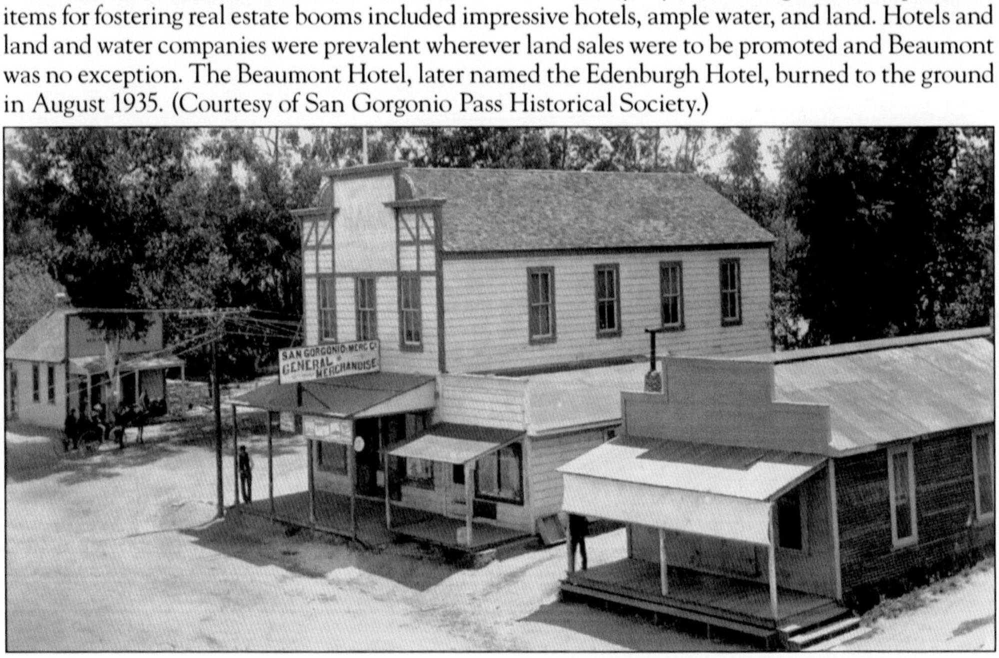

Seen here are three early businesses in Beaumont. The town had developed to some extent by this time and general merchandise stores were in great demand at this growing stage. It is interesting to note the sign on the front of the General Merchandise store advertising ice from the Union Ice Company. The false fronts on the buildings that were so typical of this time are also visible here. (Courtesy of Marilyn Vonderheide, LMS Foundation.)

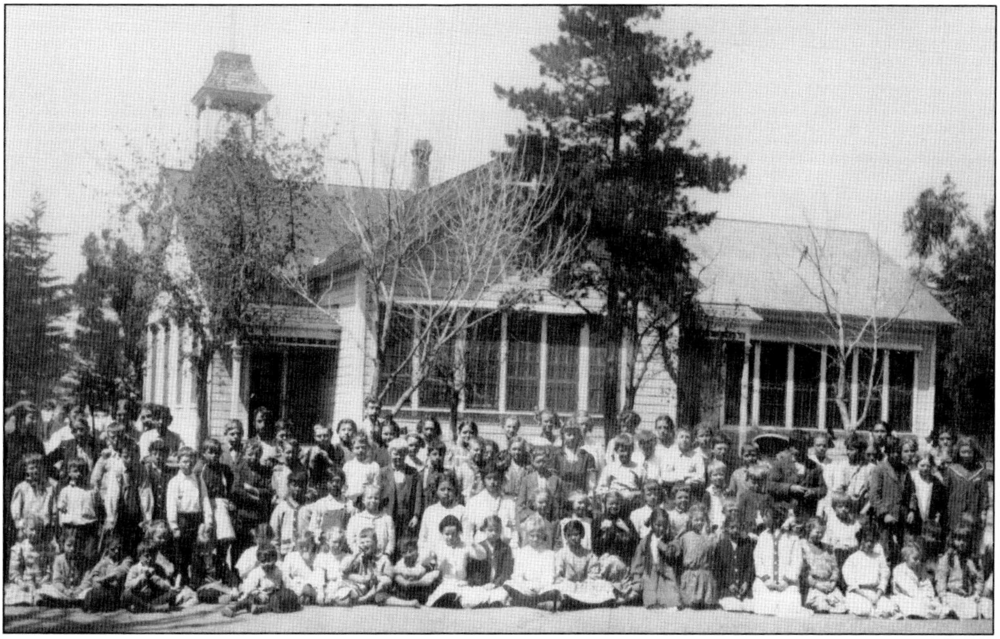

Grades one through eight and the kindergarten class are all gathered beside the Wellwood School in Beaumont for their yearly picture in 1910. At this time the population of Beaumont was growing, spurring the need for a schoolhouse such as the one seen here. A school like this was located in both towns of Beaumont and Banning. (Courtesy of Nara Haskell.)

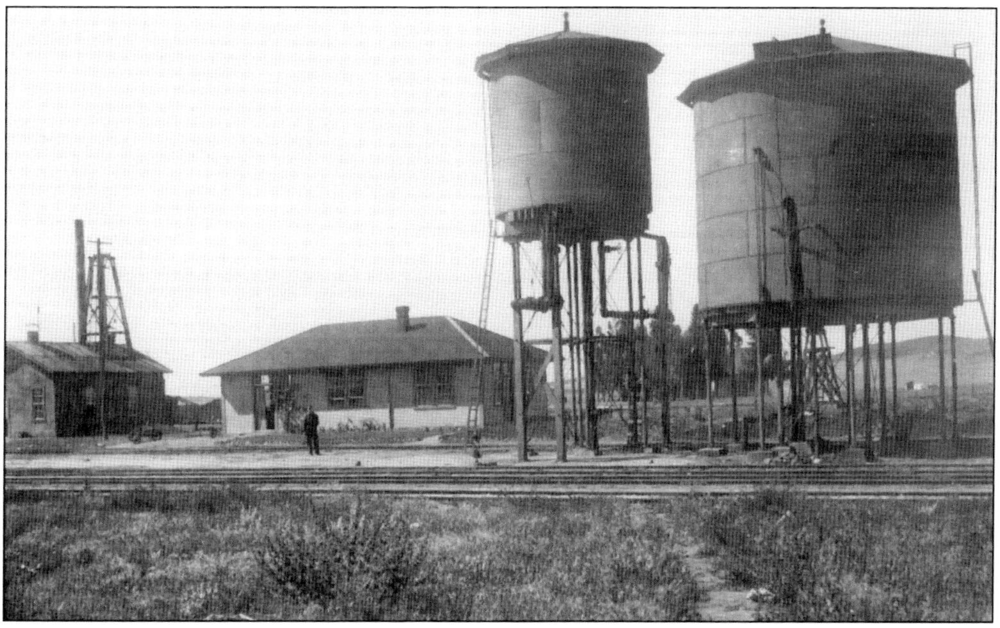

This 1910 photograph shows railway diesel and water storage tanks at Beaumont in the San Gorgonio Pass. These commodities had to be available at all times for the passing trains. The house in the center belonged to Mr. and Mrs. Roy Adams. Roy was an employee of the railroad and worked in one of the railroad shops. The railroad shop seen at the left of the photograph was still standing in 1982. (Courtesy of the San Gorgonio Pass Historical Society.)

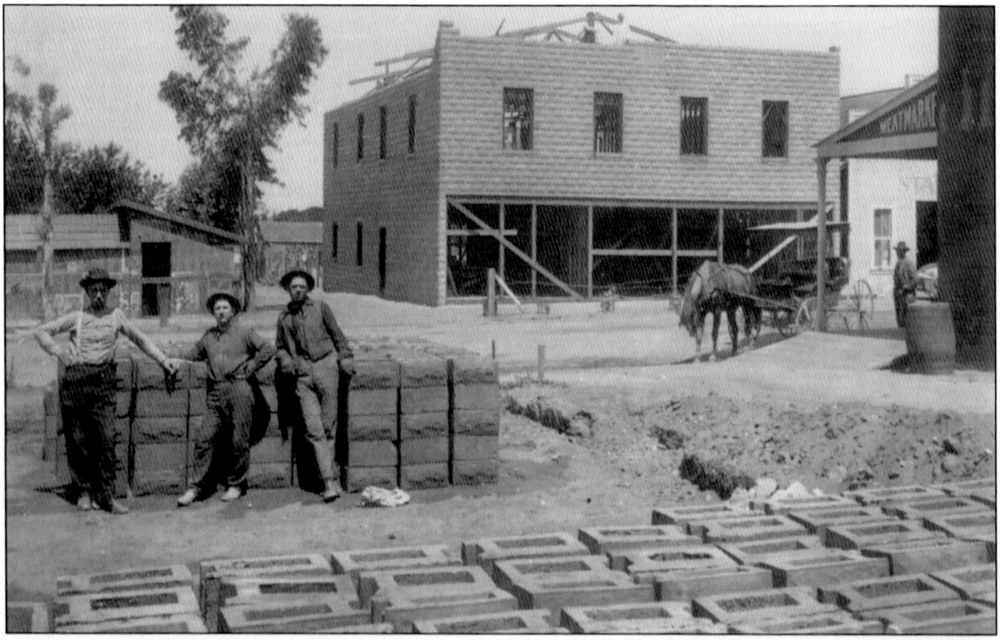

These workers have begun the early construction phase of a new building across the street from Grant's Mercantile Building on Egan Avenue. The time was the early 1900s. By this time, Beaumont had started to incorporate a more sturdy construction method when erecting new buildings, as can be evidenced by the heavy cement blocks in the foreground of the picture and the block building across the street. (Courtesy of the San Gorgonio Pass Historical Society.)

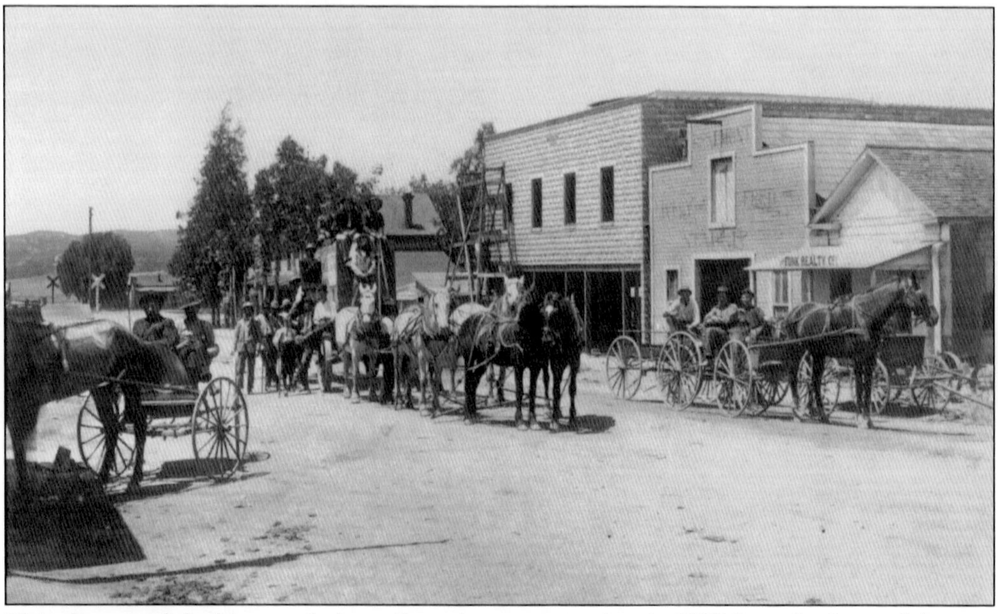

This photograph looking south down Egan Avenue was taken in 1907 from the front of the post office across the street. The buildings shown, from left to right, are Chas. Budden's hotel, Grant's Mercantile Building, Bert Curter's livery stable, and Drew Funk's reality company. In front of the mercantile building is an eight-horse team made ready to carry a wagon filled with heavy cargo. (Courtesy of the San Gorgonio Pass Historical Society.)

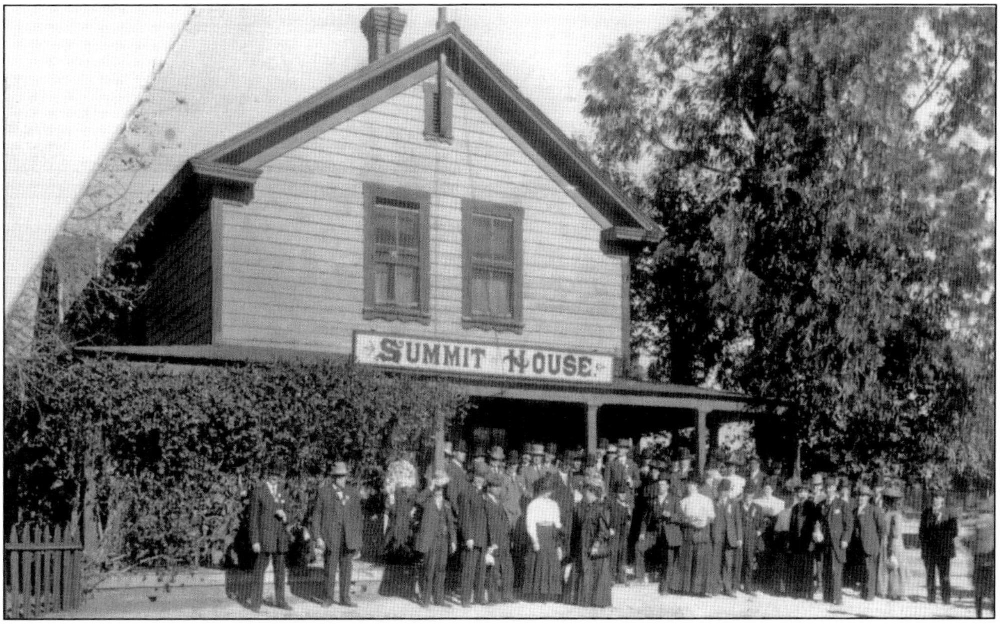

The Summit House, Beaumont's first hotel, was built in 1884 by Frank Mindeler. It became a very popular place to stop for anyone traveling though the San Gorgonio Pass area, and also catered to large groups requiring a meeting place. Members of the Southern Editorial Association who held their meeting here are pictured in front of the Summit House. The building burned in May 1925. (Courtesy of the San Gorgonio Pass Historical Society.)

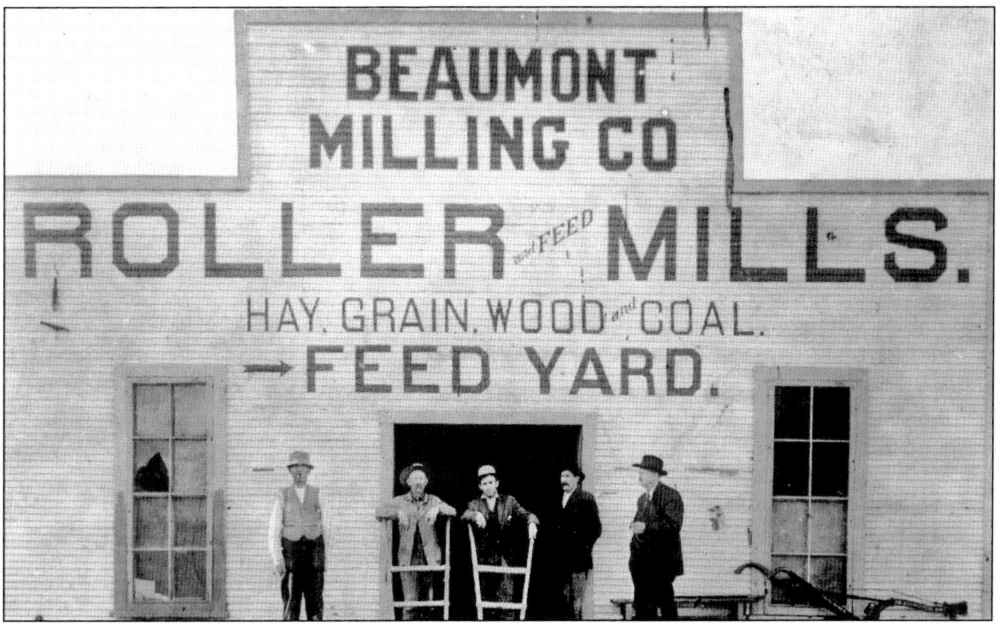

During the early 1900s, barley was a heavily grown crop, with the Stewart ranch producing a large amount of all the grain produced in the Banning and Beaumont area. The Beaumont Milling Company evolved to process the grain produced during that time. In addition, the company bought and sold hay, wood, and coal and operated a feed yard. (Courtesy of the San Gorgonio Pass Historical Society.)

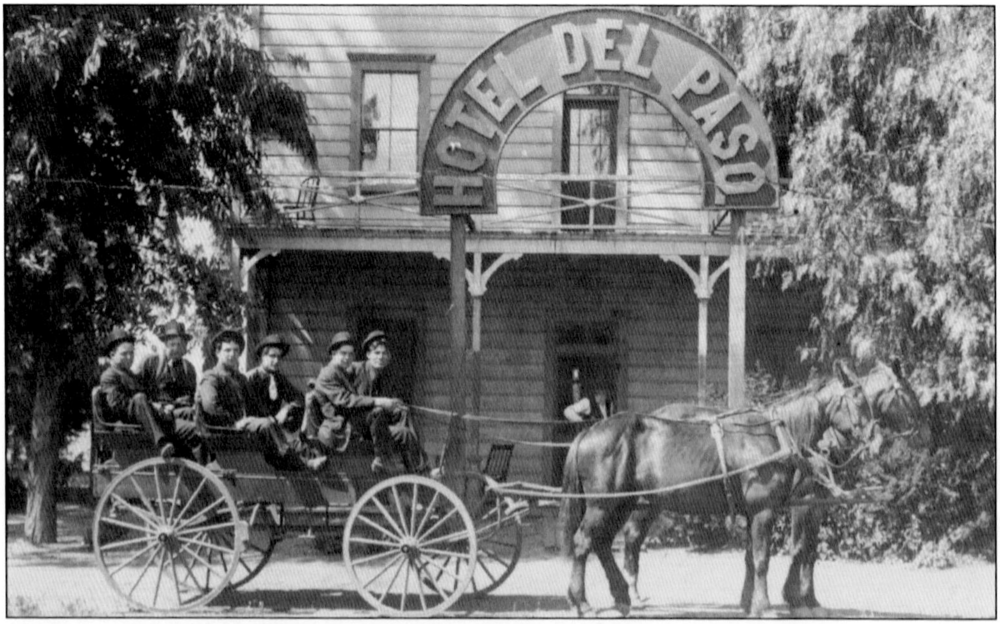

This group of visitors came to the Hotel Del Paso, Beaumont's first hotel, around 1890. Because this was the era of the real estate boom, these visitors may have been among the many that were brought here by excursion train during the time when an exuberant effort was launched by the promoters of real estate to sell their land to any interested newcomer. (Courtesy of Nara Haskell.)

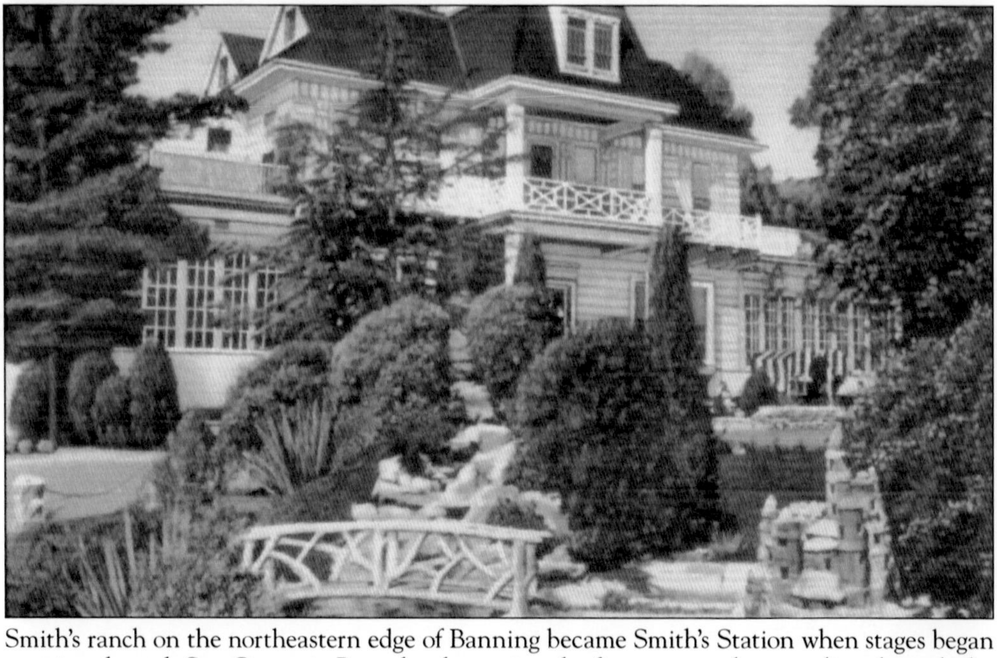

Smith's ranch on the northeastern edge of Banning became Smith's Station when stages began running through San Gorgonio Pass, thus becoming the first stop on the stage line through the pass. In 1884, Smith's Station was sold and a three-story hotel, pictured here, was built and named the Highland Home. In 1921, it was sold and renamed the Highland Springs Hotel. It since has burned down. (Courtesy of Steve Lech.)

When well No. 2 was sunk north of Beaumont and the water flow it produced proved adequate to supply substantial water to the town, a canal flume was built to bring the water to Beaumont. The complexity of such an undertaking involved the shoring up of the canal wall. (Courtesy of the San Gorgonio Pass Historical Society.)

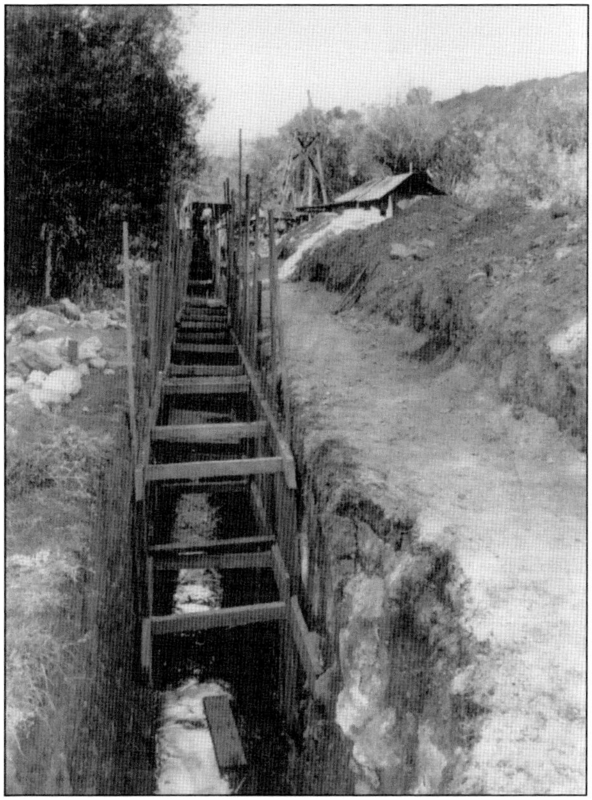

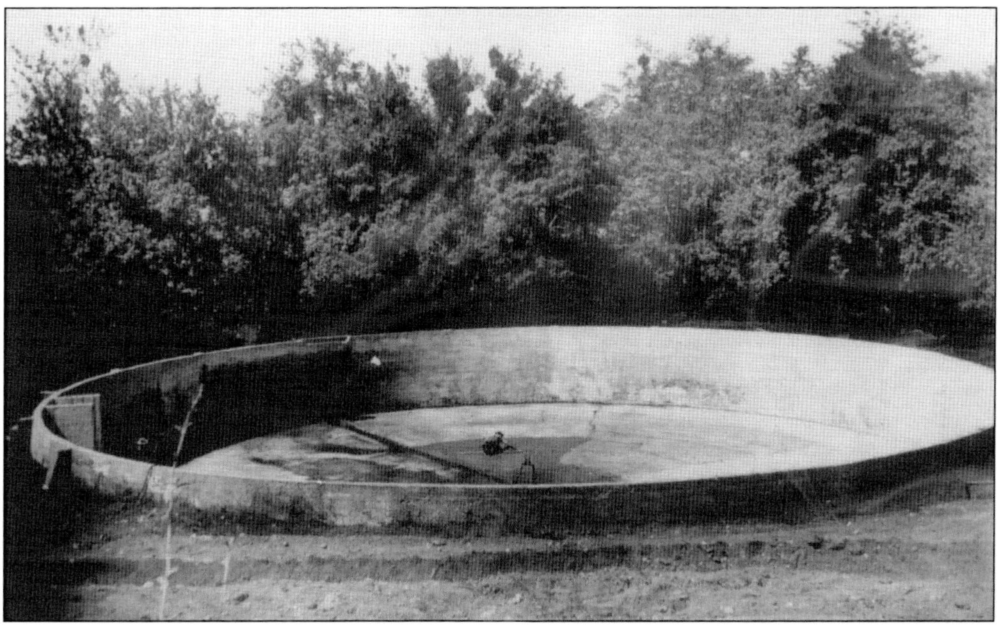

This open-air reservoir was constructed in 1911 to store water for Beaumont's water supply, which was produced by wells dug in Edgar Canyon. The size of the reservoir can be estimated by the marker, the small image of a man sitting in the center and bottom of the reservoir. Beaumont, like Banning, maintained water reservoirs to store its water. (Courtesy of Nara Haskell.)

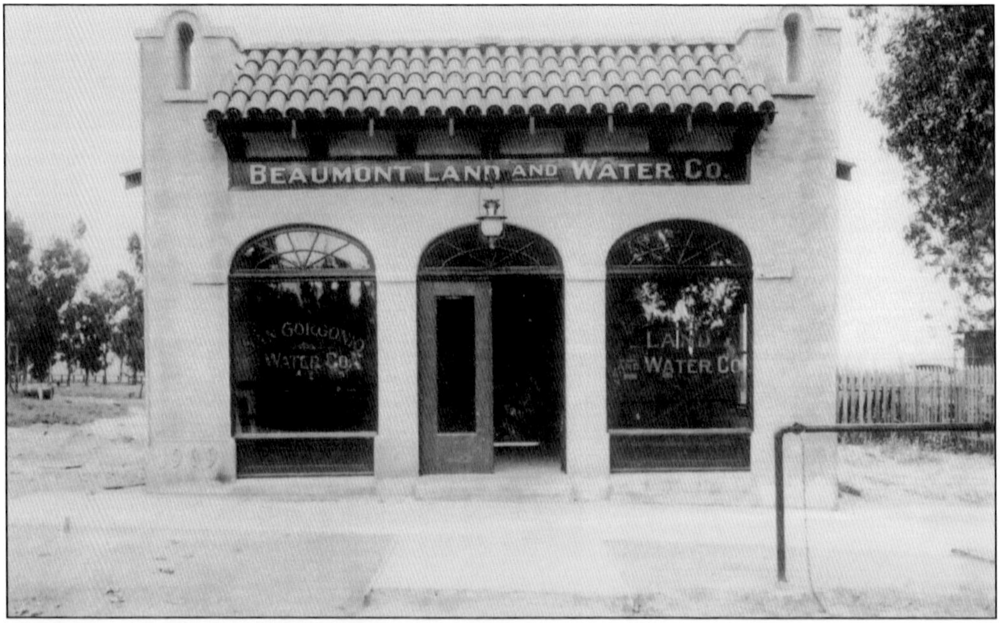

The Beaumont Land and Water Company building was constructed in 1909. During the boom years it was important for developing communities to establish both land and water companies to entice buyers and promote community growth. Beaumont, like many other towns riding the real estate boom of these early years, was no exception. (Courtesy of the San Gorgonio Historical Society.)

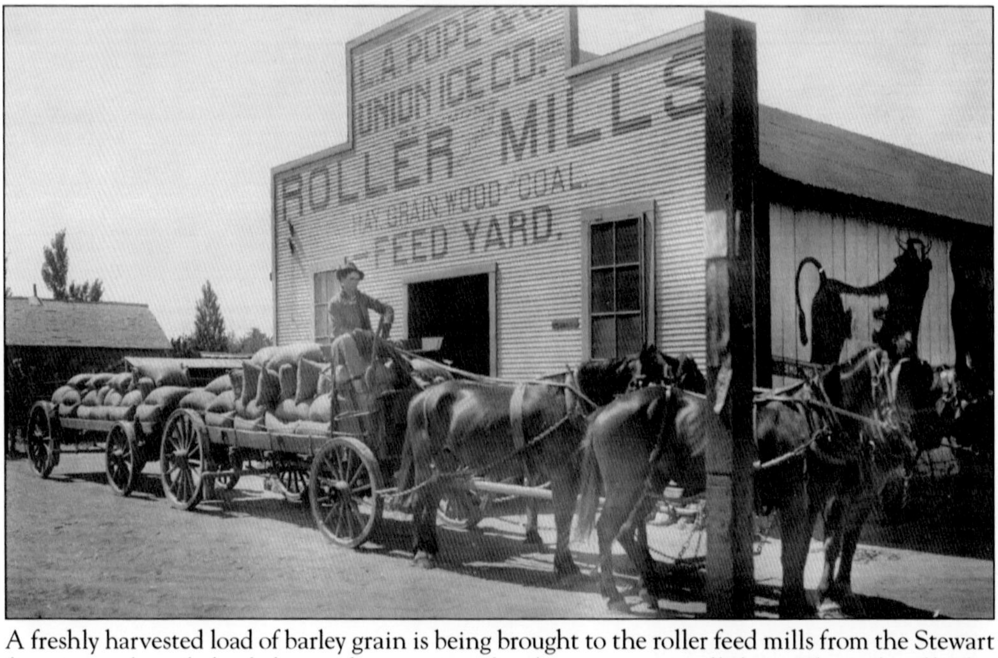

A freshly harvested load of barley grain is being brought to the roller feed mills from the Stewart farm in two heavily-loaded carts that require a four-horse team to pull them. The sacks of barley represent numerous hours of toil in the field before they arrived there, and the trip from the threshing field to the mill sometimes could be a long journey. (Courtesy of Marilyn Vonderheide, LMS Foundation.)

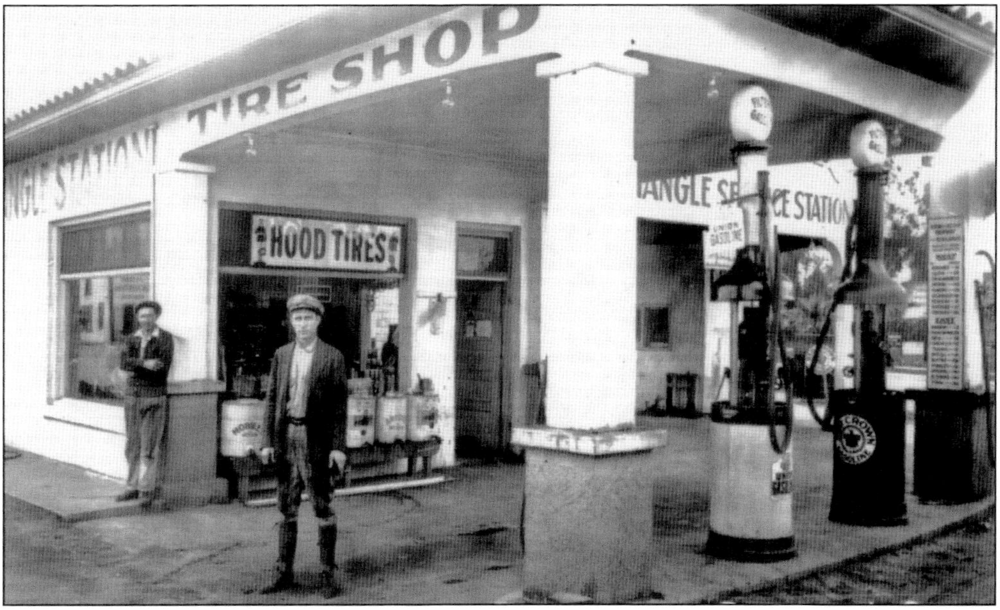

A few small gasoline stations like this one could be seen throughout the San Gorgonio Pass and adjoining areas, but were distantly spaced. Traffic in those early years was light and required few stations, quite in contrast to today's high demand. In this picture, it is interesting to note that just one brand of tires is being advertised on a sign in the window, unlike the numerous listings seen today. (Courtesy of Steve Lech.)

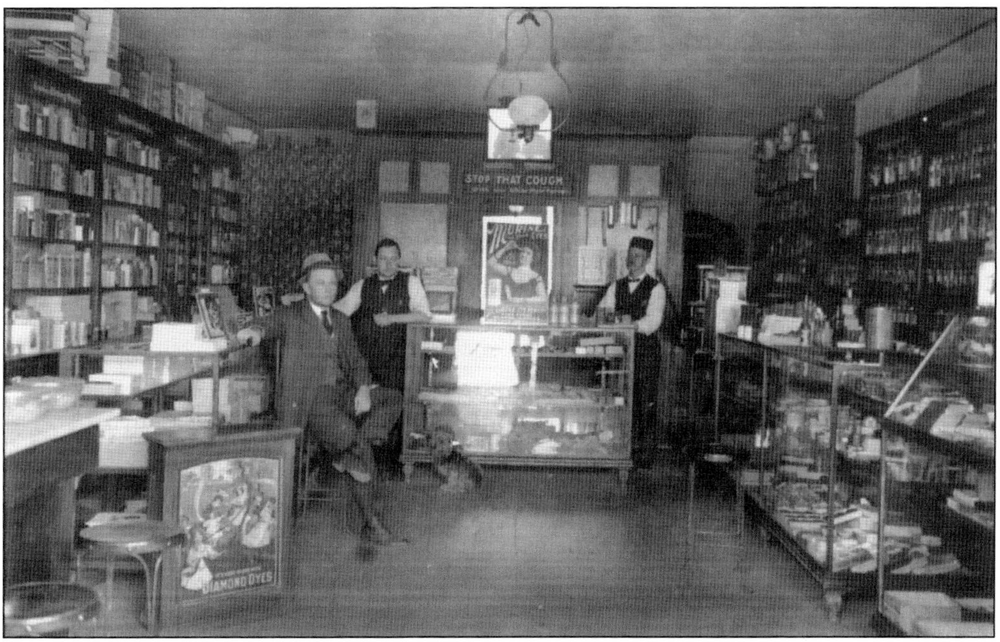

This view is of the inside of the Fulton Drug Store in Beaumont in its early years. The man standing at the counter at the right in a skull cap is Robert Fulton, the proprietor. The two other men in the picture are perhaps employees; one may be the druggist. It is interesting to note the poster on the counter advertising Murine for the eyes, an advertisement that may still be seen in today's drugstores. (Courtesy of the San Gorgonio Pass Historical Society.)

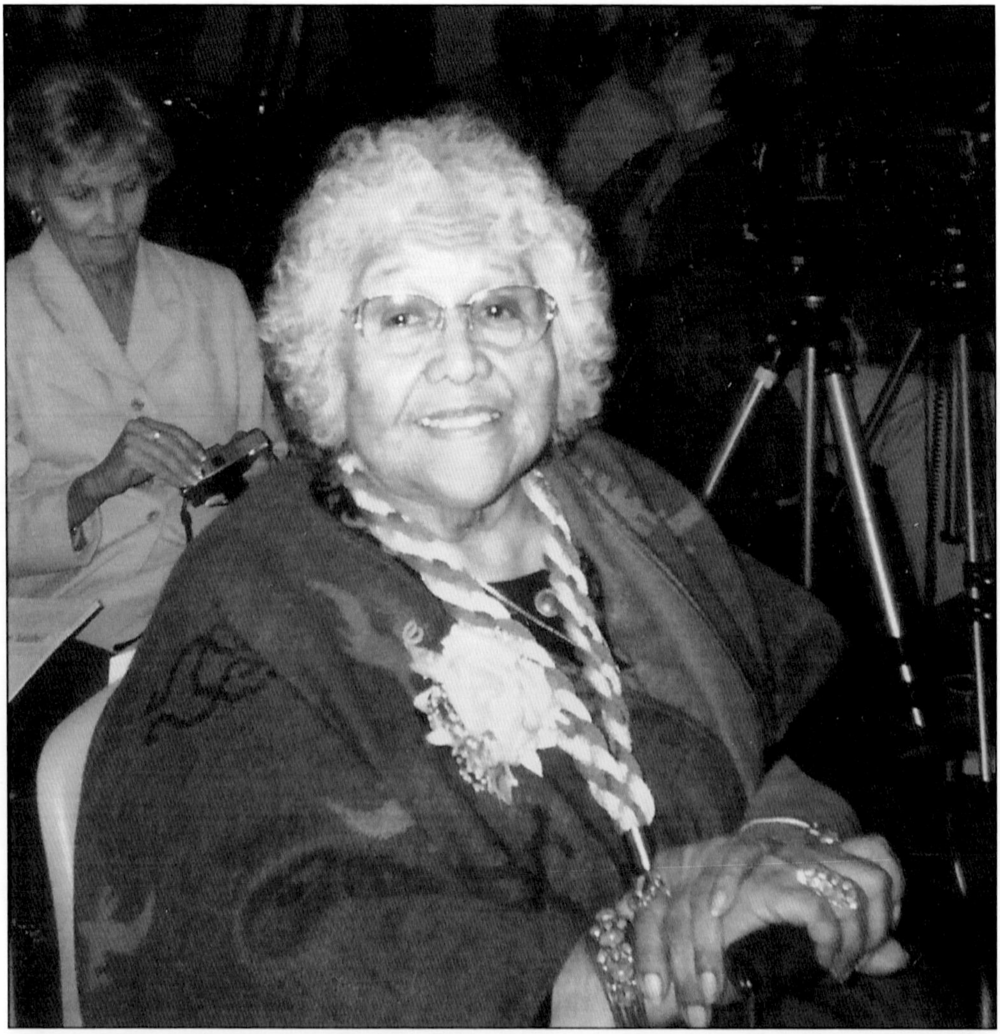

Katherine Siva Saubel was born on the Los Coyotes Reservation and is currently its tribal leader. She was the first Native American to graduate from Palm Springs High School. She married Mariano Saubel from the Morongo Reservation and lived with him there. Among her numerous honors was being the first Native American to be inducted into the National Women's Hall of Fame. Her most recent achievement was in 2003, when La Sierra University awarded her an honorary Doctor of Humane Letters for her lifetime of work to preserve Native American languages and culture. Her life story has been made into a play, *We Are Still Here*. (Courtesy of Katherine Siva Saubel.)

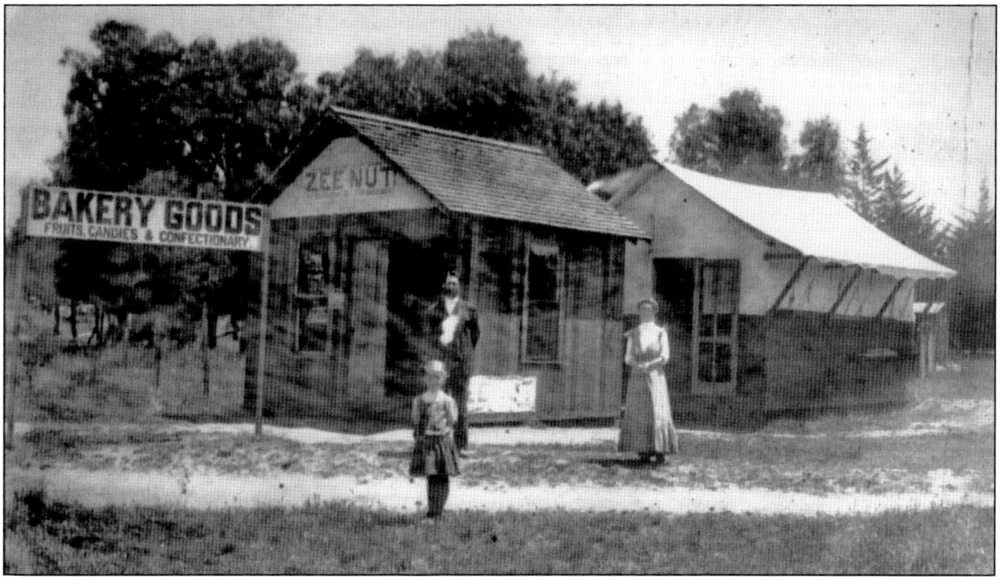

This *c.* 1907 photograph shows the business and home of G. M. Kimball near today's Sixth Street in Beaumont. The home to the right of the photograph appears to have a canvas covering for a roof. As the sign denotes, the business dealt in bakery goods, fruits, candies, and confectioneries. Kimball, his wife, and his daughter are posing in front of the store for the photograph, which appears to be in a remote area at that time. (Courtesy of the San Gorgonio Pass Historical Society.)

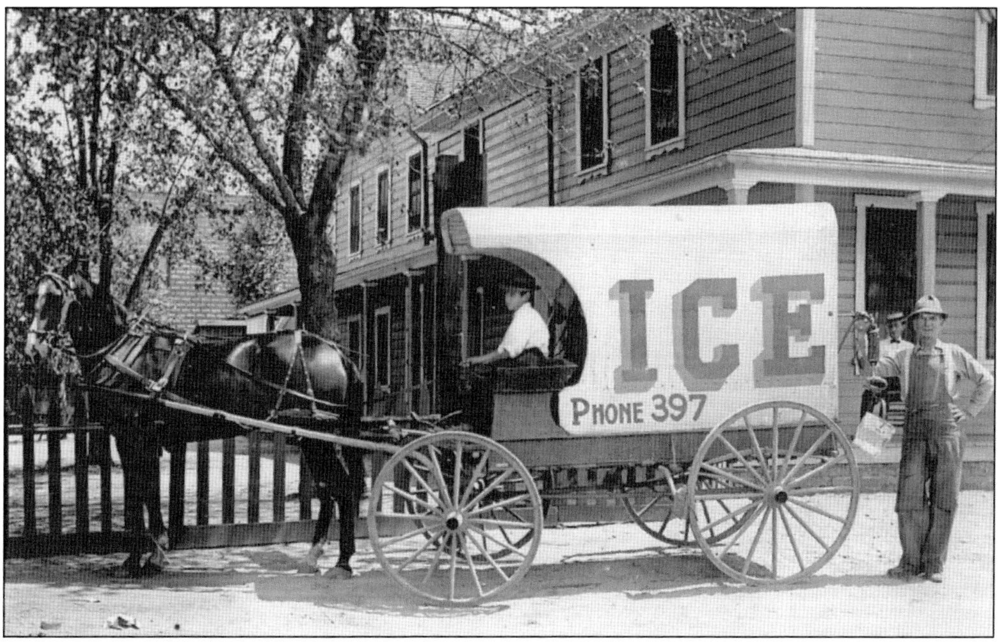

When ice became available in the San Gorgonio Pass, the ice business proved a lucrative venture. This wagon delivered ice for an agent of the Banning Ice Company in Beaumont and consisted of a driver and one-man delivery crew. Due to demand, several ice deliverers were needed to adequately supply the area. Note the block of ice hanging from the ice tongs and the scale at the rear of the wagon. (Courtesy of Marilyn Vonderheide, LMS Foundation.)

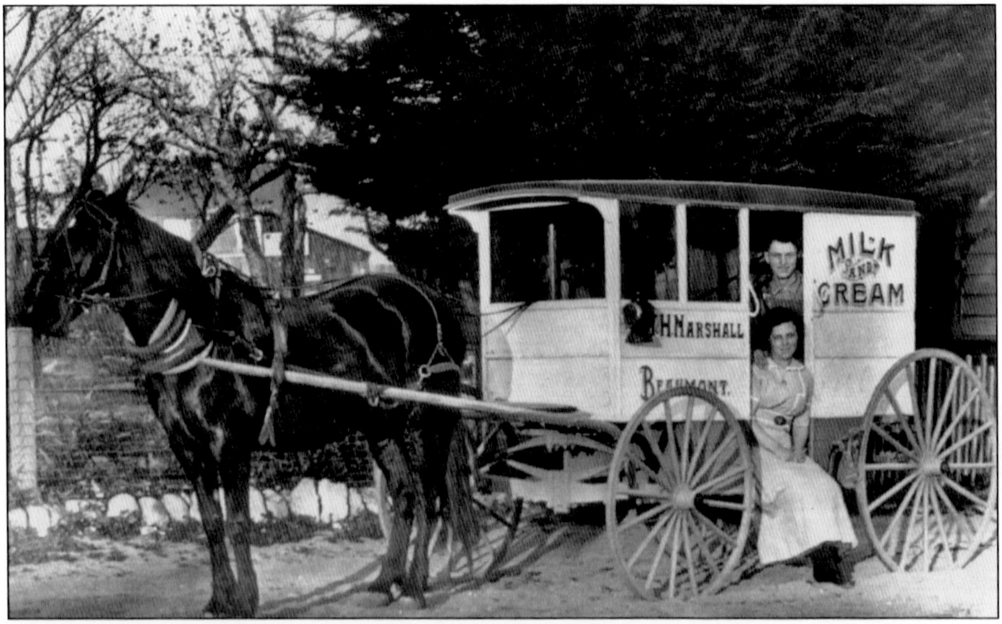

This one-horse carriage of the Marshall Company of Beaumont was often seen delivering milk and cream around the streets of Beaumont. Delivery services like this were quite prevalent for both milk and ice during the town's early years. The horse appears to be waiting patiently while the driver and delivery lady stop to pose for the photograph. (Courtesy of the San Gorgonio Pass Historical Society.)

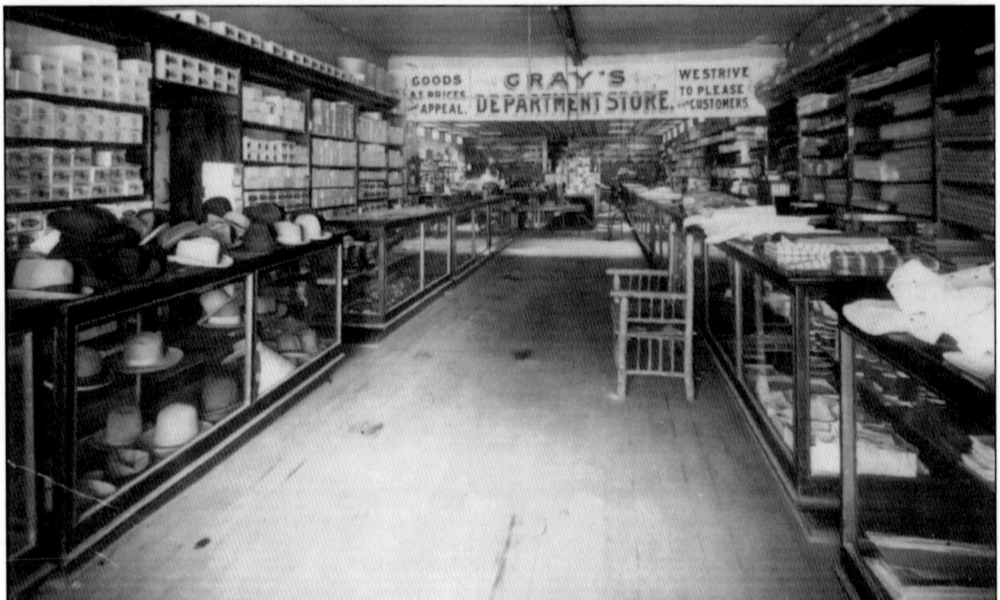

The merchandise at Gray's Department Store in Beaumont was arranged quite orderly, except perhaps for the large selection of hats. It is obvious that hats were a popular item. The store advertised "goods at prices that appeal and we strive to please our customers." Gray's was a popular department store with its closest competition in nearby Banning. (Courtesy of the San Gorgonio Pass Historical Society.)

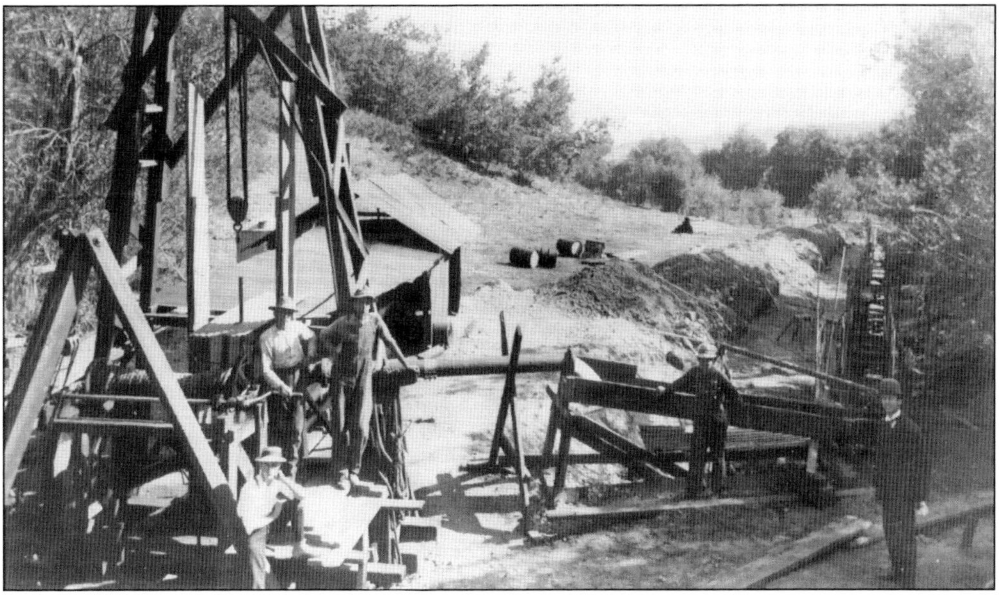

Water Well No. 2 was drilled by the Beaumont Land and Water Company in 1908 in Edgar Canyon north of Beaumont. It was 346 feet deep and 12 inches in diameter. The photograph depicts the workers proudly standing in front of a good flow of water being brought by flume to Beaumont. They were happy to have struck water here because the first drilling had been unsuccessful. Note the good water flow coming from the well pipe. (Courtesy of the San Gorgonio Pass Historical Society.)

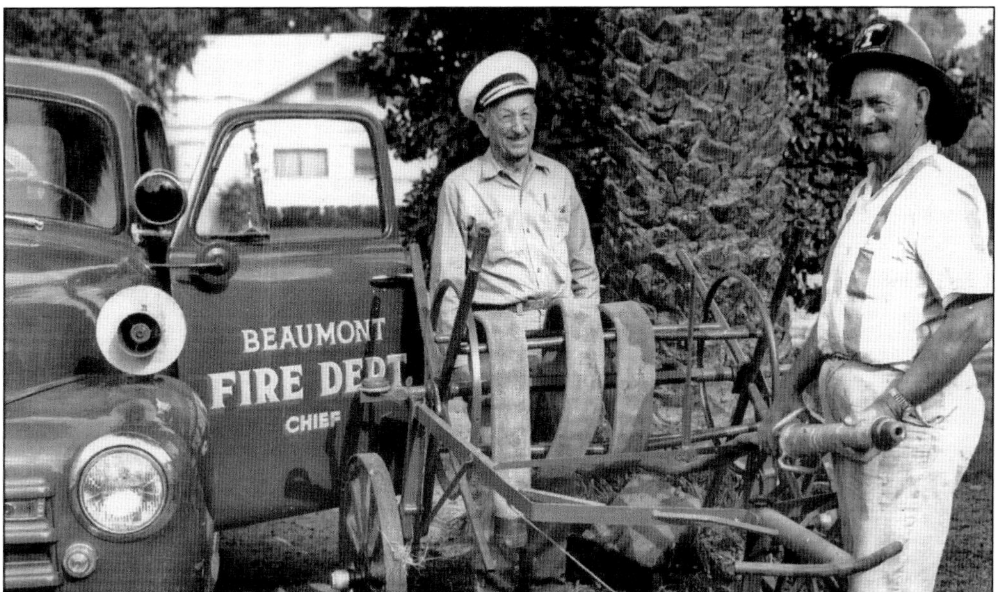

Chief Clarence Lewis and fireman Ray Samson stand beside this 1949 Chevrolet fire truck with red spotlight and fender-mounted horn. The contrast between this antiquated firefighting equipment compared to today's large trucks and elaborate hose system is obvious. Beaumont has certainly improved its fire department in the 50 years or so since this photograph was taken. (Courtesy of the San Gorgonio Pass Historical Society.)

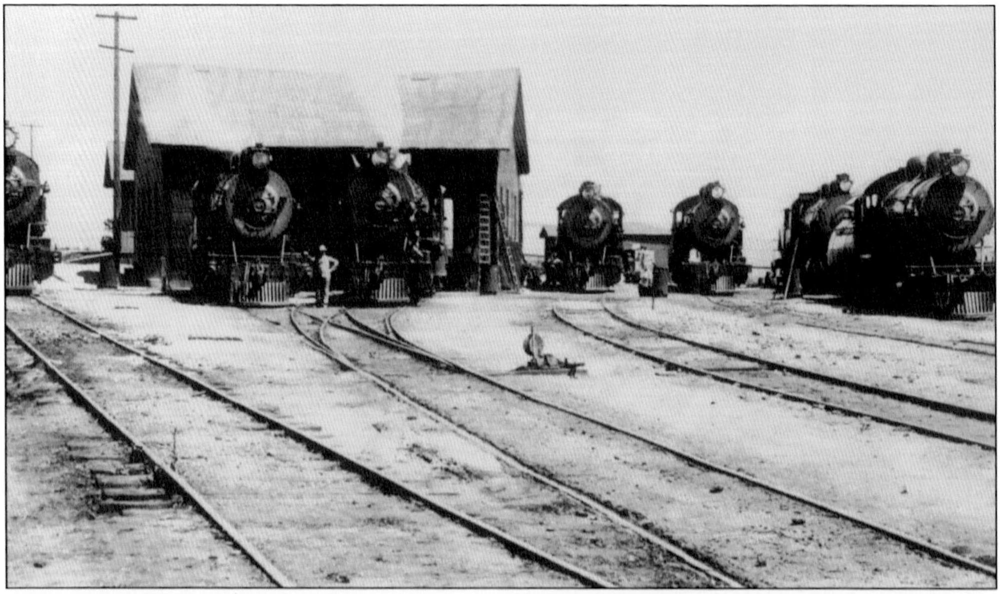

Because the railroad continued to prosper on its route through the San Gorgonio Pass, the need for a train roundhouse was required and was eventually established at Beaumont. This was the central point where engine locomotives were serviced and made ready for use throughout the line. The steep grades to and from the San Gorgonio Pass were rather extreme and often more than one engine was required to ascend the summit. (Courtesy of the San Gorgonio Pass Historical Society.)

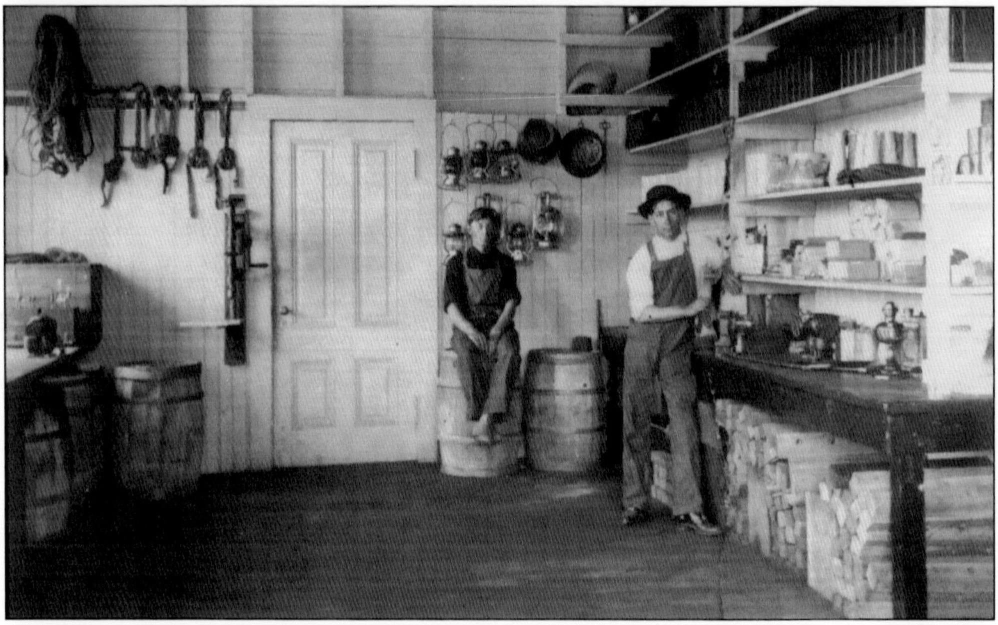

The Southern Pacific's roundhouse served an important function in keeping the trains moving efficiently through the San Gorgonio Pass. Pictured is the inside of one of the roundhouse storage rooms where lanterns and other needed items were stored. The storage rooms also served as tool sheds and work areas for some of the employees, two of whom are posing here. (Courtesy of San Gorgonio Pass Historical Society.)

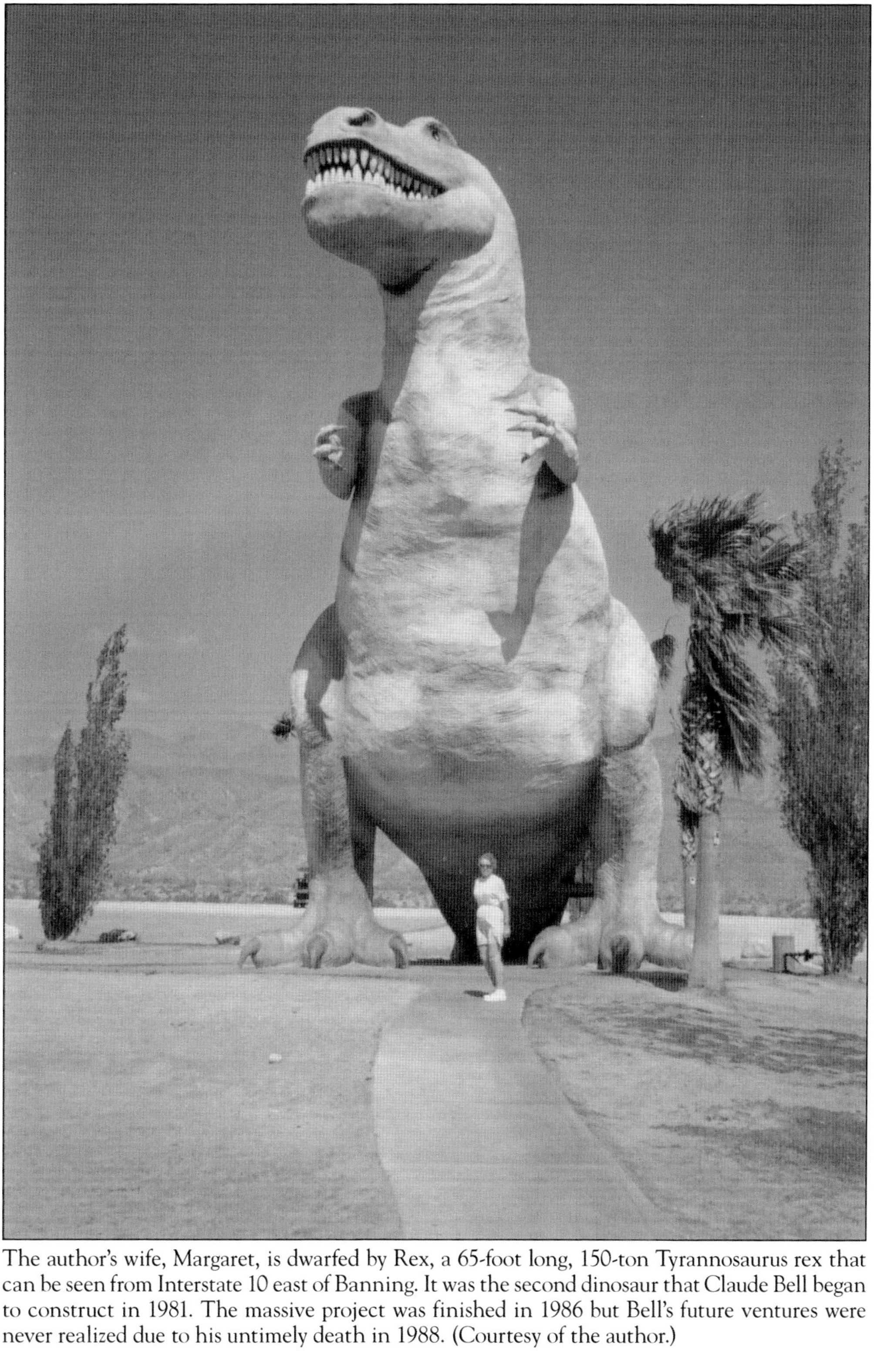

The author's wife, Margaret, is dwarfed by Rex, a 65-foot long, 150-ton Tyrannosaurus rex that can be seen from Interstate 10 east of Banning. It was the second dinosaur that Claude Bell began to construct in 1981. The massive project was finished in 1986 but Bell's future ventures were never realized due to his untimely death in 1988. (Courtesy of the author.)

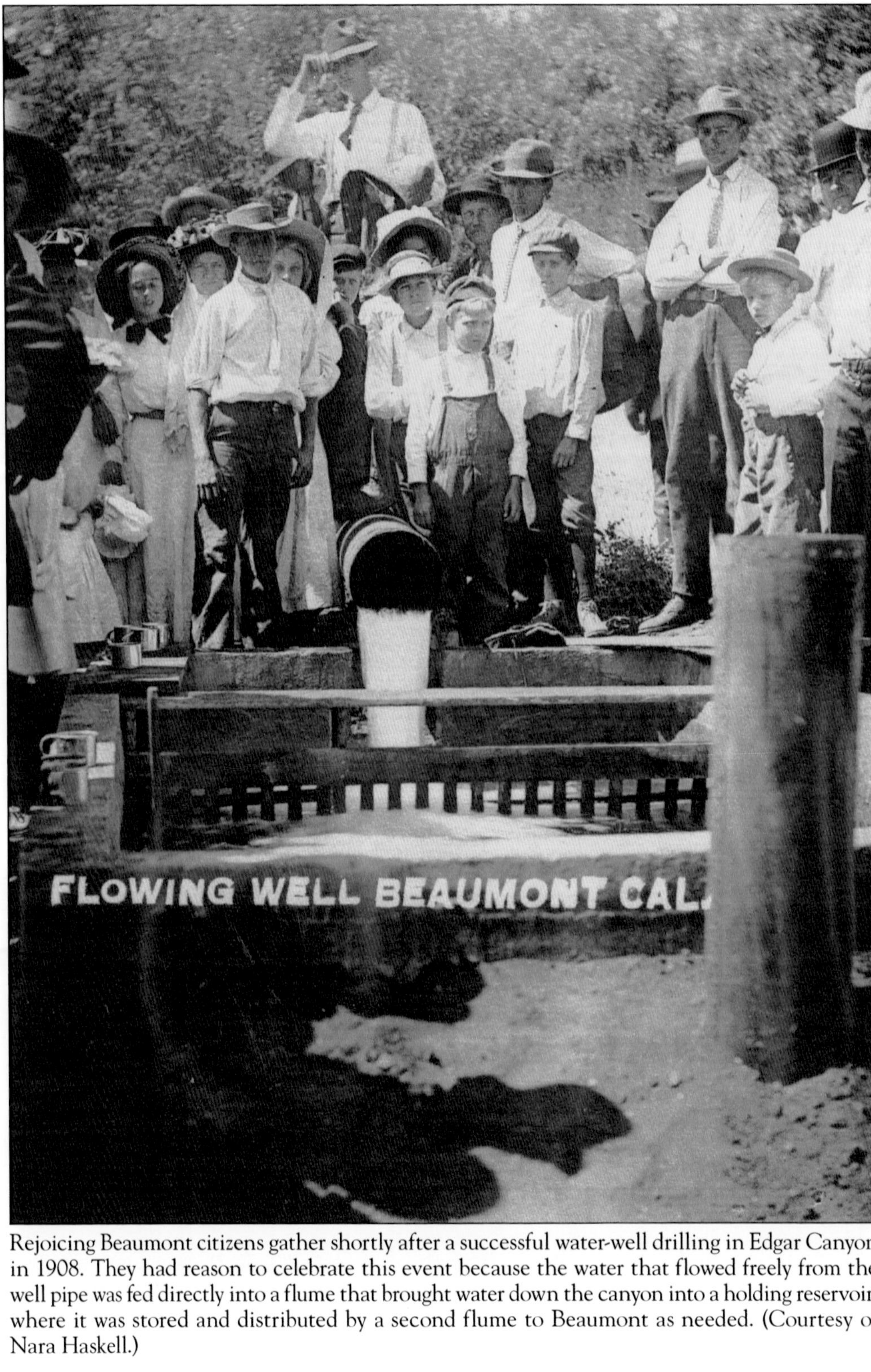

Rejoicing Beaumont citizens gather shortly after a successful water-well drilling in Edgar Canyon in 1908. They had reason to celebrate this event because the water that flowed freely from the well pipe was fed directly into a flume that brought water down the canyon into a holding reservoir, where it was stored and distributed by a second flume to Beaumont as needed. (Courtesy of Nara Haskell.)

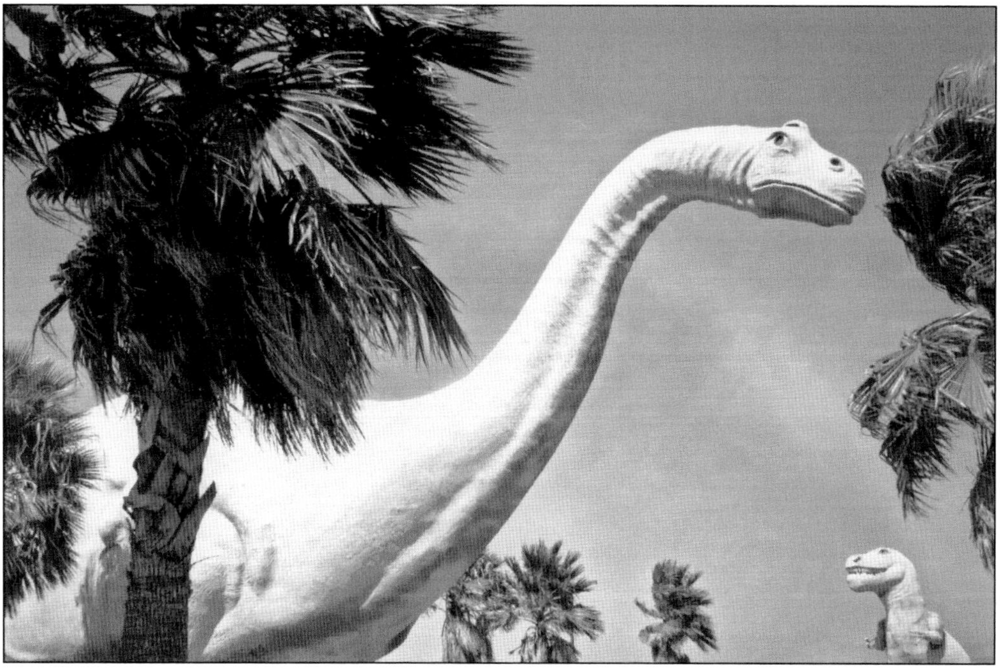

This sight certainly turns heads as travelers head east past Banning on Interstate 10 through the San Gorgonio Pass toward nearby Cabazon. Named Dinny, the massive 150-foot, 150-ton brontosaurus took 11 years for Claude Bell to build. Its domination of the landscape is further enhanced by Rex, seen in the background. This sight is a great tourist attraction that lures many into the belly of Dinny, where gifts can be bought. (Courtesy of the author.)

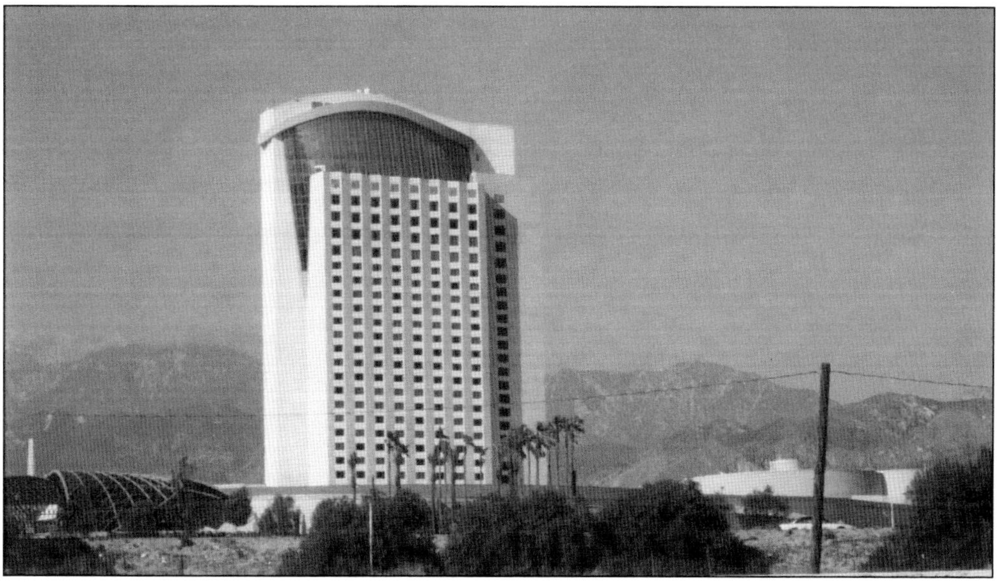

This high-rise casino recently opened on the Morongo Reservation east of Banning. The $250 million resort sits on 44 acres and boasts a 685,000-square-foot, 27-story structure with 272 hotel rooms, 32 double bay suites, six luxury casitas (each with its own pool), four nightclubs, nine restaurants, 2,000 slot machines, a 316,000-gallon swimming pool with its own beach and lazy river, and numerous other features. (Courtesy of the author.)

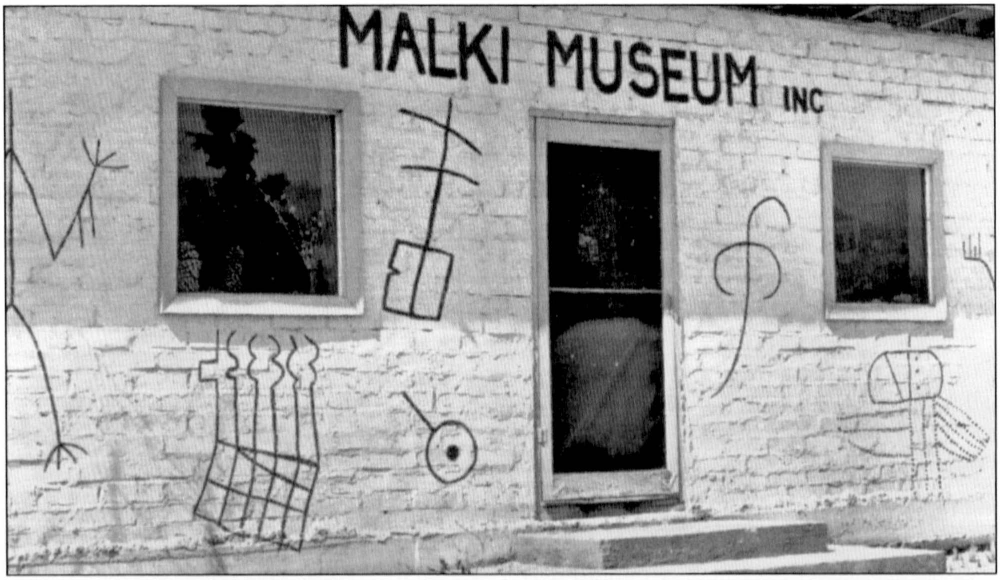

This is the original Malki Museum on the Morongo Reservation, before it moved to its new building. It is now over 40 years old, and founders Jane Penn and Katherine Saubel are still active in its operation. The museum's mission is to promote scholarship, cultural awareness, and understanding of Southern California Native American tribes. (Photo by David Ball; courtesy of Steve Lech.)

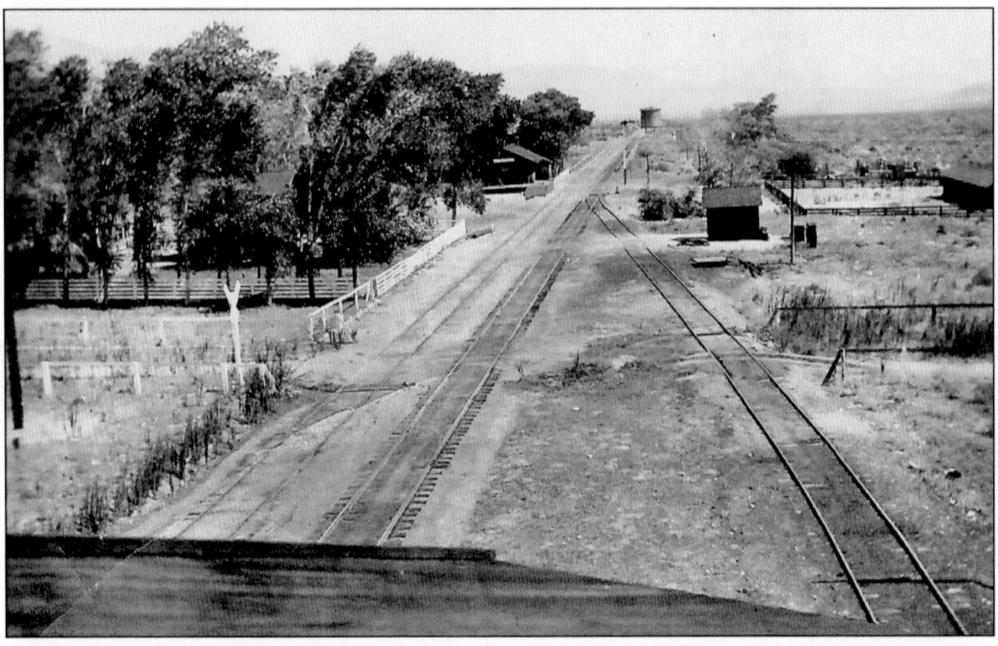

This early train station is located in what is today the town of Cabazon. It is interesting to note that even in these early years there were two tracks running through the San Gorgonio Pass, despite the fact that most of the communities through which it passed were in their infancy at that time. The railroad spur to the right in the photograph is the track that ran down into Hall City, which at this time had a better probability of becoming a town than Cabazon did. (Courtesy of Marianne Bailiff.)